November 2005

MW00803993

META-COACHING

Volume II:

COACHING CONVERSATIONS

FOR TRANSFORMATIONAL CHANGE

L. Michael Hall, Ph.D.
and
Michelle Duval, Master Coach

With
Robert Dilts

Published by: **Neuro-Semantics Publications**
                                          P.O. Box 8
                            Clifton, CO. 81520-0008 USA

Printing Company: **Action Printing**
                              Jerry Kucera, Owner
                            516 Fruitvale Court, Unit C
                              Grand Jct. CO. 81504
                                (970) 434-7701
                              Actionpres@aol.com

Cover Designed and Created by *Doug Clary*, Action Printing

Author: **L. Michael Hall, Ph.D.**
                              P.O. Box 8
                              Clifton, CO   81520
                              (970) 523-7877

Neuro-Semantics® is the trademark name for the International Society of Neuro-
Semantics. For more than 2000 pages of *free information*, see the web sites:
                        www.neurosemantics.com
                        www.runyourownbrain.com
                        www.equilibrio.com.au

COACHING CONVERSATIONS

Acknowledgments

As "No [person] is an island unto itself" neither is a book or a coaching model. Without the insights, assistance, encourage, feedback, challenge, love, faith, and coaching of many people this book would not have been written.

Without the very intimate and personal coaching sessions with our clients and participants in the Meta-Coach trainings we could not have written this book. From those coaching sessions and the thought-provoking questions in trainings we were able to construct *the Axes of Change* model. From these sources also came the many rich personal stories of the people who's searching minds and energy highlight the power of a transformational Coaching Conversation.

While we gathered the stories and transcripts from live coaching sessions, we have changed the names in the following transcripts. We do thank each one for sharing themselves with us and, now in this book, with you.

We wish to thank our *Meta-Coach Collaborative Partners* around the world:
        Anne Renew and Cheryl Lucas, Directors of the Institute of Neuro-Semantics, Africa;
        Denis Bridoux of PGPE, Halifax, England;
        Andrew and Zurina Bryant, Self Leadership International
        Reg Reynolds, Meta-Skills Institute, South Africa;
        Omar Salom, Mexico
        Liz Newman, Acumen, Sydney Australia
        Joseph Scott and Kevin Greenleaves, England

A special thanks also to Sarah McIntyre, Grant Ryan, Rod Power, Sarah Nanclares, Dr. Susie Linder-Pelz, Julianne Johnson, and Carrie Zivetz for their contributions to this book and on-going support.

And a special thanks to *Robert Dilts* for his contributions of chapters 18 and 20 in this book.

FOREWORD

- What is life coaching, executive coaching, personal coaching, business coaching, team coaching, etc.?
- How can something as simple as a coaching conversation make a profound difference, even a transformation in a person's life?
- How does coaching, as a methodology, enhance our skills in communicating as well as facilitate the change process itself?
- Why and how has coaching become a powerful change methodology in business and organizational life?
- What expertise distinguishes an effective coach?

These are but a few of the questions we address in *Coaching Conversations*. Here we do not repeat what you can find in scores of books on Coaching 101. Our focus here is much more focused and practical—it is *to describe how coaching conversations actually work.* Along the way we explore and expose their structure, reproduce transcriptions of actual conversations, and describe how to create profound coaching conversations.

After all, *coaching is preeminently a conversation.* Dialogue lies at its heart. It's an exchange and exploration that gets to the heart of a matter, mirrors current reality in a non-judgmental way, and facilitates the unleashing of hidden potentials—all of which makes transformation possible.

Coaches engage clients in a number of conversations for a variety of purposes. Sometimes the express purpose is to facilitate one's expertise, to set compelling outcomes, and/or to further one's development. The conversation may be to discover talent and resources, it may be to unleash powers that are yet untapped, it may be to fiercely expose interferences to success, or to map a new game plan.

It is precisely because coaching is ultimately a conversation that coaching offers a tool and methodology for all. Whether you are a business owner conversing with clients and team members, a mom or dad sharing your values, someone seeking to support a friend, a colleague encouraging a team member to give it his or her best, a professional lawyer or doctor communicating with clients and patients, or an entrepreneur marketing his or her products and services—it is in and through *conversations* that we seek to accomplish our objectives and bring out the best in others.

Who is this book for?
First and foremost, this book is for *professional coaches.* It is for those who already are professional life , person, executive, or organization coaches and

who want to enhance their professional skills, expand their repertoire of possibilities, and add new models to their understanding and profession.

This book is also for anyone committed to his or her own personal development. It is for anyone who wants some of the most cutting-edge tools for facilitating one's own self-actualization. It is for anyone interested in learning and developing the ability for self-coaching.

It is for anyone interested in learning and using the transformational secrets which masterful coaches use to enrich how they work with others. This includes anyone who must work with and through others—managers, colleagues, business owners, teachers, etc. and when we simply want to have the best skills to powerfully support another—as a lover, a parent, friend, etc.

Coaching for Enhancing Performance
Coaching itself is a *democratic* process for developing, learning, and adding quality to life and business. It's for anyone wanting to improve the quality of life, expand skills, relate more authentically and personally, take performance to higher levels of expertise, and unleash one's highest potentials.

In athletics, world-class coaches call forth the very best in their players to create peak performance. In that context, a coach isn't in the game the way the players are. The coach plays at a different level. The coach's game has a different purpose: to get the very best out of each player and out of the team. It is to facilitate awareness and clarity, to activate the power of talent and potential, to awaken new dreams and visions, and to access needed resources. So it is with any and every coaching conversation.

Coaching as a Conversational Dance
In these pages we compare the coaching conversation to a *dance*. The coach dances with a client to facilitate the unleashing of potentials and the experience of change. The dialogue dance creates motivation and energy in the player or the client. The dance create readiness for change, the power to change, and the leverage for the change. In this dance, new frames of mind are co-created for facilitating that change. The dialogue is a dance around support, celebration, accountability, fun, and actualizing potential. It's a dance for enabling dreams to come true. Do you want to dance?

As a conversational dance, a coach moves in and out of the conversation, listening and questioning, giving and receiving feedback. Sometimes the coach is the awakener and sometimes the explorer who probes the old matrix of frames. Sometimes the coach is the provoker and energizer. Sometimes the coach does the testing and challenging dance while at other times the coach becomes the celebrant and cheerleader to the client's dreams and plans.

In all of this, coaching involves both verbal and non-verbal skills. It involves the verbal skills of talking, exploring, probing, teasing, and setting frames; it also involves listening—active, intense, passionate, and curious listening. In other words, we coach via *the communication arts.*

Coaching via conversation facilitates a positive transformation on the inside as coach and client co-create the experience. This creative process occurs in two stages, first inwardly as a new Inner Game is conceived, and then outwardly, as the new game is given birth in the form of an enhanced performance. It's in and via the *conversation* that this magic occurs. Coaching at its best means having a different kind of conversation—a kind of dialogue that is *not* typical or common at all. In engaging in such conversations, the coach believes in and plays to the client's strengths and resources. This is why the coach will engage in a dialogue about resources, outcomes, intentions, and dreams.

Coaching as a Meta-Game about the Performance Game

We've noted that the coach's place is not at the level of the client's game; that's where the client plays. The coach plays *a higher game.* What is this higher court of play? It is the meta-court of supporting, facilitating, eliciting, provoking, cheerleading, encouraging, and unleashing potential. It is this higher, or *meta,* place where the coach plays to the structure and form of the client's game. This transforms personal, business, and executive coaching.

In this, *the best coaching is always meta-coaching.* In it a coach moves up a level above the content of a problem, issue, dream, belief, etc. creating contexts and situations where the client is able to discover his or her own powers. That's why a coach engages clients in new and different ways through a variety of means.

The meta-coach engages the client through robust conversations that enable the client to speak his or her truth. This truth-speaking is a conversation of discovery wherein a client probes the truths of his or her realities. In such conversations, *transformation* occurs organically as an expression of growth. We are changed by such robust conversations because they heighten transformative resources within us:

- *Mindfulness:* In coaching we develop a higher level awareness of things, the ability to step back and to move up the levels of mind.
- *Being in the present:* In coaching we show up in the now of this moment to be fully present with the person.

- *Passionate intentionality:* Coaching focuses preeminently on what we want and develops a clarity of our outcomes.
- *Informed choices:* Coaching puts us at choice point as we move to the executive level of our mind.
- *Increased ability to act:* Coaching facilitates being proactive and taking the initiative in making things happen in the world.

> In this, *the best coaching is always meta-coaching.* In it a coach moves up a level above the content of a problem, issue, dream, belief, etc. creating contexts and situations where the client is able to discover his or her own powers.

- *Self-celebration, trust, and passion:* Coaching facilitates us becoming more centered in our ownselves, our abilities, values, and visions.
- *Taking charge of our own choices and life:* Coaching encourages a greater sense of self-efficacy.
- *Continuous and accelerated learning:* Coaching is a learning modality for empowering resilience and optimism in an ever-changing world.
- *Peak performances:* Coaching facilitates us actualizing more of our potential so we more fully engage all of our talents and possibilities.

In this book we focus on the kind and quality of conversations that make coaching a truly transformative experience. While the context here centers on the coaching partnership, our aim is to capture the spirit and magic of transformation so you can apply it to any area of business or life.

Coaching Conversations in Two Parts
The first part of this book presents *the framework* for powerful and transformative coaching conversations. Here we will explore the meaning of conversation, the power of questions, the dialogues for meaning, and the matrices of frames in our mind-body system. As the theoretical framework, this provides the overarching frames for change and the levels of change that we move up and down as we coach to both the inner and outer games.

In the second part of the book we take you inside a variety of coaching conversations. In these key transformative conversations you will find scores upon scores of questions that empower a coach to explore, probe, celebrate, discover, and challenge.

What's New and Unique about *Coaching Conversations?*
What's new is that this book uniquely focuses on the *conversations* as the dialogues lying at the heart of coaching. For those who do executive coaching, personal coaching, business and corporate coaching, team coaching, and so on —*Coaching Conversations* establishes the framework of coaching as a linguistic

and relational phenomena that supports the client in mapping and remapping his or her internal matrix of frames that simultaneously evokes new possibilities for a fuller life and effectiveness.

This book also uniquely focuses on *the power of questions* to invite the client to new places for new transformative possibilities. How easy it is to *know* about the power of questions and to have plenty of experience in using them for transformation *and* at the same time to default to giving advice, making suggestions, and using one's expert role to solve client's problems. Yet playing the expert to a client's experience is *not* coaching. That's consulting, mentoring, teaching, and possibly therapy. In the context of coaching, advice-giving actually interferes and prevents the magic known as coaching.

How is "playing the role of an expert" a problem in coaching? It's a problem because *giving advice* interferes with empowering clients accessing their own resources and solving their own problems. Solutions belong in the mind and hands of the client, not the coach. In the long run, giving solutions dis-empowers rather than empowers. It shifts responsibility and accountability for one's life to someone outside. It implies, "Someone else has the answer, I need to find an expert."

Coaching is a twenty-first century methodology for empowering people through profound questions so they can take charge of their own life, take ownership of goals and outcomes as they become fully able to be one's own expert regarding meaning (what things mean), value (what's important), lifestyle (how to live), and empowerment (what skills and aptitudes to develop).

In *Coaching Conversations* you will find the newest cognitive-behavioral change model, *The Axes of Change*. This model will enable you, either as a coach or a person wanting transformation, to understand the change dynamics and to play the various roles of change, from *awakener* to *challenge, prober, provoker, co-creator, actualizer, re-inforcer* and *tester*.

Coaching Conversations uniquely focuses on the *states* that allow us to invent and ask the best kind of questions. Having a list of questions is the first step. Yet without the right attitude, the questions will be felt as false, as mere techniques, and not work. The wrong spirit will dilute the power of transformational questions.

Coaching Conversations puts into your hands hundreds of questions for coaching and invites you into a dozen sample conversations. These conversations invite you right into the coaching encounter and give you a front-row seat to the transformation. With that, you'll be able to model some first-class coaching that you can apply in your personal life, with friends and associates, as a parent, lover, coach, or in your professional life.

But I'm not a Coach . . . Is this Book for Me?
Yes indeed! This book is equally valuable for those interested in coaching as a change process. As such, *Coaching Conversations* offers a fantastic journey into the realm of personal growth and transformation. You will get a sense of what a personal coach does, and how coaching enables one to find his or her passion, refine critical skills, discover one's heart and values, become more strategic and intentional in living life, deal with self-interruptions and interferences from internal dragons, and experience more joy and pleasure.

Coaching Conversations will introduce you to the ways a meta-coach work in supporting, honoring, probing, and exploring the matrix of frames a person lives in. These conversations may even begin the process of self-coaching that will empower you to choose your own games and to develop the skills and qualities that will enable you to win at those games.

Coaching Conversations invites you into a front row seat to observe coaching in the raw—how it works and how it facilitates new game plans. Here you can explore the *outer games* of the things that we do in the world, our action plans, skills, and behaviors and the *inner games.* The coaching model in this book picks up on the metaphor of sports coaching and the pioneering work of Timothy Gallwey in his Inner Game books. It is derived from the *Frame Games* (2000, Hall) model and the books and models resulting from that model. So, if Love is a Game, you will be able to identify the frames or rules that will work best for you and your loved ones. If *Business is a Game,* you can now construct your own matrix of frames that will support your success and productivity.

What Can I Expect in this Book?
First, there is *the framework* for what coaching is and how you can use it as a coach or client, or use it to enrich your communication or management skills. We first focus on the power of questions as the means for coaching. Discover how questions play a formative role in facilitating transformation.

Next, there are examples of numerous kinds of conversations. There we offer a set of exemplary questions and a sample dialogue that takes you on a journey into a coaching experience. Each dialogue ends with a meta-debriefing to highlight the structure of an engaging and life changing conversation.

You will want to read this book at least twice, probably many more times. On your first read, get a sense of the models and how the fierce-probing-to-the-heart-of-things coaching conversations work. Just enjoy as you witness and observe. Then return for a closer reading to understand and comprehend in more depth. We anticipate that you will eventually dog-ear the second part of the book as you use it as a reference tool. You may want to experience the dialogue again and again as you feel the call of hope, vision, and transformation.

As you become your own coach using the models in this book, set yourself tasks for your own development, aim to learn and over-learn the questions, then give yourself lots of practice as you know that great coaching is all about *translating* what you know into actions.

Use this text on coaching to discover your own personal *matrix of frames* and those of others. After all, we were all born into a Matrix—a matrix of mental and emotional frames that we absorbed and inherited from family, school, religion, and culture. Yet that Matrix is mostly invisible to us. Because it is so close and familiar, it seems and feels real and inevitable. We can hardly imagine that it could be otherwise.

Of course, *that* is the illusion. The Matrix is not real. The Matrix is a construct of our own making. We create it by "thinking." We create it by how we use our mind-body-emotion system. It is the construct of all of our belief frames, understanding frames, decision frames, value frames, expectation frames, memory frames, imagination frames, intention frames, etc. And in the coaching conversations that follow, you will find multiple pathways of entering into the Matrix and, in doing that, transforming it. Then as you *wake up* to your Matrix, you can *master* the frames you set and the games you play. We can't tell you how this adventure will end, we can only point you to the door and tell you how it will begin—if you want the dance. Shall we dance?

End Notes:
1. The term *matrix*, as used in this book, refers to *the embedded frames of meaning* that define and govern our sense of reality. In this metaphor, we were born into a Matrix of belief, value, understanding, and decision frames of family, school, religion, race, and culture. As we grew and developed, we created thousands of additional meaning frames. These make up the Matrix of our mind. For more, see *Frame Games* (2000) and *The Matrix Model* (2002).

Chapter 1

THE ART OF COACHING

- What is *coaching* when we apply that term outside the realm of sports?
- What does a coach do, to what end, and why?
- How do the forms of personal, executive, or business coaching work?
- What are the skills involved?
- What is the theoretical framework for *coaching*?

Coaching is about one of the newest developments in the area of accelerated learning, high level enhancement of performance, and personal development. While the field of coaching has been around for three decades, only in the 1990s did it explode into public awareness as *a field for enhanced personal performance* and as a new methodology for coping and managing the acceleration of change in business.

Because central to coaching is having a focused, and sometimes fierce, conversation that leads to transformation, *coaching conversations* summarize the heart and soul of coaching. In this work we will explore how we use language to explore and map our understandings of these processes and how we use them to keep updating our maps against an ever-changing territory. In *Coaching Conversations* you will learn about the many kinds of conversations that are possible, what they are for, and you will even get to listen in to actual coaching conversations.

The bottom-line is that *coaches coach by having the kind of conversations that make a transformative difference in the mind-body-emotion system.* For that reason, our focus here is on those conversations—how they work, what makes them so magical, and how coaches can develop their expertise in facilitating conversations that get to the heart of things.

Coaching—A Sports Metaphor
Pick a sporting game, any game. Tennis, golf, baseball, gymnastics, boxing, soccer, it doesn't matter what you pick. Now see people playing that game,

having fun, developing skills, learning about themselves and others, increasing confidence, winning, losing, refining skills, winning as a team, pulling together for each other, taking their skills to the next level, being coached.

Good. Now with that movie in your mind, zoom in on the last phrase, "being coached." There you go. Now nudge it a little to the right. That's right. Now zoom in to frame just the coach and the team. Good. As you do, notice how the coaching can make all the difference in the world to the team's performance.

> *Coaches coach by having the kind of conversations that make a transformative difference in the mind-body-emotion system.*

When you take a moment to reflect on this, isn't this amazing? The coach isn't out there *on* the field or *on* the court. The coach doesn't actually *do* anything in the game like scoring points when it comes to the actual performance of the game. Instead, the coach works prior to the game, the coach works *about* the game, and by the time of the game the coach shifts to working mostly to support and cheerlead the players and team.

- Given that, how is it that a coach can "make all the difference to the game's success?"
- What does the coach actually do that makes his or her role so crucial?

Because there is someone who understands *structure and form* of the activity over and beyond *the content* and details of what's happening on the court or field, coaching works to enhance those playing. A coach operates to facilitate the ongoing development of the player's skills, states, and performances.

When we consider someone *coaching* an Olympic athlete, we clearly see that a coach does not necessarily have the expertise of that sport. The coach may be far too old to perform at that level! In this, the coach has a different kind of expertise, an expertise *about* the sport, not *of* it. This puts the coach at a meta-position to the player and the game. Top coaches are often not even in the same ballpark when it comes to being able to actually *perform* the skill or expertise.

While my (MH) daughter, Jessica, was involved in gymnastics, I decided to get involved in coaching gymnastics at the local gymnastics center. During that experience, sometimes the boys would challenge me. "Let's see you do it!" On strength moves, I would typically give it a go and still be able to do what I could do in high school, but not on the flexibility moves. The few times I was seduced to do so, I paid for it in sore muscles the next day, and sometimes a bruised ego when my body didn't respond as it did when I did gymnastics in my teens. Yet from a coaching standpoint, I did not even need to do that to coach them in their performance.

Why not? Because being an expert *in* a sport does not guarantee that the expert can coach it. Michael Jordan has clearly demonstrated that for us all. As a player with the Chicago Bears, ** he was world-class. As a coach, well, as a coach, he just didn't have the magic that he had on the court.

What a coach does occurs at a level *higher* to the overt actions in the day of the performance. Because coaching is about an expertise at a higher level to the performance, *it is at the level of structure and process.* The coach has to have expert knowledge about the content. This *about-ness* makes the coach's expertise a *meta*-expertise. Throughout this book, and the series of books on Meta-Coaching, we will use the term *meta*. This term refers to something "above" and "beyond" another thing, something at a "higher" level so that it is about it, that is, in reference to it.

Personal, Business, and Executive Coaching
Today sports coaching is the dominant metaphor for the field of personal and business coaching. In transferring this metaphor to coaching for personal transformation, executive performance, team development, etc., the coach's expertise does not lie in the performance, but in *facilitating the best performance in the client.*

This is what a coach does. He or she empowers the client in such a way that the performer develops new skills, learnings, enjoyment, and expertise. Coaching in all these areas evokes the best in a client, empowers the client to take charge of his or her state, and facilitates generating the highest quality results.

To achieve this, coaching utilizes a special kind of psychology. It does not use the old psychology models which focused on how people are broken and need to be fixed. Not at all. At best, that is remedial psychology and informs how people can be hurt and traumatized and need to be brought up to average. That's psychotherapy, not coaching.

Coaching utilizes *generative* psychology. Rather than healing hurts, or even working on problems, generative psychology focuses on healthy people, people who are already up to average and "okay," and who are ready for a challenge. It's for those who are driven to fully use their knowledge and skills as they seek to actualize their potential. This psychology is about generating new potentials, new resources, and new strengths. Self-actualization psychology is a positive psychology focused on creating the orientation that aims for excellence.

Coaching is "going for the gold" in the client by empowering him or her to actualize their fullest potentials. It is seeking excellent (although not "perfection") in a particular area, health, relationships, career success, parenting, etc. All of this describes the very special kind of coaching that we specialize in when we use the Cognitive-Behavioral and Developmental models.[1]

As such, coaching is a solution-oriented relationship. A meta-coach believes in, and uses, processes that activate the potentials of clients for developing higher level skills and for honing skills for more efficient performances. In coaching, we do not teach, train, consult, counsel, or give advice—we rather facilitate the self-discovery and empowerment of the client.

While this describes coaching, coaching is even more.

- Coaching is about taking what a person already does well to a new level of expertise.
- Coaching is about finding the difference that makes the difference between average and superior performances.
- Coaching is about moving forward through the cultivation of even the smallest refinements.
- Coaching focuses in all areas of skills for performance development: public speaking, negotiating, business acumen, relationship enrichment, health and fitness, teams, etc.
- Coaching is a person-focused conversation about success, development, and excellence in performance that empowers one to move forward.
- Coaching is a catalyst for new ideas, change, and enhanced performance.
- Coaching is transformative learning. It enables a person to create change through learning which then allows one to be more, do more, achieve more, and contribute more.
- Coaching ennobles people as it facilitates them to perform at their best, create and keep their purposes in mind, and develop a dream that becomes their life vision and mission.

How does coaching work? Coaching works by a special form of behavioral feedback. That's why a coach provides *clean and factual* sensory-based feedback thereby allowing a person to see him or herself as if in a mirror. This moves a person to a choice point for adjusting one's inner frames of mind for playing a new inner game and for adjusting behaviors for a new outer game.

Coaching operates by facilitating a very intense and focused conversation—a solution-focused conversation. While this conversation takes place *in the moment,* it has an eye on the future. It is an explorative conversation that is intense, robust, and at times, even fierce. As such, coaching is not for the faint of heart. The conversation seeks to get to the heart of a situation with eyes wide open and necessitates non-judgment awareness in both coach and client.

This robust search for patterns in the client with a non-judgment awareness describes a critical factor that distinguishes coaching from counseling or therapy. *Coaching requires a lot of ego-strength.* Generally people in counseling lack that kind and level of ego-strength; they are there, in fact, to develop sufficient ego-strength to learn to face reality without caving in. It is also the non-judgment awareness of *just witnessing* and cleanly and clearly perceiving what *is* without judgment that allows one to receive feedback. Otherwise it activates one's sense of attack.

Sometimes *coaching* takes a freestyle approach and is like a stream-of-consciousness conversation. Coaching then follows the mental-and-emotional energy wherever the client chooses. It tracks up and down the levels of the mind discovering the matrix of frames that makes up a person's mental-emotional structure.

At other times coaching uses *a process approach* as it invites a client through a specific set of experiences that, like training drills, aim to bring forth a discovery of resources, new insights realizations, and new connections between things that creates a greater sense of alignment and congruency.

Meta-Coaching
In 1972 Tim Gallwey, a tennis coach, began coaching *The Inner Game of Tennis.* It was the mental-emotional game that allowed top athletes to play the outer game more effectively. Gallwey, in fact, pioneered much of the current focus in coaching on the place where the real game occurs—the game inside the player's mind. That is where the outer games are truly won and/or lost.

Later, completely unaware of Gallwey's work, I (MH) developed the *Frame Games* model using Meta-States to articulate a cognitive-behavioral approach to human consciousness and functioning. *Frame games* sorts out the inner and outer games and provides a transformative way to work with a person's inner game or frames of mind. This has led to a series of books and trainings in Neuro-Semantic— *Games Fit and Slim People Play, Games Business Experts Play, Games for Mastering Fear, Games for Building Wealth, Games Great Lovers Play,* etc.

Neuro-Semantics is the cognitive-behavioral model upon which Meta-Coaching is based. This phrase refers to how we humans create *meaning (semantics)* and then encode those meanings into our very neurology and body (*neuro-*) so they become encoded in muscle memory. We then *feel* that meaning in how we breathe, move, act, talk, etc. This translates our inner game of frames so they become "our way of being in the world." Meaning is like that. It's an internal job. Yet because meaning seeks expression, we externalize it. This gives us the definition of Neuro-Semantic as *the performance of meaning.* As a Cognitive-Behavioral / Developmental coaching model, this framework of Meta-Coaching gives a meta-coach a well-tested model.

Meta-Coaching starts from the assumption that people already have within all the potential resources needed. The task of a coach is to *facilitate* the discovery and development which allows a client to sequence and order those resources. In doing so, a client creates better maps and strategies for succeeding. This is the inner game of our frames. In dong this, a meta-coach uses experiential learning processes to awaken each individual to find his or her way of expressing the richest meanings.

> This robust search for patterns in the client with a non-judgment awareness describes a critical factor that distinguishes coaching from counseling or therapy. *Coaching requires a lot of ego-strength.*

Gallwey (2000) defines coaching in this way:

> "Coaching is eavesdropping in on someone's thinking process. The most important part of the job of a coach is to listen well. Effective coaching in the workplace holds a mirror up for clients, so they can see their own *thinking process*. As a coach, I am not listening for the content of what is being said as much as I am listening to the *way* they are thinking, including how their attention is focused and how they define the key elements of the situation." (p. 182)

Meta-coaching uniquely distinguishes structure and content. The *structure* of an experience operates at a meta-level to the *content* of the details of a person's story. Given that it is structure that makes the biggest difference for transformation, this involves how a person thinks, sorts, codes, and perceives as Gallwey (2000) noted:

> "It is essential to the Inner Game of Coaching that the coach try to see from the point of view of the person being coached. By learning to listen to the client non-judgmentally, the coach learns the most important elements of the craft. Learning to ask questions that help clients reveal more and more to themselves is a natural outcome of such listening. The coach's questions are geared to finding out information not for the purpose of recommending solutions, but for the purpose of helping clients think for themselves and find their own solutions. Ideally, the end of every coaching conversation is that the client leaves feeling more capable of mobility." (p. 188)

Coaching Relationships

Effective transformative coaching is based upon the creation and development of an open, trusting, and authentic relationship. It works through mutuality and collaboration, when coach and client work together to co-create a new reality or action plan. Before a person can coach, he or she has to be able to create rapport—a sense of connection. For this reason, an effective coach cannot coach everybody. Just as we cannot influence everybody, win everybody, or persuade everybody, we cannot coach everybody.

That's why finding the right coach is important. Every coach is a fallible human being with strengths and weaknesses. Every coach also has his or her own idiosyncrasies. With these idiosyncrasies and strengths and weaknesses, the most successful coaches know their own, and then play to their strengths. That's also why the most successful coaches are selective in who they coach. After all, they focus on creating a coaching relationship that brings out the best as they facilitate more passion, joy, and vitality in life.

In coaching, as in the other professional domains of development (i.e., training, consulting, counseling, mentoring), *relationship is everything.* It is in and with relationship that a coach probes, explores, detects, reflects, questions, challenges, confronts, and facilitates empowerment.

Summary
- Playing off of sports coaching as a metaphor, *meta-coaching* is about facilitating higher quality performances and experiences in life and business. We do that by working with the structure and process that makes for greater skills and effectiveness.
- *Conversation* lies at the heart and soul of coaching. We converse as we use language, listening, dialoguing, questioning, etc. This means we initiate the kind of conversations that have the potentiality to transform our inner games so that the outer games are enriched and empowered.
- How this happens and the skills involved in making it happen is the subject of the next chapters.

End Notes:
1.   Meta-Coaching and Neuro-Semantics is based upon numerous Cognitive-Behavioral models including Rational-Emotive Therapy (RET, now REBT), Reality Therapy, Control Theory, etc. It is based upon the Communication model of NLP (Neuro-Linguistic Programming), the Ericksonian models of Brief psychotherapy, Solution-focused therapy, and Narrative therapy. It is also based upon the field of LifeSpan or Developmental psychology and the Self-Actualizing psychology developed by the founders and leaders of the Human Potential Movement, Maslow, Rogers, May, Frankl, etc.

PART I:

CONVERSATIONS

AS A

TRANSFORMATIVE

PROCESS

Chapter 2

CONVERSATION

AS TRANSFORMATIVE MAGIC

"Magic is hidden in the language we speak.
The webs that you can tie and untie are at your command
if only you pay attention to what you already have
(language) and the structure of the incantations for growth."
Bandler and Grinder (1975)

"Coaching is a conversation
that opens up new vistas of possibilities,
energies, forces, skills and enjoyment."
Julie Starr, *The Coaching Manual*

Transformation, the power to change form or appearance, is built into both nature and into human nature. In nature we expect transformation, do we not? We anticipate natural changes in the seasons as we expect winter to turn into spring and start looking for buds blossoming, grass growing, and leaves springing forth to fill out the trees.

Similarly we anticipate our own maturing and developing as we see our bodies change in height and shape and our abilities evolve. We see in our development of talking, walking, reading, and writing. Throughout life we continue to change in form and appearance. In this, transformation is programmed into our biology. It's in our very way of being in the world.

Transformation speaks about improvement, higher quality, moving to a higher level, experiencing something more fully and richly, and isn't that what we all want in our life, in our careers, in our health and fitness, and in our loves and relationships? We want positive transformations in how we feel, how we think, how we perform, and in the quality of our perceiving and responding, and in the results that we get.

Transformation moves us to living life at a higher level and experiencing a higher quality. That's why we buy the things we do, that's why we seek better jobs, more career opportunities, why we seek to get or stay in shape, experience richer quality relationships, buy self-help books, continue our education, join a gym, get a personal coach, see a therapist, attend cutting edge trainings, keep up with the latest developments in our field, etc.

- Is transformation truly possible or is it a wisp of a dream?
- What are the processes that create transformation?
- Why intentionally seek transformation?
- What facilitates a rich transformation of mind-and-emotion?
- What are the key variables of quality transformations?
- Who best knows about actualizing human potential?
- What are the processes governing human transformations?
- What models facilitate such transformations?
- What tools and techniques make such transformation possible?
- Is transformation painful or can it be a joy?
- Can transformation actually be fun and exciting?
- Are we made for continuous transformations throughout life?
- Or is transformation the exception to human experience?
- Is transformation only for a select few or is it for everyone?
- What models enable us to tap into the power of transformation?
- How does dialogue facilitate transformation?
- How many kinds of conversations are there?

These are but a few of the questions about transformation to be explored in the coming chapters. Here we will answer some of these questions and let the chapters that follow more fully explicate them within the coaching process.

Is transformation truly possible or is it a wisp of a dream?
Transformation is not only possible, it is built into the very nature of who we are as human beings. We are forever transforming. The entire universe is changing. We live in a world of ongoing process or change. Nothing stands still. All of our beliefs, understandings, values, frames of mind, behaviors, skills, and even ourselves are all subject to the processes of change.

Do you remember what you believed as a child? How many of those beliefs still govern your life? Do you still believe in Father Christmas and the Easter Bunny? Do you still think boys (or girls) have "germs?" Do you read and write no better than you did when you were seven-years old? Is what you valued when you left school the same as what you value today? *Transformation* is the rule, staying the same, or resisting change, or "not changing" is the exception, and mostly an illusion.

Our inner "reality" which we call our subjective experience, and then our outward expression of that reality, are derived from our frames of mind. What we think, perceive, and feel as "real" comes from our mental maps about things. We *frame* reality. This makes transformation part of our very nature. We create our "reality" by receiving and setting frames *and we alter such* as we re-frame, or de-frame, or frame things in a new and different way. This is the way it is with "mind."

To change—all we have to do is alter our frames of mind about meaning (i.e., belief frames, value frames, etc.). *When we alter frames, we change.* It's that easy; it's that profound. To this extent, we are highly malleable. Our "reality" is primarily governed by the things we believe and understand. To quote Paul Watzlawick, it is in this sense that our reality is "an invented reality." We invent it as we grow. We invent it as we map things in our own unique way or we buy into the maps offered to us in our communities as we grow up.

Is transformation truly possible? Of course it is. It is the only thing that's truly possible. Remaining static and unchanged is what is not possible. But positive, enhancing, and empowering transformation—such is not inevitable. We can just as easily change for the worse. That's why being mindful of our frames, and altering them for the best, calls upon us to become more conscious, awake, and intentional.

What Causes Transformation?
If *transformation* is actually the norm, then we will find that there are many things that truly facilitates a rich transformation of mind-and-emotion. Anything that affects our thinking, representing, believing, valuing, understanding, perceiving, remembering, imagining, etc. will influence our transformation or lack thereof. This explains the nature of transformative education. That's why reading can be transformative as can having a robust conversation with a friend, coach, or mentor. It explains why television, movies, books, radio, plays, etc. can be transformative—for the better or for the worse. Any medium of communication transmit information and it is information that *forms* us on the *inside* (i.e., in-forms).

The key variables for *quality* transformations lie in how we *represent* things to ourselves, how we *frame* things, how we *give meaning* to things, our thinking patterns, our style of processing and encoding information, our style for registering that information in our bodies and neurology, and how all of these translate into our behaviors and expressions. These are the key variables. There are others, but the magic mostly arises from these.

What does this mean? It means that the key to the matrix of your mind lies in how we construct meaning. In one of the Neuro-Semantic coaching models, *the Matrix Model* we call this the meaning matrix.[1]   It all begins with what we *reference*—that is, the references of experiences that we pay attention to, and use, as our referent events in interpreting events.   Once we have a referent experience, we represent it in the theater of our mind as we play that event as a mental movie.   Upon doing that, we then edit the movie in how we encode it, linguistically label and categorize it, associate emotional states with it, evaluate it, apply metaphors to it, and set intentions.   In this way we create our meaning structures, *meanings* that transform us.

> To change—all we have to do is alter our frames of mind about meaning (i.e., belief frames, value frames, etc.).   *When we alter frames, we change.*

What does anything *mean* to you?   What does criticism *mean* to you?   Or an "A" on a report card?   Or applause?   Or a pay raise?   Or approval of your peers? It's the meanings and anti-meanings (the meanings that we refuse) that form and construct the Matrix of our mind-body system.   Change these meanings and we change.[2]

*   Why intentionally create transformation?
*   If transformation is the norm and natural, why do we want to interfere to intentionally create change?

These questions highlight a crucial factor about growth and development. Namely, there are many things that can *interfere* with natural ongoing development.   Limiting beliefs, self-doubt, fear, inadequate coping styles, procrastination, over-reliance on others, fear of accepting responsibilities, these and many other factors can, and do, *interfere* with transformation.   Sometimes, *transformation* is as easy as removing the obstacles in the path.   Sometimes by simply clearing the path or *facilitating* the right context, transformation occurs easily and naturally.

What models are there for such transformation?
Numerous models provide us a map for managing change and transformation. There are models that are as old as the Greeks and as new as the neuro-sciences. Some are like Model-Ts in terms of effectiveness.   They will get the job done, but it will take a long time and may involve a hard and unpleasant trip.   Others are more like jet engines that can move us along the pathway of change much quicker.   It is when we know *how* something works in terms of its structure and process that we can make changes in moments, rather than years.

The fact is, we need the right tools and the best techniques if we want to effectively facilitate quality transformations. You can open a can with a knife, even a stone, but the trouble, the work, and the mess are incredible compared to having a can opener. Technology for measuring time greatly improves the accuracy and quickness of sundials, especially on cloudy days or when deep inside the earth. Similarly, *human* technology can provide us a way to more efficiently and enjoyably handle the challenges of transformation in human personality.

Neuro-Semantics is the central model used in Meta-Coaching. This model describes how we encode and frame our understandings which create the semantics, or meanings, that define our sense of reality. From these mental maps we experience corresponding mind-body-emotional states in our neurology. As a unified Cognitive-Behavioral model, Neuro-Semantics integrates the best of developmental psychology and self-actualizing psychology in detailing how we can stop performing unresourceful meanings and how we can *perform* the highest and best of meanings.

Who knows about transformation to actualize human potential?

Is this a strange question? You would think that psychologists would be the people who would know the most about this, yet this is not so. Why not? The reason is that much of psychology has accepted presuppositions and premises that actually undermine the exploration and discovery of many of the most cutting-edge variables in quality transformation of human thinking and feeling.

Yet this is not a new or strange phenomenon. In *The Structure of Scientific Revolutions* (1972) Thomas Kunn told the story of person after person who entered a field from outside and was able to bring about a paradigm shift precisely because the new person to the field could see facets that those inside could not. Those inside suffered paradigm blindness. Often our model of the world actually prevents us from seeing the means and solutions to transform things.

The Swiss actually invented and had all of the technology of the digital watches before anyone else. Yet the Swish watchmakers could not see its value or market appeal. Knowing what was required for a "watch" to be a watch, they became paradigm blind to the possibilities. So it was left to the Japanese watchmakers to win and dominate that market.

The field that deals with how humans can and do change has been dramatically and wonderfully influenced in the twentieth century by people from outside the field of psychology and psychotherapy. Some of those we have relied upon include:
- An engineer, Alfred Korzybski (1933) creator of General Semantics.

- A linguistic, John Grinder (1975) who co-created NLP along with a student of computers and mathematics, Richard Bandler.
- An anthropologist turned cyberneticist, Gregory Bateson (1972, 1979) who explored the structure of mind and consciousness.
- A sports coach, Timothy Gallwey (1972) who wrote *The Inner Game of Tennis*.

These, and many others, have offered tremendous insights in their writings, research, and trainings about how healthy and "fully functioning" people actually change and the transformational variables that make a difference.

Can transformation actually be fun and exciting?

Changing one's mind, emotions, experiences, etc. does not have to be painful. It doesn't have to "tear one up." A person does not have to "go through pain" to gain perspective or new skills anymore than we have to drag a person with a broken leg up a flight of stairs and shoved him down again as if that would undo the broken leg. Repeating a trauma is not the way to cure it. Recapitulating the steps that led to a misfortune or disaster doesn't facilitate recovery, let alone transformation.

This means that we can have fun, even pleasure, in a mind-body-emotion transformation. The degree of hurt, shock, pain, etc. does not guarantee transformation. Transformation can come with an *"Aha!"* with the shout of an "Eureka!" and even with the raised eyebrow that matter-of-factly says, "Got it."

Remedial change is just the beginning. Often we have to first fix or take care of something that has gone wrong. That is one kind of change. Yet beyond remedial change is *generative* change. When the transformation becomes generative we are talking about generating new and exciting forms and expressions for cultivating and nurturing our best, our highest potentials, and yet undreamed of capacities. Generative transformation taps into the levels of mastery and genius.

Change can actually be fun. We can discover models and technologies that allow us to enjoy the process of moving from our current level of security, and even expertise, to ever higher levels. Using cognitive-behavioral framing, we can reframe change so we interpret and experience it as fun and natural. Would you like to do that?

This is one of the unique offerings of meta-coaching. As change agents, meta-coaches are leading the field of coaching in finding ways to make change fun and challenging for those ready for the next step after "okay." Meta-Coaching is for the foremost leaders and experts who are committed to being at their best and pushing the boundaries of what's possible for themselves.

Are we made for continuous transformations throughout life?
Yes, you bet we are! Because human experience is one of continuous development in a process universe, *we are born for continuous transformation.* In other words, transformation is not the exception, it is the rule. It is the nature of life which is always changing. That is why transformation is for everyone, not just a few select persons. It is your nature and mine to move from one level to yet higher levels of experience. We only need to have the mind, the will, and the trust in the process.

Continuous improvement (*kaizen*) was discovered in the last quarter of the twentieth-century as one of the key secrets by business experts. Edwards Deming made it an integral part of Quality Control in business thereby integrating quality into the very process of development rather than an after-thought, as something to check on after its too late to change.

In human experience, *kaizen* refers to continually learning so that ongoing improvements enable us to keep refining our expertise of skills and knowledge. This allows us to become the leaders in a world where change is accelerating and where today's leaders are those who stay one step ahead of the curve. Are you ready for that game? Do you have the frames to play that one?

Can we Talk Ourselves or Others into Transformation?
Yes, indeed. Actually it is through *talk*, through a dialogue, that we primarily change. Conversation with a trusted friend, colleague, or well trained coach is one of the key transformation processes.

It was Sigmund Freud who discovered the power of language itself to affect a transformation in personality. Freud (1939) wrote about that in these classic words which today equally applies to coaching:
> "Words and magic were in the beginning one and the same thing, and even today words retain much of their magical power. By words one of us can give another the greatest happiness or bring about utter despair; by words the teacher imparts his knowledge to his students; by words the orator sweeps his audience with him and determines its judgments and decisions. Words call forth emotions and are universally the means by which we influence our fellow creature. Therefore let us not despise the use of words . . ." (pages 21-22)

This is where the term *dialogue* intriguingly underscores the process. As a term comprised of two words, *logos* and *through* (dia-logue) describes how we move through meaning in the exchanges to find or create the meaning that determines our experience and reality. The frames of meanings show up in the references that we carry in our mind, what we remember, and how we remember. All of this becomes our database for our subsequent thinking, feeling, and responding.

This explains why it is *not what* happens to us that matters most, but *how* we interpret what happens. That's why two people can experience the same event and come away influenced and changed in radically different ways. Do you remember the last time you went to a movie with a friend and your friend had a very different reaction to the movie than you? The event was just the trigger, yet the internal style of how each processed, represented, thought about, and framed the event created each person's inner and outer games.

The *logos* of the meanings attributed, and held in the mind, make up each person's inner world, inner Matrix of frames. Finding these and moving *through* (dia-) them is what we do in a dialogue. We move *into* and *through* the meanings and, in doing so, transformation naturally, easily, and delightfully transpires.

It is not just the talk in conversation that provides a key transformation tool, it is having a special kind of conversational exchange. It is an intentional and directed dialogue that allows a person to move through his or her own meanings and to choose from a higher state of mind new meanings that will empower and enhance behaviors and experiences. We describe this as a *robust* conversation because the dialogue is focused, authentic, real, lively, vital, vigorous, and strong. It exhibits a full-bodied strength that can even be fierce.

A robust dialogue touches the heart and core of things. It gets to the inner truth of our frames and exposes the truths, lies, deceptions, and misunderstandings that we have been living. And when conducted in a context of non-judgmental awareness, the dialogue invites the recipient to a meta-position wherein true choice lies.

Because *meta* refers to a *higher* level, a comment becomes a meta-comment when it comments about a comment. An emotion becomes a meta-emotion when we emote about an emotion, as when we feel happy that we have finally felt bad enough to do something to change things or when we feel excited about a feeling of curiosity. A meta-thought involves thinking about other thoughts. So a meta-state is a state (like fun) about another state (such as learning). This creates a higher and more complex mind-body state, in this case, *joyful* learning which will accelerate our learning.

The Transformative Questions of a Robust Dialogue
To have a truly robust dialogue that gets to the heart of things we have to *be present* in the conversation. This means that we fully show up, accept reality on its terms rather than ours, and use our ego-strength to develop the personal efficacy and competency to use the knowledge gained to make changes. Obviously, having a robust dialogue that cuts through the layers and layers of superficial meanings to finding the frames that are driving an experience and the

over-arching frameworks is not for the faint of heart. It takes a lot of ego-strength.

In business today, leaders who are in the forefront know that getting high quality information from their people is absolutely crucial to stay current with the speed of change. Having entered into the era of the knowledge worker where information, and especially applied practical information, separates those who lead from those who follow or are retired, having a robust dialogue with people is critical. Larry Bossidy and Ram Charan (2002) speak about this in their work on *Execution: The Discipline of Getting Things Done.*

> "You cannot have an execution culture without a robust dialogue—one that brings reality to the surface through openness, candor, and informality. . . . The reason most companies don't face reality very well is that their dialogues are ineffective." (p. 102, 103)

It is robust dialogue that increases our effectiveness in gathering information, understanding what it means, and then shaping our decisions. What does it take to facilitate a robust dialogue whether between friends, between lovers, in a business, or in a group?

1) It takes openness to reality. It takes realizing that we have nothing to fear from information or truth. Whatever *is,* is. Denying it, rejecting it, or pretending that it isn't so will not help things.

2) It takes openness to information. It takes a willingness to be open to learning new things and to changing one's mind. It takes a learning state, a thoughtful non-judgment state to just perceive and witness, the willingness to be wrong and to be corrected. Without these personal attitudes, we will not be truly open, but defensive.

3) It takes openness to candor and informality. It takes an informality and the invitation of candor. Formality suppresses dialogue whereas an informal context invites questions, encourages people to be spontaneous, and to use critical thinking skills for exploring the validity and strength of a position.

It is *the quality* of our dialogue that makes the difference. In a robust dialogue we are not afraid to ask the hard questions, the questions that force us to step out-of-the-box of our current thinking and to challenge the assumptions and presuppositions. It is this kind of dialogue that can actually alter the way we think as well as the capacity of a team for creative thinking.

In this sense, robust dialogue enables us to bring out and express our realities, even when we find it uncomfortable. Robust dialogues are tough and focused, open and inquisitive. We engage in such because we realize that while nobody knows everything, we know more together. The minds of two or more in a robust dialogue can experience an increase in intelligence and wisdom. Such conversations facilitate greater comprehensive understanding of things, especially other people.

Since leaders are the ones who set the tone of any conversation, they will be the ones using dialogue to create the culture in any given group. A leader can do this simply by going first and using robust dialogue to surface realities whether in a friendship, love relationship, or business. As they do they will use their rigor and intensity to explore the depths of the situation. They will flush out assumptions, push for goals being realistic and compelling, and invite the best imaginative and critical skills of their people. They will not be satisfied with "Yes" men.

How many kinds of Conversations are there?
What we have found is that there are a great many kinds of robust conversations that we can use to create these enlivening dialogues that lead to positive and life-enhancing transformations. In fact, we have built the second part of this book around a dozen of these. This provides a coach numerous kinds of conversations for using in the coaching relationship to facilitate growth and development toward greater expertise and mastery. You will witness the transformational magic and simplicity of changing frames of mind.

There are conversations about outcome, intentionality, focus, awareness, meta-levels of the mind, the matrix of one's mind-body-emotion system, adventure and risk taking, seeing and seizing opportunities, clarity of values, meaning, etc. It is typical of effective robust conversations that we become so engaged that we become *absorbed* in a single focus. As a result, the dialogue becomes a "flow" experience. Becoming so engaged, we get lost in the conversation. Then time and space and environment go away, our sense of self goes away as well. Only the conversation remains—the focused engagement of a coach and a client around an area that invites a profound transformation. And that's when the magic happens. That's when the dance of change and rich meaning construction occurs. Are you ready for that dance?

Summary
- Language itself is a powerful tool that influences and affects transformation of our mind-body-emotion states. Dialogue, as a dynamic form of robust conversation *cuts through* the meanings that we operate from and the meanings that we create. This gives us the heart of the human technology for transformation that we call *coaching*.
- Conversation becomes lively and vigorous when we use it to explore the Matrix of our frames. It provides us a way to explore the reality of our thinking and emoting, and to quality control the productivity of our

current frames. Doing that puts us at choice point. Are you ready to step up to that?

• Given that our consciousness is a languaged phenomenon, we can now use the magic of language and the robustness of a focused conversation to re-language ourselves and others as we invite a conversation to generate new creative maps for navigating life, business, and relationships. So, how ready are you for a *coaching conversation*?

End Notes:

1. *Matrix* refers to "a womb," a place where things are given birth, something within which something originates or develops. In mathematics, matrix refers to a rectangular array of mathematical elements as the coefficients of simultaneous linear equations. In Neuro-Semantics, Matrix refers to our mind-body-emotion frames from which our reality and experiences originates.

2. For more on the construction of meaning, see *The Matrix Model* (2003), *Frame Games* (2000), or *Mind-Lines* (2002).

3. The Cognitive Psychology Movement began in 1956 with George Miller's work and his paper, *The Magic Number 7 plus or minus 2.* He then co-authored *The Structure and Plan* (1960) with Karl Pribram and Eugene Gallenter. Another key pioneer was Noam Chomsky and his creation of Transformational Grammar. Howard Gardner was commissioned to write the history on this movement. Cognitive-behavioral psychology emerged at the same time with Aaron Beck, Albert Ellis, William Glasser, and many others. It now leads the field of psychology and psychotherapy in terms of effectiveness in meta-analysis reports of effective modalities.

The Cognitive Revolution in psychology is dated from the work of George Miller, Ulrich Neisser, Bruner, *et al.* in 1956, who established the idea that our internal maps govern our experience. At this time also Chomsky (1957) delivered his death-blow to Skinner's Behaviorism by his analysis of language acquisition and demonstration of the complete inadequacy of the association theories as an explanatory model about "verbal behavior."

Chapter 3

THE MAGICAL POWER

OF *QUESTIONING*

*"Judge a man by his questions
rather than by his answers."*
Voltaire

"The coach's job is to ask questions, not give answers."
Whitworth, et al. *Co-Active Coaching*

*"You can tell whether a man is clever by his answers.
You can tell whether a man is wise by his questions."*
Naguib Mahfouz

"The uncreative mind can spot wrong answers,
but it takes a creative mind to spot wrong questions."
Antony Jay, *Management and Machiavelli*

Asking *the right questions* lies at the heart of a transformative coaching conversation. When we ask the right questions we set a framework that allows discovery, transformation, and empowerment to occur. This power of questioning is a key component in effective coaching.

Through *conversation* we gain entrance into the matrix of a person's "reality" because of the very nature and power of dialogue. In this, it is *conversation that calls the matrix into existence.*

We speak our world (our internal universe or matrix) into being. No wonder language itself plays such a crucial role in our mental-and-emotional

experiences. Language is the primary
mechanism that we use in forming the
matrices of our mind. Yet while language
plays a central role in our conversations, it is
not merely the fact of language, it is *what we
do* with language, with words, and with how
we express our ideas.

> It is *conversation that calls
> the matrix into existence.*

What do we do with language and words in the coaching context? Ideally, we
dialogue. We dialogue by cutting through (*dia*) the meanings (*logos*) encoded
in words to get to the heart of things. In dialoguing with each other, we explore
what each person means and the meanings that we didn't know we meant (e.g.,
our frames by implication). And it is this that enables us to discover the
structuring of our matrix. By our language we explore, share, and/or invent
meanings. In this way our conversations construct our matrix of frames and co-
create those of the person with whom we are in communication.

What is the primary context in which we create our meaning frames? Is it not
in the contexts of *conversations?* Yes, in conversing with each other we invent
the meanings that form the structures of our lives. Are there not many kinds of
conversations? One conversation is the internal conversation which we call
"thinking"—our internal dialogue. It's the conversation we have with ourselves
as we talk to ourselves and reason through something to make sense or make a
decision. Another involves our external conversations. Then there are the
conversations we have with our culture as we receive and interact with the
stories, frames, meanings via the media.

Even today, as we continue to relate and converse with self and others, we
continue to create and re-create our matrix of meanings "one conversation at a
time." In this way we literally *talk our "realities" into being.* Susan Scott
(2002) says we succeed or fail "one conversation at a time." I like that. We call
our Matrix into being one conversation at a time, we load and reload our Matrix
one conversation at a time.

All of this began with the first conversations that we experienced in interaction
with our parents and others. What they said, how they said it, the quality of the
relating that the words elicited, and the states they came from and those induced
in us—these factors critically influenced our first definitions of self, life, and
others. These were the original conversations from which we constructed the
first fabrics of reality in our matrix. Given that, then—

- What was the quality of talk that you received from your parents and
  early home life?
- What is the quality of conversation you engage in today?
- How does it affect the quality of your Matrix?

- What conversations would you like to have to generate new possibilities in your internal universe?
- What conversations would you like to install to influence and govern your internal dialogue?

The Communication *is* the Relationship

There are two words that we banter around without much thought that are important here. These two words are critical for how we create and keep refreshing our Matrix of frames. The two words are "communication" and "relationship." At first glance communication and relationship sound like two very different words describing two very different things. That's the illusion; they are not. It's only a trick of language, it is not the reality.

In reality they refer to the same thing. I noted this in *Communication Magic* (2001). To create a communion between two people, we communicate. Yet how do we create that communion? We do by relating—by the sharing of ideas, emotions, hopes, dreams, fears, joys, etc. In this, the "communication" *is* the "relationship." And, conversely, the quality of the relationships *is* the quality of the communication. We *relate* by how we *communicate* and how we communicate. As we *communicate*, so we *relate*.

Given that the communication we have with each other *is* how we relate (i.e., our "relationship"), and that through relating of ideas and words we create our Matrix one conversation at a time, we can more fully appreciate the magic of *high quality matrix conversations*, can we not?

Once upon a time, it was considered revolutionary for there could be such a thing as "the talking cure." Sigmund Freud was celebrated as a genius for this discovery. Today this is so much a part of our cultural knowledge that we know it almost intuitively. Scott (2002) notes this in these words:
> "Our lives succeed or fail gradually, then suddenly, *one conversation at a time.* While no single conversation is guaranteed to change the trajectory of a business, a career, a marriage, or a life, any single conversation *can.*" (p. 1)

That's the magic, is it not?
> *Any single conversation has the possibility of changing the very direction and trajectory of our lives. It has the potential for changing the meanings of our life.*

Certainly you have had a conversation like that, have you not? Life-changing dialogues typically occur with a therapist, coach, or mentor. Yet it can also occur with a friend or associate who participates in co-creating a new reality with you as you "cut through" with each other the layers of the meanings in both the front and the back of your mind and, in that unlayering, get to the heart or truth of what's most important to you. Because that is where we are able to make new choices, that's the source of the magic. Scott describes this kind of a conversation as a "fierce conversation,"—a robust, intense, powerful, passionate, unbridled, uncurbed, and untamed conversation. That's what makes it especially powerful.

In a robust conversation, we come out from behind ourselves into the dialogue in such a way that we speak authentically from what we are and how we experience things. It is in the coming out that we are invited to create and load our Matrix with a new reality, one with more useful, enhancing, empowering, and magical frames.

> Our lives succeed or fail gradually, then suddenly, *one conversation at a time.*

The Magic of Just Asking Questions

Regarding asking just the right question, Julie Starr says this:

> "The ability to ask fabulous questions consistently is uncommon enough to seem like a rare talent. It's actually a skill that can be developed, with concentration and practice. With coaching, a beautifully timed, perfectly worded question can remove barriers, unlock hidden information and surface potentially life-changing insights. In other words, to be a great coach you need to be able to ask great questions." (*The Coaching Manual*, p. 147)

For years, I've (MH) been searching for and creating lists of *great questions*. What drove this was my desire to develop a repertoire of questions that would *cut right to the heart of a matter* when interviewing, researching, intervening with a client, gathering information, modeling, and coaching.

I learned this from my studies and trainings in NLP. This cognitive model based on Noam Chomsky's work in transformational grammar enables us to ask precise questions for generating communication precision. The set of linguistic distinctions lead to a set of precision questions called *the Meta-Model*. These questions provide a tremendous resource for inviting a person inside the matrix and re-mapping that matrix. It's also a set a questions that can be used for precision in business, for modeling the structure of experience, and for creating therapeutic "magic." So impressed with this I eventually wrote an entire book on that model of precision questions (*Communication Magic,* 2001).[1]

This also describes the very heart of *coaching* as a model for working with people. That's because coaching is not about solving a client's problems or doing therapy, it is about *facilitating* new levels of mindfulness by which a client takes full responsibility for his or her responses. Doing this enables the coach to empower clients to really listen to their inner desires, their heart, and to clarify their desired outcomes, and then to make things happen in the real world.

My (MD) highest intention as a coach is to cut straight to the heart, the truth of my client's reality. By using questions I step inside their internal world to see their experience through their eyes. This lets me lead an exploration to find the *leverage* frames of mind— the frames of mind with the most power in them to create *self-organizing* change. After all, with just the right kinds of questions and enough energy motivation for change, transformation occurs almost magically. This is the power of only asking questions. And in Meta-Coaching, when we only ask questions, we call this "pure coaching."

In modeling some of Michelle's coaching sessions, I have typically counted 100 to 150 questions, and sometimes over 200, during which she will not make any statements.[2] There's a wondrous power in questioning. On the surface, making statements and sharing our brilliant ideas seem more powerful than asking questions. Yet that's the illusion. It may make the speaker feel more powerful, yet it does not do the same for the recipient. And while showing off our knowledge and expertise is seductive, it does not empower the recipient.

Yet when we ask questions, questions that probe and explore an experience, the questions elicit internal responses. It facilitates an active response. The listener goes inside. The listener revisits his or her matrix of references and frames. Frequently this will elicit an original referent experience from which the person mapped something and in questioning the linguistic mappings, it invites the person to re-map more resourcefully. This is "the magic" of the precision questions of the Meta-Model.[1]

Similarly, we have extended this magic by developing many other searching questions in Neuro-Semantics. In fact, we have identified a whole series of *meta-questions* designed for flushing out higher level frames. You will discover these in the next chapter. These meta-stating[3] questions get to the thoughts behind the thoughts, the feelings beyond the feelings, and all of the references that a person uses in filtering and thinking about the immediate experience.

Yet there are many other sets of powerful questions for unveiling the meta-levels of a person's structure of contextual meaning. The list of meta-questions in the next chapter and frame game questions do that. These meta-questions flush out a neuro-semantic network of embedded frames and allows us to get to the heart of a person's truth or reality. The same holds true of fierce conversation questions (also in the next chapter).

Robust conversations of the kind we're describing are actually a collaboration of two people, both signed up to explore the Matrix. A true "fierce conversation" can only occur through the collaboration of the people in it and must be directed to an agreed outcome. In this way there is consent from those in it, given by the nature of the contribution they make to the conversation. One person puts a statement out there . . . and the other responds with a question. I (MD) will pre-frame at the beginning of the coaching relationship that our conversations will be co-created one question at a time and, in this way, both of us will be *making it up* as we go. There is no right or wrong in such conversations. In real time conversations we will follow the energy in our exchange until the desired outcome emerges or until other conversational adventures beckon us.

What is the *Power* of Asking Questions?

There are several *powers* activated in the process of just asking of questions. By asking questions we can explore thoughts and ideas, we can probe feelings and emotions, we can make explicit the structure of an experience, identify the thinking patterns, and discover the referent events and the internal contexts of a person's thinking and feeling. By questions we can facilitate the invitation for a listener to go inside and become reconnected with the referent events from which that person has created the maps that limit and sabotage. By questions, we evoke listeners to become engaged in their own reality, to listen to their own inner voice, and to discover their true heart. By questions we can hold another accountable and elicit an experience of being real with self and other. By questions we can witness another's subjective experiences and behaviors and support that person in discovering or re-discovering the frames that make it so.

Questions are our tool par excellence for entering and exposing the matrix of our frames. What's so empowering about questions arises from how they *engage*. A well designed question can be captivating, compelling, and even spell binding. You have experienced those kinds of questions, haven't you? The kind that cause you to stop, right where you are, and really search inside. They seem to turn our mind inside out. Have you noticed the *engagement power* of questions? Reflect on what the following questions evoke in you, how they work in you, where they send your brain, and which ones invite you into more resourceful states.

On the surface, asking questions may seem to be a neutral thing. Yet it is not. When we ask questions, we create, invite, evoke, or reinforce various *frames by implication*. And when we ask the right questions in the right spirit within the explorative context of coaching, people typically *go inside* their matrix and call forth the belief frames that empower them to transform. This is the magic of questioning.

It's the Questions that Drive us

At the beginning of the Movie, *The Matrix*, Trinity finds Neo in a dark club. He "followed the white rabbit," like Alice did, to find this place. But it's dark and the music is blaring. We only get glimpses of what seems like a subversive sub-terrestrial place. There Trinity approaches and into his ear she whispers,

> "It is the question that drives us, Neo. It is the question that brought you here. You know the question, just as I did. The answer is out there, Neo."

This elicits Neo to pose the question that drove him, "What is the Matrix?" And metaphorically, this is the first question for us all, *What is the matrix?* Yet after that comes even more fascinating questions:

- Is the Matrix I live in enhancing or limiting?
- Does it support my humanity or sabotage my hopes and dreams?
- What do I need to become aware of my matrix?
- How can I learn to master my matrix?
- What is the range of possibilities for designing a new matrix?

The Power of Meta-Questions

If powerful questions of the first level give us with a powerful technology for generative transformation due to how they engage and captivate our mind, doesn't it make sense that meta-questions, at a higher level, will be even more engaging?

- What questions could you ask about the questions you ask that would take your questioning to a new level?
- What are you not asking yourself that would transform your very thinking style and way of being in the world?
- If your life was the answer to a question, then what is the meta-question that you have been trying to answer by your life?
- What one question could you ask your coaching client that would be the most empowering and transformational question possible?
- What would you have to do or experience or feel in order to create that question?

Meta-Questions (questions about our questions) enable us to formulate even better questions and to quality control our questions. Meta-questions invite us into the realm of questions and questioning itself.

Indications that you have Question Power

I love it when I ask someone a question, and the person stops, and says,

> "You know, until you just asked me that question, I have never thought of that!"

This reveals the power of that particular question in that person's life—the power to engage and send his or her brain in a new direction. Questions of that sort is what make transformation possible.

Awareness Questions are those questions which direct us to become aware of something, perhaps just to wake up to live and to experience sensory awareness. Sometimes, however, the question invites us to became aware of the critical variables in a process which allows our natural learning skills to rise to the occasion and make learnings that will lead to new levels of mastery.

This is what Timothy Gallwey discovered from his years of tennis coaching. As a sports coach, he began asking *awareness* questions, questions that simply directed a player's attention to the moment and to the experience. He would ask about the seam of the ball, "Which way the ball is spinning, clockwise or counter-clockwise?" These awareness questions invited the player to enter into a new relationship to the ball. The person would no longer view the ball as a "threat to success" or any other semantically-loaded concept or feeling. Instead it would bring the tennis player into the moment—into viewing the ball *as simply a ball* with certain features and qualities. In *The Inner Game of Tennis*, Gallway describes this as one of the turning points for him in learning how to coach.

The amazing magic of awareness questions is how they invite us into that new relationship to meaning. They do so by inviting us to *suspend* meaning, even if just for a moment, so that we can see, really see, what's happening in the world outside of our mind. Awareness questions invite us to expand our awareness in a non-judgmental way. By them we "lose our mind and come to our senses" in a fresh way.

The Power of Questions
What is the *power* that we feel and experience with questions? How does this *power* influence us?

The heart of this power lies in *the experience of discovery* itself. When a question is asked that engages us, it does its work by evoking in us the process of discovery. As we use our minds and emotions to begin exploring something—and while the final result of discovery is often insight, rejuvenation of our energy, and new processes—the discovery process itself can just as well be one of struggle, frustration, confusion, ambiguity, and fatigue.

It is because of the question that discovery occurs. If the question is a powerful one, it evokes in us a search. It is the question that creates the channel and opportunity for the discovery. Because our brains seem to be answer-seeking and answering computational devices, plant a question and the brain gets activated to find an answer. This is what facilitates a client to become animated and engaged. It also facilitates the *owning* the results. The principle is simple. When we find our own answers, we remember them, we keep them, we feel more committed to them, and we feel more satisfied with those answers. After all, they are our babies. For these reasons, we will be more likely to follow through to implement the discoveries we've made.

Kinds of Questions

As there are many different kinds of questions, there are many different things we can do with questions. Among these are the following:

1) Awareness questions. Questions that open our mind to become aware of what *is* are especially powerful and useful in coaching. Change almost always depends upon developing this kind of awareness. We describe awareness of what *is* as non-judgment awareness. This awareness notices, observes, and witnesses without evaluating, interpreting, or judging. The best kind of questions to elicit this kind of awareness are sensory-based questions and open-ended questions.

> When you begin to feel shy and anxious about meeting new people, how do you breathe? What do you do in terms of your gauge and countenance? Do you look the others in the eye? How steady is your gaze?

2) Gauging questions. Questions that gauge degree, extent, amount, and probability are questions that invite us to make these kinds of distinctions. These questions break up and interrupt either/or questions with their black-and-white answers. These questions recognize that many things (perhaps most things) occur along a continuum as a matter of degree. So we ask,

> To what extent? How much? How does this rate? How does this compare to X?
> How much does that thought or emotion disturb you?
> How much does that feel real to you?
> How much more real would you want it to feel?

3) Designing Questions. There are questions that invite us to construct, engineer, and create. Outcome questions and resource questions perform this function. To answer these questions we have to come up with ideas, hopes, dreams, resources, and construct a vision of life in terms of a preferred future or the resources we need to move there. These engage us so that they set a mapping function in motion within us. We begin to construct life apart from a problem or constraint. And even if we cannot answer the question in this moment, the question continues to engage us in the search for a solution.

> If you develop the skills to transform you life the way you want and follow your passion, what will life be like for you in five years? What

will you be doing and experiencing?

4) Strategy Questions. "How" questions are generally questions of strategy or tactics. They involve exploring the processes involved in accomplishing something. These are typically questions that begin, "How would you . . .?"

> How do you maintain your solution focus when the world's coming down around you?
> How do you know to shift to negotiating at that point?
> If you were to find the courage to explore where you are with Jim in terms of your career path, what personal resources would you do so that you can do so comfortably and effectively?

5) Accessing Questions. Some questions operate in such a way that they seem to access information, experience, feelings, or resources. What they do actually is invoke, excite, or provoke us to do the accessing. Yet the power of these questions is that once accepted, even superficially, they worm their way in and won't leave us alone until we have accessed their target. What are some of these questions?

> How much would you feel really curious if you knew that the curiosity would help create the very resource that you want? If X resulted from that, what would you then do? How does this make you feel?

6) Modeling Questions. The questions that evoke us to look around in our mental world for other examples, templates, or models are especially fascinating in how they work. Frequently when a person comes to the edge of his or her map and doesn't know something, doesn't have a clue about how to do something, a modeling questions loosens the mental blocks.

> Do you know anyone who can do this, can handle criticism without taking it personal? Yes, you do? How does she do that? What must she be thinking or feeling in order to do that? What would it be like if you could be her for a day?

7) Solidifying Questions. While some questions gather information and expand our mental maps, other questions drive a point home, confirm an understanding or feeling, and so solidifies the map that we have built or begun to build. These are especially useful for enabling someone to sustain a new direction, to remember a new insights, and to install a new frame as their frame of mind. In doing this it turns the mere thought into an energized belief.

> How would you sustain this thought or feeling?
> How could you remember X?
> Does that make sense?
> Do you like that?
> Would that support and enhance you as a person?
> So you'd like to keep this one with you?

You'd like to make it yours? Really?

8) Inventive and creative Questions. Some questions put us into a creative mode so that we begin brainstorm ideas, playing with alternative ways of dealing with something, or even thinking outside the box. "What if" questions are like that, so are possibility questions which explore other options. We can also use "suppose" statements and turn them into questions that will also do this.

> What if you had already achieved this goal, what would that do for you?
> What if you viewed this as an opportunity rather than an obstacle, how would that change things for you?
> Suppose you woke up tomorrow and this obstacle was no longer there, what would be different? How would you know? What would be the first sign? What clues would others be able to pick up regarding the difference?
> While I'm not asking you to do this, if it were possible to be straight with your manager, and calmly share with him your ideas, how would that be of any value to you?
> What resourceful states would you need to pull that off?

9) Choice questions. Questions that pose multiple choices and/or that elicit the listener to identify various options can open up possibilities and invite creativity, and give or deepen the sense that a person is not stuck.

> Which of these three ideas do you like best?
> What else would you like to achieve? And what else? And anything else?
> What would you prefer to believe? To say to yourself?
> What lessons would you like to learn from this and take with you for the rest of your life?

10) Emotion questions. There are also questions that explore what we feel and probe the heights and depths of our emotions. These questions enable us to use our body sensations (feelings, kinesthetic states) and our full-fledge emotions, as well as our meta-feelings for exploration in our matrix of frames.

> What is your feeling behind that thought?
> What are the emotions driving that behavior?
> As you just stay with that emotion for a minute, let whatever thoughts and feelings come to mind and as you notice them, what is the taproot of this emotion?
> How much permission to you have in yourself at this moment to feel or experience this emotion?
> How would you prefer to feel about this?

11) Suggestive questions. It is possible to ask a question that is not really a question, but a statement. These can be dangerous and manipulative, *and* they can also be insightful and powerful for establishing a productive direction. As such they make points as much as inquire about things.

> Since "wonderful" is actually made up of thousands of tiny things that come together, what are some of the tiny things that you could begin to count and to appreciate that, when later viewed from another perspective, you might see the whole as more valuable than you ever imagined?

12) Open-ended questions. While some questions search for single answers and "the right answers," you cannot be wrong in answering an open-ended questions. If we ask, "How do you best like to relax that rejuvenates your spirit?" and the person speaks about running, we cannot say, "No, that's wrong, running is active and has nothing to do with relaxing, try again." Open-ended questions invite the respondent to explore within and offer whatever he or she finds there.

> What's happening inside as you hear this?
> What's could you find wonderful about yourself if you allowed yourself to?
> What's the best quality of your compassion?
> Is there anything that's a little bit wonderful that you could value?

13) Frame questions. We can ask questions that flush out the frames that are implied by various thoughts, emotions, memories, and imaginations. We can explore the higher level implicit *frames by implication* above and beyond a given level which support it. These enable us to move up through the labyrinth of the matrix and to identify the frameworks that are either supporting or sabotaging our success.

> What did you learn from that experience?
> What negative lessons did you learn from that, which may have been useful at the time, perhaps as survival lessons, but which no longer support your success?
> Are there any lessons in the back of your mind that need to be unlearned, that when released, will free you for going after your dreams?

14) Self-Organizing questions. In a system of interactive parts, various energies and dynamics can be established so that a facet of the system can govern the operation of the system. When this happens we say that there is "self-organization" occurring within that system. We can even build cybernetic systems that self-organize.

We can set up a feedback loop within non-living, non-sentient materials that self-organize. The simplest example is that of a thermostat in a home. When we set the bias of the thermostat for a particular temperature, the feedback loop of information to the thermostat registers that data and compares it against the bias of the thermostat. If the temperature is within the range, nothing happens. If it is less than the bias set, the thermostat activates the furnace to add warmth to the home. If it is more than the bias, the thermostat activates the air conditioner to cool things. In this, the thermostat operates as a self-organizing influence. It governs the temperature in the home.

In the human mind-body-emotion system, our highest *valued belief frames* function as self-organizing attractors. They move out us into the world seeing, expecting, wanting, feeling, acting, speaking, etc. in terms of the bias that the value sets. If you believe that human nature is evil and that people will trick and deceive you, hurt and manipulate you, that you are powerless against it, and that playing it safe is the best strategy—that frame will self-organize all of your powers of mind-and-body so that it becomes your "reality."

Conversely, if you believe in the goodness of people and value making a difference and enjoying life to the full, that frame will operate as your self-organizing attractor, and make it so for you. Given the presence of self-organization as part of our neuro-semantic nature, we can now ask questions that can become self-organizing attractor frames and powerfully invite clients into a more productive orientation.

> What are your highest intentions and dreams?
>
> If you wanted to live with joy and giving joy as you move through your everyday life at work, with friends, in your health, etc., what would you need to believe that would best support that?
>
> Sounds like being appreciated is really important to you, so I wonder what you best appreciate about yourself? What could you appreciate that you haven't, but if you did, would enable you to make a bigger difference in the lives of others?

Summary

- Questions provide a powerful way to explore, understand, and even construct new realities, new strategies, and new ways of functioning. In this questions are much more powerful that statements that give advice.

- *Questioning is an art.* It involves so much more than just posing a question—it involves the mind-body state of the one asking and the kind of intentions that facilitates the experience.

- What would you have to realize about questions that would excite you to use more questions in your conversations?

End Notes:

1. The Meta-Model will be described more fully in the next chapter. It is essentially a model of 22 linguistic distinctions and 22 sets of questions to elicit high quality information so that statements can be expressed in a fuller and more well-formed way.

2. For see a live "pure" coaching session, see the video-tape of Michelle Duval during the 2005 Meta-Coach Training in the USA, www.nlp-video.com.

3. If a meta-state is a state about another state as playful can be a state about how we experience our curiosity, hence playfully curious, then *meta-stating* is the process of bringing or applying one state to another. When we *meta-state* as a verb, we embed one state inside of a higher state that operates as it's frame.

Chapter 4

QUESTIONING *MODELS*

FOR COACHING POWER

"Those who control language control people's minds.
Sloppy language invites sloppy thought."
George Orwell

"Coaching questions compel attention for an answer,
focus attention for precision
and create a feedback loop.
Instructing does none of these."
John Whitmore

"A prudent question is one-half of wisdom."
Francis Bacon

- If questioning is as powerful as we have suggested, are there models for the questioning art? What are they?
- Are there models that we can use that will empower us in our coaching?

How do we efficiently tease apart *structure* from *content? How* do we find the leverage points in a conversation that leads to change and know precisely when to ask the right kind of question?

If we had a well-formed questioning model, it would give us the technology for achieving all of that and much more. Effective models are created by modeling excellence in any given field. Models make it possible for others to replicate the behaviors and magical strategies of a talented expert. We are able to do just that by putting those distinctions together in *one* framework that can function in many different contexts, which we call a *model*. And there are several powerful questioning models that put into the hands of a coach *profound transformative questions.*

The following models are especially critical for coaching. We will introduce these will be the models and overview them in this chapter.

> The Precision Questions of the Meta-Model
> The Meta-Questions of the Matrix
> The Questions of Appreciative Inquiry
> The Questions for having a Fierce Conversation
> The Questions of the Frame Game model
> The Questions that structure a Well-formed Outcome

The Precision Questions of the Meta-Model

Every time we open our mouth to speak, we articulate some linguistic map about some facet of reality. As we do, we use words to sketch a map about things. Or to shift metaphors, we put into words the screenplay of the movie playing in our mind. As we do so, to some degree the words accurately or inaccurately map things. And the words are comprised of linguistic structures and forms that enable us to remember things that have been, describe things that current are present, or imagine new possibilities. These words are also how we "make sense" of the world.

There is "magic" in such words. That's because the words and linguistic structures are symbols that *stand for* something else. Even when we speak about a dog, something "magical" happens in our minds. We create a movie in our mind of a dog. We may see the dog, hear it bark, feel its coat, smell it or have any combination of these *senses* in our mind. Yet there is no dog in our brain. Nor is there a movie or a movie theater in our brain.

We *represent* the "dog" and we can even make a movie of a brown dog with white spots, a friendly, wanting to lick you in the face dog. How does that happen? How did you just create that movie in your mind? You read these words and ... *presto!* ... suddenly a movie begins.

When we take words and track from them *referent events* and represent them on the theater of our mind, we "make sense" of the symbols. We call this comprehension. Knowing the symbol system of English (or whatever language we speak), we use the words as a screenplay of what to see, hear, feel, smell, and even taste on that inner movie theater. In Meta-Coaching, we call this internal state a *primary state*.

But when our words are vague, when our words are fuzzy and not clear, then we have to invent the rest of the story. For instance, what kind of a dog did you represent? How big is it? What kind of ears does it have? Where did you see it? In your living room, yard, or in a park? Whatever your answer to these questions, your answers make up what *you* invented and hallucinated about the words.

This is where the precision questions of the Meta-Model are profoundly useful. By asking about everything that you cannot literally track from the words to your mental screen in your mind (representational tracking), you are able to hone in on the specific and precise information in the speaker's mind that's crucial to your understanding. All you have to do is to ask about anything that seems fuzzy to you.

The Meta-Model is an exceptional questioning model for coaching fuzzy, ill formed thinking-and-feeling into concrete, clear, focused and well-formed strategies. This model is most useful in coaching outcomes and goal specificity, modifying or changing behavior and for developing skills and strategies.

The Meta-Model sorts the questions out in terms of 22 linguistic distinctions. The first ones are obvious and natural; you already have your intuitions trained to inquire about them. The higher ones are less obvious and are more likely to seduce us to project our own ideas and understandings. This is where the precision questions helps us to *not* do that, but to inquire and to meet another person at his or her model of the world instead of our own.[1]

Figure 4:1

Questions for Precision

Linguistic Distinction	*Description*	*Question for Precision*
1. Simple Deletions	Deleting or leaving out information	What specifically? Who specifically?
2. Comparative Superlative Deletions	Comparisons left out	Better than who or what? Faster in what way?
3. Fuzzy Nouns Verbs (unspecified references)	Details about subject and actions left out.	Which man? How did he reject him?
4. Unspecified Adverbs	Descriptive details left out.	How or in what way did that happen?
5. Unspecified Adjectives	Descriptive details left out.	What is that like?
6. Universal	Things describes in	Always? Never?

Quantifiers	universal terms: all, never, always.	Has there never be a time when X?
7. Modal Operators	Mode of operational *modus operandi* must, have to, get to, can, can't, want to, etc.	Do you have to? Who says you must? What if you didn't? Are you truly able?
8. Lost Performatives	Evaluative statements mapped by unknown person.	Who says that? Where did you get that idea?
9. Nominali- zations	Actions frozen in time as if it a static thing.	What is the action within X? If I were to see Y, what would I see?
10. Mind- Reading	Knowledge asserted about another's thoughts, feelings, motives without stating how one knows such.	How do you know? Did the person actually say that?
11. Cause- Effect	Causation statements of relations between events, stimulus-response beliefs	What causes X? Does X always make Y? What else contributes to Y?
12. Complex Equivalences	Equating an external action with an internal state.	Does X always equal Y? Does X only equal Y?
13. Presupposit- ions	Assumptions about things not expressed.	What are you assuming as true without questioning?
14. Over/Under Defined Terms	Terms that we over-define in terms of concepts and under-define in terms of empirical evidence.	What does X look like in real life actions and behaviors?
15. Delusional Verbal Splits	Words that split interactive facets of a system.	How can you have "mind" apart without body?
16. Either-or Phrases	Phrases that map things as in an either-or choice.	Does it have to be this *or* that? Is X ever *both* X and Y?
17. Multi- Ordinality:	Words we can use reflexively on them- selves	Can you *love* love? Could you be *afraid* of fear? Is there science of science?
18. Static Words	Processes that have been frozen into a	What is the action or process that you are referring to?

global label.

19. Pseudo-Words:	Words that commit linguistic fraud due to having no actual or logical referents.	Is X even a real word? What does it refer to in nature or in logic?
20. Identification:	Over-identifying with something in treating it as always the same.	So he *is* a X and that's all? Is Y just a trait or quality or action of X?
21. Personalizing	Interpreting actions and words of others as one's own reality or problem.	Is this really about you? How are you identifying with this experience or these words?
22. Metaphors	Talking about one thing in terms of another.	What is X like? What does Y remind you of?

The Linguistic Distinctions and Precision Questions

Deletions:
1. Simple Deletions:
"They don't listen to me."
Who specifically doesn't listen to you?

2. Comparative and Superlative Deletions:
"She's a better person."
Better than whom? Better at what? Compared to whom, what? Given what criteria?

3. Unspecified References:
"I am uncomfortable."
In what way are you uncomfortable?
"He said that she was mean."
Who said that? In what way is she mean?

4. Unspecified Adverbs:
"Surprisingly, my top salesman lied about his drinking."
What surprised you about that?
"She slowly started to choke up.."
How do you know she started to choke up in a slow manner?

5. Unspecified Adjectives:
> "I don't like unclear people."
>> *What were they unclear about? In what way where they unclear?*

Generalizations:

6. Universal Quantifiers: generalizations that use "all" terms which exclude exceptions.
> "She never listens to me."
>> *Never? She has never so much as listen to you even a little?*

7. Modal Operators: operational modes of being, modus operandi.
> "I have to take care of her."
>> *What would happen if you didn't? You have to or else what?*

8. Lost Performatives: Evaluative statements mapped by someone unknown.
> "It's bad to be inconsistent."
> *Who evaluates it as bad? According to what standard?*

9. Nominalizations: processes and actions turned into "nouns" as if a static things.
> "Let's improve our communication."
> *Whose communicating do you mean? How would you like to communicate?*

10. Mind-Reading: claiming knowledge about another's internal thoughts, feelings, motives without identifying how you know such.
> "She doesn't like me."
> *How do you know she don't like you? What evidence leads you to believe that?*

11. Cause-Effect: causation statements of relations between events, stimulus-response beliefs.
> "You make me angry."
> *How does my behavior cause you to feel anger?*

12. Complex Equivalences: equating an external action with an internal state.
> "Her yelling means she doesn't like me."
> *So you equate her yelling as not liking you? Does yellow always mean that to you?*

13. Presuppositions: silent assumptions.
> "If my husband knew how much I suffered, he wouldn't do that."
> *Does your husband hold the same values that you do about suffering? Does he have the same beliefs about what constitutes suffering and its*

degree?

14. Over/Under Defined Terms:
"When we married, I thought he was a good husband.
In your view, what behaviors make a good husband? Is this term under-defined in specifics in the real world and over-defined in ideals in your mind?

15. Delusional Verbal Splits:
"You don't understand! I suffer from clinical depression and it has nothing to do with my thoughts."
Are you saying your "mind" is separate from your "body?"

16. Either-or Phrases:
"We can only either succeed in this endeavor or fail, so let's go for it!"
You have no other alternative except success or failure? Can you imagine anything in between those two choices?

17. Multi-Ordinality: words that we can reflexively refer to themselves.
"I just love. It's my nature?"
At what level are you referring to "love?"

18. Static Words:
"Science says that..."
> *What science specifically?*
> *Science according to whose model or theory?   Science at what time?*

19. Pseudo-words: words that have no actual or logical referents.
"My biggest fear is that I might become a failure."
What do you mean by "failure"

20. Identification: eliminating differences and identifying with something in a way that treats it as always the same.
"I'm not a good learner."
Are you more than or different from the skills that you bring and apply to learning something?

21. Personalizing:
"His little digs in the meeting push my buttons. I hate that."
Are you personalizing his actions and words? How are you bringing what he does out there so that they enter into your inner world of thoughts and emotions?

22. Metaphors:
> "I felt as lost as Hansel and Grettle in the woods and my path back seems as no more secure as bread crums in a woods."
> *How does this story relate to the point you want to make?*

The Meta-Questions of the Matrix

All levels in our mind are made up of the same "stuff" that governs the *primary level*: thoughts, feelings, and physiology. We *use* our see-hear-feel representations and words to build up meanings at the meta-levels to create the matrices of our mind. The following set of questions in various categories offer lots of ways to explore and elicit these higher level structures in the mind. These are *meta-states* because they are states about our states. As you use these, remember the different categories are *not* different things—just other ways of expressing the same thing, different ways of expressing the meta-frame.

Meta-frames arise as we construct layers of meanings by how we think-and-feel about things. This is an active process even though the words we use words *freeze* that action. We call these frozen words, "nominalizations." The problem with these is that by naming (nominalizing) verbs and actions, they start to seem like nouns (persons, places, things—actual *things*). In this way we stop seeing the *action* and we begin to hallucinate "concepts."

Over the centuries, we have invented all kinds of terms and "concepts" to describe our layers of thoughts-and-feelings about things. We create these *layers* of thoughts and feelings as we reflexively think-and-feel about our thoughts. The terms that we use to describe these complex layered thoughts include such everyday terms as beliefs, values, decisions, models, expectations, identification, understandings, etc.

Now the trick is to realize that these terms are *frames* (mental contexts for our thinking and feeling) and that every one of these terms refer to the same thing —the experience. Each offers a view from a different perspective. This means that every frame that we layer contains within it *every one of these categories*.

Each layer of thinking-and-feeling about an idea is simply our way of framing or categorizing experience. This creates lots of confusion about the higher levels of our minds. When we nominalize (or name) these categories, "Beliefs," "Values," etc. we actually mis-cue our mind-body system so that we begin to think of these layers as *actual* "things" and as *different* things. Yet they are not. All of these words are expressions of various *mental processes*—the framings that we do which create our neuro-semantic reality or matrix.

Meta-Questions are to a Developmental and Transformational coach what a paint brush and canvas are to an artist. Artfully designed, these questions invite our clients to *step-back* from their internal and external experiences to explore the meanings they have in "the back" of their mind and the effectiveness of those meanings in achieving desired experiences or outcomes.

Meta-Questions are used purposefully to awaken a client to the highest visions and intentions, probe and tease out empowering and limiting frames of mind, provoke to find leverage for change and co-create transformation through building empowering new frames of mind.

Think of the following questions as 26 ways to move around the *diamond of consciousness* and see, hear, feel and explore the many *facets* of perception and focus. These *facets of focus* give us multiple ways into the Matrix of our mind. So if you use one word or term and it doesn't elicit more information, then use another. When we coach to the matrix, we use many questions in each of these categtories. In a later chapter we have lots of specific examples. This introduces the set of *meta-questions.*

    1. Meanings:
        The ideas that we hold in mind.
    2. Beliefs:
        The ideas that we affirm, validate, and confirm.
    3. Frames:
        The ideas that we use to set frame of reference, structures of context in our mind.
    4. Generalizations:
        The ideas that we draw as summary conclusions about things, ideas we have about other ideas.
    5. Realizations:
        The ideas we develop as new insights, understandings, and even eureka experience. (Denis Bridoux)
    6. Permissions:
        The ideas that we allow and permit which open up new possibilities from old taboos.
    7. Feelings:
        The emotional ideas and feeling judgments that we bring to other ideas.
    8. Appreciation:
        The ideas of appreciation or value that we use to frame other ideas.
    9. Value / Importance:
        The ideas that we value, treat as important and significant, esteem.
    10. Interest:
        The ideas of fascination, curiosity, interest, etc. that we bring to other ideas.
    11. Decision / Choice / Will:
        The ideas that we separate and "cut off" (cision) from other ideas or choices so that we say *Yes* to some and *No* to others.
    12. Intention / Want / Desire / Strategy:
        The ideas you have about your motive, intent, desire, wants.

13. *Outcome / Goal:*

> The ideas we have about goals, outcomes, desired ends.

14. *Expectation / Anticipation:*

> The ideas we have about what we anticipate will happen

15. *Connection:*

> The ideas we have about our connection with other ideas, experiences, and people.

16. *Causation:*

> The ideas we have about cause, influence, contributing factors, what makes things happen, etc.

17. *Culture:*

> The ideas we have about our cultural identity, definition of reality, and cultural ideas.

18. *Presupposition / Assumption / Implication:*

> The ideas that we use as higher frames that reflect our assumptive world and understandings.

19. *History / Memory / Referent:*

> The ideas that we bring with us about previous experiences and use as our "referential index" for making-meaning.

20. *Rules / Demands / Shoulds / Musts / Authorize:*

> The ideas that we use that set up the Rules of the Games that we play out in our lives, the modal operators that generate our *modus operandi* (MO) in the world.

21. *Definition / Language / Class / Categorizes:*

> The ideas that we have that set the frames and categories for our minds.

22. *Understanding / Know / Knowledge:*

> The ideas you have that "stand" "under" you as the mental support for your world.

23. *Identity / Identify / Self / Self-definition:*

> The ideas we build up about our "self," the ideas we use in self-defining.

24. *Paradigm / Model / Map / Schema:*

> The ideas we have that come together as more complex mappings about things.

25. *Metaphor / Symbol / Poem / Story:*

> The ideas that we form through stories, analogies, and non-linguistic forms.

26. *Principle / Concept / Abstraction:*

> The ideas that we treat as guidelines, laws, settled conclusions.

The Questions of Appreciative Inquiry

One change management approach that developed in the field of business during the 1990s is known as *Appreciative Inquiry*. Rather than approaching things from a problem-based orientation, it uses two powerful states or approaches—appreciation and inquiry. It uses these states as a new approach for leading change. Appreciative inquiry is the cooperative search for *the best* in people, organizations, and the world. It's a systematic discovery of the very things that give a system life and heart and is most effective in terms of economics, ecology, and human well-being. To do that, *appreciative inquiry* involves the art and practice of asking questions that strengthen a system's capacity for higher quality performance. By appreciation we seek to mobilize the imagination and creativity of people

Appreciative Inquiry is based upon several empowering beliefs about people, systems, and business. What are the key beliefs or premises this approach?

> Human systems grow toward what they persistently focus on, and focus is governed by the questions we ask.
> A solution-oriented approach focuses on resources and on making a positive difference as it aims to create what we believe is possible.
> The seeds of change are implicit in the very first questions we ask.
> Questions set the stage for what we find and discover.
> Inquiry itself is an agent of change.
> Questions can elicit new possibilities, hope, and inspiration.
> Words create worlds.
> Deficit language and vocabularies are often the source of our problems.
> People and organizations are mysteries to be embrace**d**.
> Sharing best practices, magic moments, and life endowing experiences enables us to grow toward these things.
> Appreciative stories give us wings for flying.
> Inquiry is intervention.

Appreciative inquiry sets up a new game, *the game of evoking appreciative states*. We play the game with language as we ask about and evoke appreciation about the best of what is, envisioning what might be, and dialoguing about how to make that happen.

Appreciative Inquiry Questions:

> What are some of the high-point experiences you've had in this organization?
> What was it like when you are most alive and engaged in what you do?
> Without being modest, what do you most value about yourself, your work, your company?
> What are the core factors that give life to this business, without which the business would not be the same?
> What three wishes do you have to enhance the health and vitality of your organization?
> What are some of the magic moments you've experienced in life?

From such questions, the *appreciative inquiry* approach enables us to create a narrative-rich culture in a business, family, or even personal life. It uses storytelling as a way of setting new and more exciting frames.

The Questions of the Frame Games Model

In *the Frame Game model,* a "frame" refers to the mental context we use to represent our thoughts. It is how we mentally frame thoughts. A frame may be a belief frame, an understanding frame, a value frame, or a frame of expectation, intention, etc. A *game* refers to how we express ourselves as we interact with others and the world, how we talk, act, relate, behave, feel, etc. The questions that follow are those that first diagnose a toxic game and then those that engineer a new game.

Diagnosing a Toxic Game
Game identification:

        What's the game?

        How would you describe the game that's being played out in terms of how you think, feel, act, and talk?

        What's the script of the game?

        What sub-games are part of it all and that make it operate as it does?

The cues and clues of the game:

        What are some of the cues (i.e., linguistic, physical, environmental, etc.) that indicate the presence of a game?

        How do you know? What cues you?

Players:

        Who plays the game? With whom?

        Who else has games going on?

        What's the larger social system of the game?

Hooks (triggers and baits that recruit one to the game):

        What hooks you into the game?

        How does the game hook others to play?

        How are you recruited to play? What gets to you?

Emotional intensity of the game:

        How intense from 0 to 10 is the game?

        Are there any somatic responses or symptoms?

Rules of the game:

        How is the game set up?

        How do you play?

        What commands or orders are in the rules?

        What taboos and prohibitions are involved in the rules?

Quality control:

        Do you like this game?

        Is the game limiting or sabotaging to your effectiveness?

        Are you ready to transform it?

        Does it serve you in a positive way at all?

The agenda of the game:
> What's the intention, motivation, or payoff of the game? What's the payoff?

Name the game:
> What's the name of this game?

The style of the game?
> What is your frame of mind or style of thinking as you play the game?
> What attitude drives the game?
> What meta-program distinction influence the style of the game?[1]
>> ___ Matching / Mismatching
>> ___ Reactive/ Thoughtful
>> ___ Fast/ Slow
>> ___ Aggressive/ Passive/Assertive
>> ___ Rigid / Flexible
>> ___ Options/ Procedures
>> ___ Self / Other
>> ___ Global / Specific

Leverage points in the game:
> Where is the leverage in this game that allows you to interrupt it or stop it altogether?
> Where is there leverage to change or transform the game?

Design Engineering a New Frame Game
Preferred game:
> What game would you rather play?

Target of the new game:
> In addition to yourself, who else do you want to influence in playing this new game?
> Who else will be involved or affected?

The agendas and motivations of the new game:
> What concerns the players most?
> What values will drive and inspire the players?
> What's really important to the persons involved?
> What will hook the players into the game?
> What vested interests will they have?

The new game's larger systems:
> What's the larger social system of the new game?
> Who else is involved?

The objective and outcome of the new game:
> What do you want in this?
> What do you want for the others?

Description of the new game:

> How will the new game be played out?
> What frames will be involved?
> How will the new game be played?

Leverage points:
> Where is the leverage to influence or to set it up and install the new game?
> What frames will best leverage yourself and others in it?

The process for installing the new game:
> How can you set up these frames?
> How can you implement the persuasion process?

Check list the stages of the new game:
> Will you need to interrupt, shift, loosen, and/or transform the frames?
> Which patterns or techniques would provide the most leverage?

Patterns for installing the new game:
> Which neuro-semantic patterns could you use to install the new frame games in yourself?
> What other patterns could you use?
> What frame of mind do you need in order to play the name game?

The Questions for a Well-Formed Outcome

The primary role of an effective coach is to facilitate individuals moving from where they currently are to achieving their desired outcome. Yet how do we know when our clients have achieved their outcomes? How do we know what our client *really* wants from the coaching? How do we know when to stop the coaching? How do we influence our client to be excited, self-motivated to do their tasks on time, and to be enthusiastic even when it gets tough?

A well-formed outcome designed at the beginning of the coaching relationship is the critical key to outstanding coaching. It not only gives you and your client the evidence procedure for achieving outcomes, it also creates a self-motivating push away from what is not wanted, and an energetic inspiring pull towards a most compelling vision of the future.

While we will later explore the Well-Formed Outcome Conversation in detail (Chapter 10), the following questions elicit a compelling well-formed outcome.
> Where are you now? (Present State)
> Where do you want to be? (Desired State)
> What do you want to experience in that desired state?
> What do you want to positively achieve or experience?
> What are you going toward?
> What will you see, hear, feel, etc., when you have it?
> What steps or stages are involved in reaching this outcome?
> Have you used all of your senses in this description?
> Where, when, how, with whom, etc. will you get this outcome?

In what context or contexts is this outcome appropriate?
What are the most fitting and appropriate contexts for this outcome?
What are the steps involved in reaching this goal?
What are the stages involved?
Is this goal chunk down into small enough bits so that you feel that each piece is actionable, that is, something you can *do*?
Does the size of this outcome seem overwhelming to you?
Is the outcome something that you can initiate yourself and maintain?
Do you have it within your power and ability to reach this goal?
Can you initiate the actions to get started?
Can you maintain the actions or are they dependent upon what someone else needs to do?
What resources will you need in order to get this outcome?
Who will you have to become?
Who else has achieved this outcome?
Have you ever had or done this before?
Do you know anyone who has?
What prevents you from moving toward it and attaining it now?
How will you know that your outcome has been realized?
What will let you know that you have attained that desired state?
How do you know when to exit? When are you there?
When will you feel satisfied?
Is the outcome compelling?
Does it pull on you?
Will it get you up out of bed in the morning?
How much do you want this?
How much do you feel this as compelling (from 0 to 10)?
How much do you need this to feel motivating?
What do you need to do to make it more sparkling for you?
What would make this really sparkle?
Is the desired outcome ecological?
What will you gain through it?
What will you lose?
Is it achievable?
Does it respect your health, relationships, etc.?
Are there any parts of you that object to actualizing this desired outcome?

Summary

- If questions drive coaching, then *high quality questions* drive *high quality coaching*. It is the quality of our questions that enable us to coach so we get to the heart of matters and invite the listener into a new reality.
- There are numerous models for questioning, in this chapter we introduced several of them. From the precision questions of the Meta-Model that allow us to index specific details to the Meta-Questions that enable us to open up a matrix of frames of embedded beliefs, questions best lead the internal journey.

End Notes:

1. Meta-Programs refer to perceptual filters, the thinking lens that filter how we process and input information. For more about meta-programs, see *Figuring Out People* (1999) or the Meta-Program Board Game, *Meta-Detective.*

Chapter 5

THE ATTITUDE AND SPIRIT

FOR

QUESTIONING EXCELLENCE

"While the techniques of these wizards are different,
they share one thing:
they introduce changes in their clients' models
which allow their clients more options in their behavior.
What we see is that each of these wizards has a map or model
for changing their clients' model of the world,
i.e. a meta-model
which allows them to effectively expand and enrich
their clients' model in some way
that makes the clients' lives richer
and more worth living."
The Structure of Magic (1975, p. 18)

"I remember that when we started to talk you asked me a lot
of questions and that got me thinking. It gave me the feeling
that you were really interested. Guess that's why I felt so
free to open up to you."
J.K., Business Owner, reflecting on a Coaching Session

Asking questions is one thing.
Asking empowering questions that lead to robust conversations which
become dialogues for cutting through surface layers to the inner reality
of a situation and getting to the heart of things, and creating
transformation—that is an entirely different thing.

What makes the difference? How do we explain the difference? What
transforms a question that simply asks a question, or worse, that uses a question

as a technique or gimmick? What transforms a question so it suddenly takes us into a person's inner reality and opens up his or her matrix of frames to both our gaze and the person's?

The difference is attitude or state—our state of mind-and-emotion as questioner. The difference is our frame of mind and attitude in relationship with the client, an attitude that makes it safe to go there, that makes it fascinating to go there, that makes it exciting to make the journey, and that makes the encounter an experience that we jointly co-create.

In the final analysis, it takes a very special *attitude* to ask such questions. This is a non-trivial matter. While it seems like anyone could ask profound, getting-to-the-heart-of-the-matter questions, that's not strictly true. Questions do not work apart from the questioner and the context of the relationship. Actually, it is *the relationship* that drives the question and the power of questioning.

This is not an unknown factor. A moment's reflection reminds us that the power of questions does not lie merely in the fact of questioning. A person could question using the most empowering questions, yet if he does so with the manner of a district attorney—drilling, demanding, and forcing or with an arrogance know-it-all attitude, he will get an entirely different result from the one who asks with curiosity and compassion. Or if she questions with a lethargic and bored tone and demeanor, the question will not elicit the magic that occurs when asked with genuine interest, respect, and love.

In communication research and theory, we know the importance of gaining rapport, attentively listening, being present to the other, and of relating in a personal way. These qualitative factors introduce the importance and critical factors of context, style, and heart. In coaching, these qualitative factors are *the critical variables* that make the difference between success and failure, effectiveness and non-effectiveness.

One of my (MD) Executive Coaching clients, Jeremey, recalled his experience of going back to the workplace using the same questions which I had asked him during his coaching session that day.

> "When you ask me questions I feel myself getting really curious and excited about finding my answers. I get so curious that I just *have* to answer them—for myself. But when I tried the very same questions that opened me up with my team, they crossed their arms and just stared at me blankly! I couldn't get them to answer them. They went no where. I couldn't believe it! What's your magic, what else are you doing when you ask coaching questions?"

The Magical Attitude
Knowing that the power of questioning arises from the combination of engaging, probing, and eliciting questions *and* the right attitude that create rapport, trust, interest, engagement, care, heart, and even love, we need to know two things. First, we need to know the specific variables that make up that attitude. Second, we need to know how to cultivate it in ourselves.
*   What is the best attitude for questioning as a coach?
*   What are the factors or variables that make our attitude magical?
*   How can we cultivate those qualities in our own skills of questioning?

A Curious Fascination
It all begins with a simple attitude of curiosity. You can remember those times when you have been super-curious about something, can't you? When has there been a time when you were completely engaged, on the edge of your seat, hungry to explore, to prob and to discover new things? Remember feeling that anticipation and expectation that something extraordinary was about to occur, so much so that you turn up all yours senses just to make sure you don't miss a thing.

Curiosity is the open-minded attitude of wonder. We know that when we have the attitude that arises from, and expresses, *the questioning state,* it makes for an incredibly powerful experience for both coach and client.

Opposite to that attitude is the one that arises when we seem tired and bored with life, with ourselves, and/or with others. Such an attitude can grow from deadening of dreams and visions, from assuming a know-it-all attitude, from over playing the expert role, from the need to be right and never wrong, from failing to nurture passion in other parts of life, from the lack of exercise, from the lack of reading and exploration, and from other life-deadening choices.

The occupational hazard of developing expertise in a field frequently leads people to become non-curious as their *modus operandi*. Perhaps they think that the more they can parade their expertise and play *the Expert*, the more they'll be respected, acknowledged, and rewarded. The problem is that the know-it-all non-curious state dulls creativity and deadens the passionate state that calls forth life in others. To the extent that it comes across as arrogance, it puts others off.

Curiosity enables us to deliver powerful questions because our fascination with the client, with the client's world, with the possibilities before him or her, and with the wonder at what will emerge in the process infuses *life* and *energy* and *vitality* into the questioning. We ask on the edge of our seat. We ask with a glimmer in our eye. We ask with a holy wonder that's ready to be surprised at any moment. This questioning spirit par excellence marks top coaches.

The Know-Nothing State
When we are curious in a simple child-like way, we ask the best questions. Just pretend for a moment that you are a child again, that you have yet to fill your mind with all the knowledge you now possess. How did you know what to ask and when? Didn't you just ask questions about whatever you didn't know? Wasn't it that simple? Plus, you didn't care what people thought of your questions. And why not? Because people expected you to ask questions. And you, in turn, expected they would want to answer them, did you not?

Sometimes we don't have a clue as to where we come up with our questions. They are just there as the natural and organic thing to say. Because of the innocence of the state and the honesty of our curiosity, we get by asking them. To ask them without that state makes them seem like a gimmick. It's our authenticity that makes them real. It's authentically wanting to understand that enables us to probe our client's reality.

Among the best questioning for gathering high quality information and exploring the matrix of a person's frames is the *know-nothing state.* Along with curiosity, this state enables us to ask the most innocent, naive, and dumb questions.
- What is this?
- Is that what you *really* want?
- Do you hear what you're saying?
- How will that affect your vision and dream?
- Who says you have to do it this way?
- Where did you get these ideas?

The detective Columbo on the TV series is the epitome of asking know-nothing questions. These questions allow him to probe into the murder mystery cases and to get through barriers that stopped others. He used the persona of his wrinkled overcoat, scuffy hair, two day-old beared, and seeming incompetence to distract the murderers from considering him a threat or danger. He appeared as "out-of-it" and therefore harmless. Yet his wondering know-nothing questions would get through the rehearsed lies to probe to the truth.

Asking from the know-nothing state enables us to put aside our assumptions, blinding paradigms, self-fulfilling beliefs, and deluding filters so that we can freshly think outside of the box. It's a strategy for creativity that enables us to facilitate a new kind of thinking, different from the kind of thinking that created any given situation or problem.

Honoring the Sacred in the Client
How privileged do you feel to sit at the feet of people each day and have them unveil their greatest dreams and most secret desires to you? How special is this

relationship as you hear the most hidden fears of people, and that which holds them back from being their most magnificent selves? How do you think and feel about this honor, this privilege?

When at our best, we ask our questions driven by our curious fascination and know-nothing innocency as we bring a sense of awe and honor to our client's situation. With respect and an expectation of moving into *mystery* itself—into the mystery of another person's mind-and-heart-and soul. We move forward with our questions that honor that which is sacred in the client.

Because so many people (perhaps most people) do not stand in awe or honor their own selves, there's a fear and even dread of exploring inside. Rather than esteeming and valuing themselves, they have an internal critic that's ready to insult, discount, disparage, judge, condemn, contempt, and shame themselves at any moment for a wide range of mistakes or imperfections. With an internal critic like that, no wonder they don't want to engage in any kind of self-reflection. It's too dangerous—too threatening, too painful.

This challenges a coach in initiating the process by bringing a non-judgmental awareness to the client that can counter-act the poisonous bite of the critic. As a coach, we need to totally believe in the inner dignity and sacredness of each person, esteem and value the mystery and possibility in every client, and able to distinguish person from behavior. Only in this way can we bring a sense of awe and honor to the client in the face of failures, errors, and mess ups.

Doing this gives the client a taste and experience of how he or she can take a kinder and gentler approach to him or herself. It models a gracious respect for oneself. On this very factor turns a critical variable in asking questions. If our questions contain even the slightest sense of judgment, they will not only *not* perform their magic. Instead our questioning will shut the client down.

When our questions come from the higher frames of respect for a client as a person and honor for that which is uniquely sacred in the person's life, we can ask the most pointed questions that deal with hurts and failures *and* the client will feel supported. It's essential that we convey our belief in the other's potential and possibilities rather than quote that as a theoretical idea. We live it as a felt reality and convey it in our tone and look.

The Hutzpa to Boldly Ask What No One Has Asked Before
Add these qualities together. Add curious fascination, know-nothing state, and honor of the sacred in the client that enables us to ask bold and daring questions. Now bake them in the oven of human passion and compassion. Then you will be able to courageously face what the client may not have been able to face, and to "hold" it *and* the person so that he or she can begin to take the first glimpses.

Graham Richardson, an Executive Meta-Coach in Sydney Australia, calls this *ruthless compassion*. This means being loving and caring enough with a person to ask the questions that get to the truth and the heart of things without flinching. Then the truths of a situation can be faced and mastered.

This facilitates in a client the development of the ego-strength to face reality on its own terms. Doing this develops the courage and willingness to ask anything and everything critical to understanding or changing an experience. In this, our questions and questioning will become fierce in the sense that it will be real, even vigorously real. We will robustly not avoid the very issues that have to be addressed as we provoke the person to higher levels of success.

Where does such boldness come from? How do we develop such courage? First from the realization that we grow, stretch, and become capable of evolving to the next level when we face reality and encounter its truth. It comes from the realization that the client, and all of his or her life, has conspired mostly to defend against truth, yet such protection cuddles and weakens one's resolve and personal strength. It dis-empowers.

Transformation for vitality in life comes from having faced such truths in our own life through fierce conversations which discover the white-hot center of some truth. Only in that way do we discover that it is in facing what we have avoided that allows transformation to occur. It is in continual robust conversations that we come to know the power and transformation of such.

Being Totally Present in the Moment
Another empowering attitude when questioning is being *totally present with a client*. Being fully in the moment with a client is a rare and unprecedented gift, a wonderful gift. The intensity of a mind which is totally focused on coaching the best resources for a person is not something that can easily be ignored. Such engagement invites a corresponding engagement.

As a species who can live in the matrix of *time* (as a concept), we can engage in "time" travel with such ease and speed that we can be gone in an instant. We can, and do, travel to past experiences and memories and we can, and do, travel to future worlds. We use memory for one and imagination for the other. In both we travel to, and get lost in, our mental movies that only exist in the mind, and not in reality.

In reality, we only have *this moment*. There is none other. It is in this moment that we time-travel to other places and times. Of course, when we do, we are no longer here. We are no longer present. No longer available. It is a demanding skill to come out from behind ourselves, and to be in this moment, yet one that develops with practice.

Similarly, we need to raise our appreciation of the critical importance of questioning. *Questions coach.* By questions we invite and facilitate experiences in ourselves and others. Questions teach, train, influence, and provoke. By questions we are more fully

> Only in that way do we discover that it is in facing what we have avoided that allows transformation to occur.

able to guide the process rather than the content. It allows us to empower our clients to supply the content.

Summary

- The key variables that make up a powerful questioning attitude include a curious fascination, a know-nothing innocence, a willingness to discover, an honoring of the sacred, the hutzpa to boldly ask what no one has asked before, being totally present in the moment, and truly caring for the client.

- *At the heart of coaching is questioning.* A coach who doesn't know the magical power of questioning has not yet entered this field, but is still giving advice, consulting, training, doing therapy, or entertaining.

- To develop a questioning attitude, first set that as your goal and then access each of the critical states as the space you come from. Then monitor your progress as you ask questions and notice the responses that you get.

Chapter 6

MIRRORING

AS THE BASIC COACHING SKILL

"Iron sharpens iron,
and one man sharpens another.
As in water face answers to face,
So the mind of man reflects the man."
Proverbs 27:17, 19

"The first act of courage
is to see things as they are.
No excuses, no explanations,
no illusions of wishful progress."
Peter Block, Management Expert

"Lose your mind and come to your senses."
Fritz Perls, Gestalt Therapy

- Is there *a mirror* for our mind and heart?
- If we wanted a human mirror so that we could see ourselves more clearly, where would we go for that mirror?
- How do coaches provide a mirror for clients?
- How can we make sure that the mirror we present is clean, accurate, and useful, rather than like a distorted mirror from a circus sideshow?

Why do you look into the mirror in your bathroom each morning? Is it not to watch the process and the effects as you sahve or put on your make-up? Is it not to compare your intentions with your results? Is it to see that you are not leaving your home with something sticking to your face?

What if you were able to look into a mirror that would reflect more— that would show you a reflection of your actions and behaviors, of your attitudes and presence? What if you could see yourself as others see you? What would seeing yourself in this way open up for you?

The Magic of Mirroring

We have all had conversations with close friends that allowed us to see ourselves, perhaps for the first time, clearly and without pretense, have we not? Such conversations are usually rare and special events . . . and scary. Yet we have had them. They often occur late at night, sometimes in the wee morning hours, perhaps with a friend we haven't seen in a long time, as a way of catching up and renewing old friendship, or when life isn't working in a certain way, and even at times after we've had a few too many drinks.

It is then that we find ourselves relaxing, dropping our guard, and sharing our heart—and experiencing our friend simply reflecting back what he or she hears with curiosity and interest. It's in those moments that sometimes we catch a glimpse of ourselves in the mirror of the other's eyes, mind, words, and heart.

This is where and how we can experience *a human mirror*. The mirror for our soul—our inner heart and mind and values and hopes and dreams—occurs in the presence of a non-judgmental friend or associate who engages us in the conversation without any agenda of his or her own. There's no agenda except to *be*, to share, to disclose, to discover.

For the professional coach, *a mirroring conversation* has so many of the features and components of a mirror.
- Non-judgmental acceptance
- No agenda except to see what *is,* to be and to experience
- A safe environment and context
- Relaxation and the dropping of one's guard
- A willingness to be truthful to what *is* rather than trying to impress

Mirroring Tools

The mirroring conversation plays a critical role in coaching precisely because it is through mirroring back that we give our clients a safe sense of themselves, their lives, their heart and soul. This offers a rare and unprecedented opportunity for most of us. Few of our associates, loved ones, family, or friends can do this for us. They're too involved, too emotionally invested, too over-identified.

To accurately *reflect back* as a coach to a client without judgment, without an agenda, and without evaluations either good or bad, we have to move into a know-nothing state. Only then can we "lose our mind and come to our senses" sufficiently so that we can operate in the see-hear-feel world of *sensory acuity*. To become and experience sensory awareness is to momentarily leave the world of evaluations, judgments, understandings, meanings, knowledge, and assumptions, and to return to the innocence of experiencing through only seeing, hearing, and feeling.

This is much easier to describe than to do. Only through mindful and rigorous practice can we become skillful in sensory acuity. Yet for a coach, it provides one of the most powerful and one of the most fundamental skills that allow us to use the more advanced skills. Without sensory acuity, we are meeting our coaching client *at our model of the world* rather than his or hers.

This is the danger and problem with most coaching, counseling, consulting, and other forms of helping. Instead of truly and accurately hearing and seeing a person *on their own terms*—we encounter them through our filters. We encounter them through our belief frames, expectation frames, value frames, history, understandings, emotions, prejudices, etc. It is this "mind," the higher mind of all our frames, that we have to lose in order to come to our senses. When we do that, we can then begin to use our higher mind. But until we experience a client on his or her terms, in the light of the client's frames—we are really not dealing with that person for his or herself.

This speaks about *the contamination* of communication. We contaminate our communications with our frames. We see and hear people through the lenses of *our* history, fears, desires, outcomes, identity, etc. Our coaching clients need us for this reason—the people in their lives *cannot* see them as they *are,* but through their love and hopes, their histories and expectations, as well as their assumptions, angers, fears, etc.

Non-Judgmental Awareness

As a coach we actually have a great advantage in *not knowing* our client. This does not say it is best to coach people we do not know, only that it gives us a fresh advantage that all of their friends, associates, colleagues, lovers, employers, employees, and peers do not have. They *know* them. At least they *think* they know them. They have built belief maps bout them that now color their perceptions. We don't. We can curiously explore afresh with respect, honoring their uniqueness, and asking the most obvious and dumb questions and then, through the use of non-judgmental awareness, simply *reflect back* what we hear. This describes the mirroring conversation.

Accepting a person on his or her own terms is the prerequisite for this. We take their words and gestures and body language and begin by assuming that it all makes sense to the person. We then begin to explore *how* it makes sense. By acknowledging the person as unique and as having the absolute right to forge his or her own way through life—we bring a respect and honor that makes it safe for the person to *be* and to *become.*

This also is a rare and unprecedented encounter. Typically, our friends and loved ones cannot do this. They care too much. They also are too quick with evaluations and judgments. Because of their own investments, they are too ready to frame as good or bad, right or wrong, and so they don't make it safe for the client to just *be*. And without that, they cannot feel safe to *become*.

Non-judgment awareness brings us back to the empirical world and sensory awareness. Timothy Gallwey, first a tennis coach and then an executive coach, discovered quite by accident that if he asked his clients to just watch the ball, to watch the seams of the tennis ball as it came to them, to observe the trajectory of the ball, the ball once again became a ball. Prior to that the ball was "a challenge," "a threat," "the possibility of embarrassment," "a make or break event." Seeing the ball in those ways semantically over-loaded the ball so that they could not see the ball. Not really. Judgments, evaluations, fears, worries, angers, self-contempt and a thousand other concepts clouded their minds, and so blinded their vision. These negative states activated dragons within.

Non-judgmental awareness allows us to *see again and afresh* at the primary level of what we see, hear and do with a heightened sense of sensory awareness. This bring a new focus and relaxation. Without the judgment or agenda, the negative emotions of fear, anger, dread, etc. melt away. This releases the interference and allows more resourceful states to arise: playfulness, interest, curiosity, wonder, learning, engagement, fascination, etc.

Megan, a Senior Executive, experienced the power of sensory acuity after being coached by Michelle on her presentation skills.

> "That is so true, I do breathe in sharply and play with my fingernails just before I go to speak to my team. When I do speak to them, my voice raises in volume and I don't look anybody in the eye. Do you know I have had people try to tell me this many times over the last six years, but all I heard from them were judgments that I was 'not good at speaking to groups,' that I 'looked nervous,' and 'sounded as though I did not trust myself.' I had no idea what I was *actually doing* that put that across. Now, finally, I get it! Thank you so much!"

In the coaching relationship with Megan, Michelle pointed out only what she *saw* and *heard* regarding what Megan was actually *doing* at the primary level. She gave her the kind of neutral feedback similar to what a video recording would have recorded of her speaking with her team. Michelle specifically mirrored back to Megan her actions and behaviors that interfered with her best performance. Megan immediately identified the key elements and easily changed her voice tone, her hand movements, and was able to make eye contact with her audiences.

Levels of Awareness

Because the mirroring conversation involves sensory awareness we have to *recognize and distinguish between the levels of awareness* to develop this state as a skill and tool for coaching.

The first level of awareness is the most natural because it is the level of awareness we were born with. This is the primary state of seeing and seeing, hearing and hearing, feeling and feeling, smelling and smelling, and tasting and tasting. It's a pure and innocent state—one that we see in babies and small children. They don't "know" what to put their hands, fingers, toes, and bodies in or what to avoid, so they explore everything. In socializing them, we teach them what smells and tastes "bad," what to avoid touching, rubbing on themselves, etc. They are just seeing, just hearing, just smelling—just in sensory awareness. They have awareness without any judgment.

When we develop opinions, ideas, associations, learnings, etc. we develop a higher level of mind. Now we have thoughts and feelings *about* the first level thoughts and feelings. By so moving to a higher or *meta* level, we have moved to a meta-state (a state about a state). This represents a higher level of awareness that's directed at our state (and so it is an inward focus) rather than an empirical sensory focus. For example *loving learning* is a meta-state of love *about* learning. *Fear of rejection* is a meta-stated fear *about* being rejected.

The ability to distinguish between primary awareness and meta-awareness is critical for coaching. It's critical for being able to conduct any of the coaching conversations. This distinction enables us to know whether to go inward to work on the inner game or to stay outside and work on the outer game with a client. How do we make this distinction? The most fundamental questions for making it are these:

* What is the client referring to?
* Is it something "out there?"
* Or is it something "in here?"

Mirroring Via Feedback

In mirroring back the raw data to a client regarding what we see and hear we activate the skill of giving feedback. At first glance most people assume that "giving feedback" is simple and obvious. It is not. In fact, it is perhaps the most challenging coaching skill of all.

If that statement seems preposterous and an overstatement, then consider what true *mirroring feedback* is and is not. It is *not* evaluations or judgments. It is *not* opinions, intuitions, or mind-reading. It is definitely *not* emotions or feelings.

Mirroring feedback is reflecting back to a client *cleanly* the empirical data of the stimuli they actually offered—the raw data of what you saw, heard, felt, and smelled sensory awareness. To do that we have to cleanly discern the difference between what we actually experienced in sensory awareness and how we interpreted, evaluated, and judged such. This is not an easy discernment to make.

Why not? Because *we live most of our life inside our own matrix of mental frames, interpretations, evaluations, values, beliefs, etc.* How does that influence our feedback? It influences everything because our matrix colors the world we see and experience. We see the world and others through the lenses of our meanings, beliefs, and mental frames.

Giving feedback is *not* offering our evaluations, interpretations, or meanings about things. When we cheer our client on about a success, that's not feedback, it is our evaluation of approval and so it operates as reinforcement. When we disapprove, ignore, or judge, that's not feedback, it's our evaluation of dislike, disagreement, or disapproval and may operate as negative reinforcement.

The difference is the difference of "logical levels." *Feedback occurs at the primary level of experience.* When we give feedback, we give back to the client see-hear-feel data similar to the feedback we get from the mirror in our bathroom. It's *clean* data in that sense.

Evaluation, judgment, interpretation, and meaning occur at meta-levels of experience. It's not that these are bad. Sometimes, even in coaching, we offer these in supporting and empowering a client. But when we do, we recognize that we are not giving feedback, we are doing something very different from feedback. We are *leading* a client from our model or matrix of the world.

Coaching the Mirroring Conversation

To coach a mirroring conversation we must first create and establish an atmosphere of *safety* so that primary level "truth" can be spoken. Without safety, the mirroring process will feel threatening, even insulting and attacking to a client. Safety is our first emotional need. John Burton (2003) speaks of this using Maslow's hierarchy list of needs in his work on *States of Equilibrium.*[1] Throughout that work, he focuses on the conditioning process that leads to meta-stating any state with fear so that a person learns to fear his or her states.

> "Safety acts as a sentinel for all other procedures. Applying this priority of safety to any and all states, we find that safety is the critical criterion we must satisfy in order to utilize any given state. *If* we believe a given state becomes *unsafe* while utilizing it, we then disconnect from that state." (p. 51, italics added)

> "Once determining a state or states to be safe, she will then move on to

accepting these states and forming a more comfortable relationship within. She reclaims any formerly rejected states, and a deeper understanding of self happens as she gains full self-acceptance . .." (p. 52)

After we have established a safe atmosphere for ourselves and a client, then we need to *the courage to speak* what we see. In this, the coaching situation differs radically from the typical conversations that we have in "polite society." There we do not say what we see.

> *Feedback occurs at the primary level of experience.*

There we use the social graces to be cordial, polite, and respectful. There we do not utter reality or truth as it appears—instead we say what is prescribed to say, what is expected that we say, what is politically correct and safe to say. There we speak to please, yet in that pleasing our speech becomes shallow and superficial.

The mirroring conversation in coaching seeks a higher authenticity—an authenticity that seeks to get to the heart of things, identify key issues and concerns, and use feedback for accelerating learning and transformation. All of this takes courage. It can be quite demanding. It demands that as a coach we face our own fears about confrontation, conflict, and intensity. It demands that the coach face beliefs and feelings about criticism, rejection, and displeasing. Yet if, as we mirror, we respect, honor, and believe in the highest good and development of a client, then the mirroring feedback offers a way for the person to jet propel him or herself into higher levels of achievement, performance, and being. That is the intent and goal.

The Magic of Robust Conversations

Robust dialogues are not for the faint of heart. It takes a lot of ego-strength to dance with that level of self-awareness, self-acceptance, and self-responsibility. The majority of people fear reality in the raw, and so avoid it. They think of it as they would of handling lightning —explosive, hot, and dangerous. They fear what they will find within. And from that fear they quickly jump to judge it and to judge anything regarding it which they dislike. Meta-stating such self-fear stops us from engaging in the adventure of entering the Matrix in the first place.

That's why we prepare ourselves and others on entering the matrix by reminding ourselves and the other person that, "It is just frames" and that "there is no spoon."

> "There's nothing to be afraid of. Whatever we think-and-feel is a function of our frames, and *we are more than our frames*. It's all our mapping, and the map is not the territory. *The person is never the problem, the frame is always the problem.* Our matrix at any given

moment is only as good as its frames. It only works as well as those frames work to empower us and accurately direct us in navigating life. And awareness invites us into the process of learning to master our matrix."

Once we know this, we can enter the matrix and elicit the kind of robust or fierce dialogues that allow us to master our matrix. The principle is this:

> The matrix *has* you and will have you until you develop the mindfulness to engage it, to know that it is yours, and to have an intense and passionate conversation about the frames of your matrix.

The adventure begins with frame awareness. From there we move into frame exploration which allows us to interrogate the frames, challenge them, provoke them, set new and more empowering frames, and thereby transform our matrix of frames. We call this process and what it does to us, *becoming the master of our matrix.*

What conversations do we create, and engage in, with our fierce conversations? There are several. We will highlight them in the coming chapters. In all of them, we engage in conversations that interrogate reality. In these we probe the reality of things and seek to describe reality so simply and compellingly so the "truth" becomes inevitable. We engage in awareness conversations; we engage in strategy conversations, and transformative conversations.

Summary

- While *mirroring* is one of the most basic coaching skills and is fairly simple to explain, understand, and see—typically, it is not a natural or common skill.

> Whatever we think-and-feel is a function of our frames, and *we are more than our frames.* It's all our mapping, and the map is not the territory. *The person is never the problem, the frame is always the problem.*

- Effective mirroring in coaching necessitates a non-judgmental attitude and the advanced ability to pace, create rapport, and create a safe environment for exploring the inner and outer games.

- Mirroring is demanding to the extent that it challenges the coach to step out of oneself, to get the ego out of the way, and to be fully *present* to and for the client.

- From mirroring we can then engage in a robust and even fierce conversation that makes for positive transformations.

End Notes:

1.   John Burton (2003) *States of Equilibrium* uniquely combines NLP, cognitive psychology, and Meta-States with developmental psychology. He synthesizes many other models in psychology. Maslow's hierarchy moves from the lower primary states of safety and security, and then love and belonging, to the higher meta-states: esteem, cognitive, aesthetic, self-actualization.

Chapter 7

INVITATION TO
EXPERIENCE

*"You don't need to take drugs to hallucinate;
improper language can fill your world with problems
and spooks of many kinds."*
Robert A. Wilson

"The limits of my language are the limits of my world."
Wittgenstein (1922)

*"Language is what bewitches,
but language is what we must remain within
in order to cure the bewitchment."*
Henry Staten (1984, 91)

Why do we ask questions?
While we can ask questions for gathering information, discovering current understandings, and exploring preferred futures, there is yet another reason—and a much more important reason. Above and beyond these reasons, we ask questions *to initiate experience.*

Experience—living through a situation or event and participating in something—experience is that which enables us to feel alive, to be touched, to think, reflect, and know something from the inside. It also facilitates a special kind of "knowing." Experience is the kind of *knowing* that makes something truly ours. We coach by questioning for the purpose of inviting people into *the experience of life and emotion.*

Why? Because the occupational hazard of learning is that we only learn *about* things, and fill our heads with lots of good and useful ideas without developing the experiential knowledge that can transfer from brain to body, from mind to muscle. It's precisely that kind of knowledge that creates the Knowing-Doing Gap in the first place wherein we *know* much more than what we *do*. Yet this undermines skill, performance, success, and most important—passionate engagement in life itself.

So we ask questions. We engage the client's mind-and-emotions so that the new knowings and learnings do not just fill up their heads, but also touch and activate their bodies and emotions. This makes the learnings *neuro*-semantic (mind-body) in nature. In this way we commission our neurology to feel the ideas that rattle around in our heads. We ask questions that grab our clients by the lapels to use their inner powers to make adjustments, refinements, or transformations within their own matrix of frames.

While we typically use questions to elicit information, that's really of secondary importance to *experience*. The information is not for the coach to use as much as it is for the client to focus on and to use to facilitate transformation.

The Magic of "Experience" via Questions
Because questions *engage* us, they invite us into experience—into thinking, feeling, wondering, remembering, imagining. Some questions will engage by provoking and irritating. They get a hold of us in a way that elicits the emotions that warn us of potential threat or danger. Other questions seduce and tempt. They allure us into inviting preferred futures, dreams, hopes, anticipations. They engage our positive emotions and fire up our passions so that we become more alive, so that we wake up to life.

Even the exploring questions that seek for information, if they are open-ended enough and evocative enough, send us inside our stored memories. There we pull out the old video arcades of past events and experiences and step back into them, re-experiencing them anew. Then we can invite to experiences also by suggesting such things as:
* Be with that emotion.
* Bring that picture closer/ farther away.
* Welcome that feeling in, breathe it in.
* Do you need to take counsel from this feeling? No? Then release it.
* Allow yourself to just notice X.
* Because there are two kinds of tears, those of sadness and those of joy, it's critical to not confuse the two, is it not?
* Maybe you can Y.
* Close your eyes and let your future glow and feel inviting.

Emotions—the Pathway to Reality
In inviting clients into *experiential life and passion*, we ask questions not only about what they think, understand, value, identify with, expect, etc. (all of the meta-questions that send them upwards), but we also ask a different set of questions. We ask questions that engage and ground our clients in their present state. We do this by asking questions about how they feel in their body and emotions.

We experience the phenomenon of *emotion* whenever there is a sufficient *difference* between map and territory (or more accurately, between our mental constructions and our experience of the territory).

- *"Map"* is one thing. It's our framing and interpreting of what we think is "out there" and how we represent it, understand it, value it, and frame it. "Map" summarizes all of our ideas, beliefs, myths, paradigms, etc.

- *Experience of the Territory* is an entirely different thing. It's the *interface* in our body of how the world out there impinges on our senses. As we input the things we see, hear, and feel from out there and as we receive the actions of the world, this experience of the territory either fits or doesn't fit with our map.

Figure 7:1
Emotions Zone

Extremely High

                              Positive Emotions

High

- -

Middle   *Comfort Zone*

- -

Low

Extremely Low

If it precisely fits with the map, and there's no difference between our mapping of things and our experiencing of the territory that we've mapped, then there is really little to no "emotion." We feel that things are matter-of-fact and not emotional at all. We register things as "normal," "as expected," "just as I thought," and so no motion is generated within. That's why we do not *move out* (ex-movere). If we were to diagram emotions as positive and negative energy from high to low, then these emotions about normality would be right in the middle—in the middle of our comfort zone.

When we feel that we are *getting more* than we had mapped, or feeling delight about getting what we had mapped, our emotions tip the scale upwards so that we feel positively charged. That's when we feel good. And the more the scale tips upward, the more positive we feel. When we move beyond the normal range of positive feelings, and way beyond what's common for us, we may even feel ecstatic.

When we feel that we are *not getting* what we had mapped and wanted, we feel another emotion, one that has a negative charge to it. We don't feel good. In fact, we feel bad. We feel miserable, frustrated, scared, or angry. We feel terrible and wish we could die or wish we could make someone or something else die!

We can compare this up and down nature of our "positive" and "negative" emotions to the up-and-down movement of a scale. On one side is our *mapping* and on the other side is our *experiencing of the territory*. As we receive in experience the things of value in our map, the experience side of the scale tips *up*. We feel "positive" as if things are going well, going great. Our map of the world is being validated, confirmed, supported.

When we do not receive the things of importance, the *experience* side of the scale goes *down*. We feel "negative." We register the sense that things are not going well, but going bad. We feel threatened, endangered. Our map of the world is not working, it is being dis-validated, dis-confirmed, negated, and we feel confused, disoriented and stressed. "Positive" and "negative" emotions are only positive and negative in the relative sense of fitting or not fitting with our map, validating or dis-validating our mental mapping of things.

Let me use another metaphor. These experiences are similar to the brakes and accelerator in a car. The accelerator pedal provides us *energy to go*—to move forward toward our goals, to keep going, to propel ourselves forward. The brake pedal provides us a counter-energy, an energy that restrains the vehicle, that slows it down, that brings it to a stop, that halts our progress.

In moving or not moving forward toward our destination, the accelerator operates as a "positive" influence or energy and the brakes as a "negative." We don't get anywhere by riding the brakes. The person who rides the brakes *and* uses the accelerator will only create counter-productive wear and tear on the engine. That's not the way to travel the highway of life.

Yet as we need both the accelerator and the brakes to navigate the highways of life safely, so we need both the positive and negative emotions. We need the confirming and validating positive emotions of joy, love, hope, desire, compassion, excitement, acceptance, appreciation, courage, confidence, etc. These provide the energy that gets us going to take effective action. We also need the dis-conforming and dis-validating emotions that signal for us to slow down, to be alert to potential dangers, to stop completely to avoid an imminent threat, and to navigate curves and slopes.

Because emotions are just *signals* about *the difference* between our map and our experience of the territory, they are neither right or wrong, good or bad. They are neither moral or immoral. That's why we have no need to fear or dread them, hate or dislike them, judge or condemn them. Instead, there is every reason to accept and appreciate them, to stand in awe of them, and to fully explore and enjoy them. Is that a new perspective or what?

> *Because emotions are just signals about the difference between our map and our experience of the territory, they are neither right or wrong, good or bad. That's why we have every reason to accept and appreciate them, to stand in awe of them, and to fully explore and enjoy them.*

We can now feel really positive about the most negative of our emotions. We can rejoice and celebrate our angers, dreads, fears, sadness, disappointment, frustrations, stress, hatreds, etc. These are not "bad" things— just *signals of difference.*

As signals of difference, emotions give us an entry point into our inner world and a pathway into our inner "reality" of frames. For the coach, it is *not* therapy to talk about emotions, explore them, or follow them wherever they take us. It is rather an exploration that facilitates more life, wholeness, and performance. Exploring our emotions gives us entrance to our matrix of frames and unleash new potentials.

> *Because emotions are just signals about the difference between our map and our experience of the territory, they are neither right or wrong, good or bad. That's why we have every reason to accept and appreciate them, to stand in awe of them, and to fully explore and enjoy them.*

Questioning as following the Pathway of Emotions

As a coach, how do you feel about exploring the emotions of a client? How easily, naturally, and gracefully can you ask the most basic feeling questions?

- What do you feel about that?
- What are you now feeling about an exploration conversation about emotions?
- What does that remind you of?
- Have you ever felt this before?
- What does it mean to you that you're feeling X?
- How do you experience your anger (or your fear, sadness, tenderness, love, joy, etc.)?

Through asking questions about body sensations (kinesthetics, "feelings") and somatized meanings ("emotions," meta-feelings)— we are able to enter into a Matrix. Following them is like following the white rabbit in Alice's Wonderland into the rabbit hole and as we do it enables us to discover "how deep the rabbit hole goes."

- What is it like to feel that emotion in your body?
- Where do you feel it? And what is that like?
- What intention drives that emotion?
- What would you like to do about that emotion or with it?
- What thoughts are in the back of your mind supporting ,and creating, and feeding that emotion?
- How does that emotion affect your sense of self?

You may not know *what* you will find, but you can know this, it will all be human stuff. It will be nothing other than human stuff. If you find any feeling, memory, awareness, idea, belief, fear, etc. that you don't like, remember, it's just a thought, just a frame, just a representation, and it only has as much "reality" as you give it. It will continue to have so much reality as you keep giving it.

The emotion we feel is never "the reality," it is rather a sign of a reality, a sign of the life of that mapped reality. It is the felt sense of the reality that we have mapped. That's why every emotion is appropriate. It is appropriate to the thought and map out of which it arose. This describes one facet of the inner logic to our emotions. If we are feeling fear—we can count on the fact that there are some fear thoughts creating it. If we are feeling anger—there are some thoughts of anger and hostility generating that emotion. Emotions correlate to the thinking that calls them into existence.

That's why if we hate, reject, or judge our emotions, if we set out to squelch our negative emotions, our fear, anger, sadness, guilt, shame, vulnerability, etc., we end up squelching our positive emotions. We repress our entire ability to register feelings and to know our emotions. We squelch our passion, love, joy, fun, playfulness, and openness.

For the most part, as a coach, asking about emotions is unnatural, strange, uncustomary, politically incorrect, and outside the comfort zone of many people. Yet it is also the source of human power, passion, vision, and creativity. It is the heart of getting to a person's reality and facilitating accelerated transformations for greater meaningfulness and peak performance.

When we ask, "How do you feel about X?" we are searching for the data of emotions, the emotional facts of a situation or experience. This enables us to facilitate our client's discovery of their "felt truths." What is true for our client about rejection or criticism? About taking the risk of courting someone's displeasure? About speaking up to someone in a position of authority? To not know these emotional truths is to not know the heart of that person's Matrix and what makes that person tick.

We call this "emotional intelligence." The work of Dr. Daniel Goleman and others has now made it fashionable to ask about, gauge, and even train the emotional intelligence of employees and leaders. Leaders, managers, sales people, those in customer service, and so on must be able to work with their own emotions and the emotions of others to communicate effectively, negotiate win/win deals, handle disagreements and conflicts, discover the truth of things, deal with mistakes, etc.

- How do you feel when someone is being defensive?
- What does that mean to you?
- What do you feel about the feelings you have?
- What feelings arise in you when someone seems manipulative and has a hidden agenda?
- How do you feel about your own fallibility and mistakes?
- How do you feel when you feel confused and disoriented about things?
- How do you feel about being inefficient or indecisive?

The Experience of Seeking Truth

All coaching conversations are searches for truth, not *the* Truth with a capital T, but for the truth of a given situation, the truth of a moment, the truth of a particular feeling. In this, we all know and own certain truths. Only you know what you think and feel about anything. Only you know what an experience feels like to you. In our search for truth we are really asking for a multitude of viewpoints, "What is true for you about this?" In this, each of us owns a piece of the truth. No one owns it all. It is by sharing our truths and exploring our truths to see what matrix of frames from which they come that we are able to expand our understandings to seeing more and farther.

When we are coaching a team, committee, or group, we will want to facilitate the discovery of each person's truths and what is real for the group as a team. We simply request that each person describes his or her point of view as best as possible.

What is all of this designed to obtain or create? It's to bring us to the compellingly resourceful experience of authenticity—*to being real.* We experience a moment of truth. In such moments flashes of reality shine in and we experience an *"Aha!"* Most of us find this incredibly compelling because it contrasts so starkly with the world of controlled impressions, of roles, masks, pretensions, lies, and deceptions. Yet because it is "truth that sets us free," it is in pursuing what's real (in contrast to what is false and superficial) that we get to the heart of things, deal with the real issues, find solutions that satisfy and that last, and create new insights that can revolutionize a life, a family, a company, or a world.

Laura, a general manager in an international publishing corporation, expressed her emotional experience from coaching with Michelle this way.

> "It was the simplest question she asked when I got the promotion to general manager. She asked me, 'What did it mean to me to get this promotion? And how did you feel about it?' Nobody else had asked this! Everybody else assumed I was over-joyed and while I was, when Michelle asked me that question, my eyes filled with tears. She invited me to welcome in the feelings that came with the tears . . . and I discovered that I was scared, that I felt like a fraud, and that I did not know if I could really do the job. Oh, it was such a relief to admit those feelings, and to have the safety to say them aloud. As we explored the reality, I realized for the very first time that I really was and am the very best person for my job. I can't tell you how strong I feel inside!"

These moments of truth occur when we face our true thoughts about something, our true feelings, our sense of self as we are this day, our relationships as we are currently experiencing them. This kind of truth seeking governs science and technology, and when we translate it to ourselves, it's about facing ourselves and facing each other openly, honestly, and forthrightly. This is the foundation and basis for having fierce conversations.

The Experience of Being Real

To search for what's real necessitates that we become real . . . and that means being real about our pretensions, fears, masks, inauthenticitie s, etc. What does it mean to be real? To be an authentic human being?

The words we have about being authentic speak about being open, receptive, response, honest, sincere, forthright, etc. Being real arises when we know that we are a fallible human being and are willing to accept responsibility for being oneself and for living one's own life according to our own values and visions.

To be real we have to be willing to risk living our own lives within our own skin regardless of whether it pleases others. It's willing to be accountable first and foremost to ourselves.

Summary

- Because coaching offers experiential learning and transformation, an effective coach knows how to elicit and induce experiential states that will enrich the client's life.

- Experiential coaching involves *emotions*. The mere fact that a coach works with human emotion, even strong and negative emotions, does *not* make it therapy. It is *emotion* that makes us alive and vital and passionate, so we coach for greater emotional intelligence and management.

- Emotions are important signals that gauge the difference between our maps of the world and our experience of the world. This elevates them above being moral issues or indicators of what we should to being signals of information.

End Notes:

1. For the neuro-semantic approach and understanding of "emotion," see *Secrets of Personal Mastery*. For NLP patterns dealing with emotions, see *The Sourcebook of Magic* and the chapter on emotions.

Chapter 8

THE CONVERSATION

DANCE

"Dancing is the only pure art form."
Snoopy

Can you remember the feelings of dancing with somebody for the very first time? Even now, do you recall the excitement, anticipation, and nervousness of not knowing how well you will move together, the trepidation for getting the moves and steps right, not wanting to tread on toes, not wanting to fall over, and not wanting to make a fool of yourself? That desire to find yourself in the zone where others float away and there is only and the sound of the music and you and your dancing partner on the dance floor.

Most of us have observed at one time or another a seemingly magical extravaganza of Ballroom or Latin American dancing, whether in person or in a movie. We have seen the energy grow and move between the couple dancing, each taking their steps gracefully, elegantly. and authentically with their own natural rhythm and style. While we know that within these traditional forms of dance one is always leading and guiding, when we look closer, they appear in perfect union. Eventually, we cannot tell who is leading and who is following.

While dancers have specific dance steps, once together they co-create a unique dance by blending and sharing their natural energies, styles and talents creating more than they could by dancing alone or by simply just following the steps. Once in the dance they let go, they stop focusing on their steps and they simply follow the rhythm in their bodies, the energy of their dance partner and the music in the air. The collaboration becomes smooth and seemless. The couple seems to be making it up as they go, as each bring their unique styles to the experience.

Just as a dance is made up of steps, each *coaching conversation* is a dance. Each conversation is made of up many different coaching dance steps. These include awakening, challenging, probing, provoking, co-creating, actualizing, reinforcing, and testing. We have many different kinds of dances or conversations that we move through as a coach: the Outcome Conversation, Metaphorical Conversation, Resources Conversation, etc. Within these we dance in and out of outcomes, resources, responsibilities, frames, possibilities, potentials, frames, expectations, beliefs, awareness, engagement, focus, commitment, learning, and more.

In dancing, we generally think about one person leading and the other following, yet when we closely observe the movements of dancers sometimes it becomes difficult to tell which person is playing which role. Sometimes the movements of the dancers become so closely matched that the collaboration is utterly smooth and seemless. We could even say that the couple seems to be making it up as they go and each bringing their unique styles to the experience so that the emergent property is something more than the sum of the parts.

In the next section, you will get to explore in depth these conversations one at a time. That we present the different conversations in this way does *not* suggest that they are separate or that you should only use them one at a time in some "pure" fashion. Not at all. We separate them simply for the purpose of distinguishing the uniqueness of each conversation as a *step*.

In a coaching conversation, the coach will dance with the client's *energy* of desires and needs, of attractions and aversions, understandings and decisions, and anticipations and hopes. In this dance the coach will continually lead out by creating a safe space, inducing states, inviting intentions, hopes, and dreams, confirming, validating, challenging, quality controlling, briefing and debriefing, confronting, and questioning. In this dance, it is an *art*, not a science.

The science that backs up and provides the theoretical framework are the cognitive-behavioral sciences which sets forth many of the change mechanisms and processes. Yet the theoretical framework does not teach the spirit or the art of the dance. If coaching is all about unlocking a person's potentials and maximizing performance, then the coach must lead out in being real and authentic as a person. The coach must also lead out in facilitating a conversation that's real enough to get to the heart of things. Shame and pretense will not work.

The coach will inquire about the things that are obvious, sometimes so obvious that they

> *To engage in a coaching conversation is to dance.*

are not see, and about things that are not so obvious, things that are only vaguely felt or sensed.   It's only then that people change, that minds are transformed, that hearts are inspired with energy, and that bodies are ready for actions. Because authentic conversations transform people, including the coach, the beginning place is *openness*. When the coach is open, to this adventure is, the dance can begin.

In the coaching dance, we use questions, reflections, and various conversations to invite the emergence of *the coaching moment*. For example, such a moment might arise in coaching when a front-line supervisor might present her fear and negative interpretation about her manager, "He just wants to control me."

There are perhaps a thousand ways to respond to such a statement. We could ask, "How do you know that he just wants to control you?" We might ask if he has a history of controlling people. Yet the most powerful question in the coaching dance will be the one that, providing a little surprise and shock, opens up of new possibilities. And, of course, learning that is itself the art.

Suppose the coach responds by saying,
> "Okay, so he wants to control you. Does he want to control you for some evil purpose, a purpose that's totally malevolent and destructive, or could this be just his clumsy way of trying to re-connect with you? Could it be that?   And if it was, how would that shift your perceptions?"

We actually asked this in a coaching conversation. The question captured the woman's attention to such an extent that it created within her *a coachable moment.* She became receptive and curious in a new way. It enabled her to step out of her paradigm of male managers and opened her to new possibilities. And with that, the dance began.

Learning the Art of the Dance
If a coaching conversation is a dance made of different dance steps, what states do you need to enter the dance, to stop focusing on the steps, and to simply follow the rhythm and the energy of your client? What states do you need to be in so that everything else just disappears as you and your client co-create magic?

In the next chapter we will introduce the coaching conversation dance itself. For this dance, we will need the ability to access certain states of mind-body-and-emotion. Among the states empowering us for the conversation of change dance are the following:
*   Flexibility
*   Openness
*   Focusing on the client as a person with needs, hopes, dreams

- Stepping back to get the ego out of the way
- The willingness to be wrong
- The willingness to not take credit
- Compassion, genuine care

To begin learning the dance steps, and to track where you are in the dance, you will need a higher level of awareness—an awareness that we call *meta-cognition.* We call this *the Step Back* skill. By stepping back we can entertain a witnessing position over our own internal thought stream and that of the other. We can watch how our collaborative meanings unfold in the ongoing conversation with our client. In dialogue, this meta-awareness moves our Socratic exploration to a higher level.

The coaching dance calls for lots of flexibility in the coach. *Flexibility* in the dance allows a coach to detect where the client is and to respond in the most powerful and appropriate way—in a way that meets his or her needs and leads to the client's desired transformation. Flexibility enables us to step in and out of many kinds of coaching conversations in a fluid and graceful way so that it seems to be of seamless.

Openness enables us to receive the information that we detect as we calibrate our client. This state can be frightening, even terrifying. It means letting go of controlling or even of knowing what to do prior to a session. It means *being present* to the current moment of the client's thinking-and-feeling and open to whatever emerges. To do this, the coach will need to be able to embrace ambiguity and tentativeness.

When we are open and flexible, *focusing* balances us. It balances the firmness that's required for holding the client's person and needs front and center in the ongoing conversation. By focusing we can set a relevancy frame to challenge whatever comes up,

> How is this relevant to who you are, who you want to become, and to the needs and desires that you've presented?

Stepping out of our own ego investments enables us to be fully present to a client. We have to get our ego out of the way for the singular reason that the coaching is *not* about us. It's never about how clever, great, insightful, brilliant, or important we are. It's about the client. So, in order to focus on the client's person, needs, and objectives, we have to be so fully centered in ourselves, grounded in our own sense of self and value, that the issue is *not* whether we succeed or fail with a client. The issue is, What's in the best interest for the development, learning, and growth of the client?

Willingness to be wrong puts us, as the coach, to the test. It tests us to see if our ego is strong enough to handle this or whether it is in the way, and if it is, to what degree. There are times when the most creative and empowering thing to do in the presence of a client is to acknowledge that the direction we had suggested, or some process, is not the right one. Needing to be right in the eyes of our clients demonstrates that we have too much of our own ego-investment involved.

Willingness to not take credit tests us about whether we are ego-driven or whether we truly care about the client. "Do I have to take credit for the client's success?" Without question, it is pleasant to take credit when a client succeeds. Yet if our need to take credit gets in the way and "defeats" the client from taking full ownership, responsibility, and celebration for successes, then our willingness to step aside from that need may be a significant factor in coaching the client to success.

Dancing as Dialogue

Since dialogue refers to "cutting through" to *the logos*, or meaning, the dance of the coaching conversations is always and ultimately a dialogue. It's a dance to cut to the heart of things, to find and converse about the client's meanings and to cut through to co-create the most empowering and enhancing meanings possible.

All of this takes courage. It's much easier to talk about all of the pulsating and powerful things around "the heart," and to not touch *the heart* of an issue, objective, challenge, or development. Yet that's when those coachable moments appear. When they appear, how they appear, and the structure of them is more of a mystery than a formula. They typically appear when we least expect them . . . when we are cutting through to the heart of something of importance.

Summary

- There's an art to coaching conversations, and that art involves learning *how to dance in the conversation.* This means moving with and alongside the client, calibrating to his or her needs, objectives, and person.

- It also means cutting through to the heart of things to have a real and robust conversation. To do that we need to be able to be well-practiced in several steps: flexibility openness, focus on the client, willingness to be wrong, to not take the credit, and to get our ego out of the way.

Chapter 9

THE CHANGE DANCE

"Coaching is about fostering directed purposeful change."
Antony Grant (*Coach Yourself*)

What do we do when we coach? Ultimately, *we coach to facilitate change.* Coaching aims to invite, evoke, and inspire *change*—an alteration in how we are thinking, feeling, speaking, behaving, and relating. Sometimes we coach to facilitate a change of thinking or feeling, at other times we coach to facilitate a revolutionary change. Sometimes we seek to unleash new potentials for a new way of life. At other times we seek to disrupt an inner—outer game that doesn't work. These are some of the facets of change.

There are also *levels* of change. There is first level change when we change our thoughts and actions. Yet we can even change a change that we've made. A coach dances between many kinds of conversations in order to explore with a client the right kind of change and the resources to make it happen.

If we want things to remain the same or to continue in the direction that things are currently going, we don't need a coach. Change is what calls for a coach. We need a coach when we want to change things—when we want to grow, develop, make an alteration, learn, evolve, or transform. Change is what coaches study; change is the domain of a coach's expertise; it's the domain of the coach's highest skills. After all, *coaches are change agents.* So, with all of that in mind, we can now ask such relevant questions as the following:

- What do we mean by *change* in the first place?
- What are the mechanisms that actually create change?
- How do we facilitate change?
- What are the levels of change?
- What are the axes of change and how the Axis of Change model provide a systemic approach for working as a change agent?
- What are the coaching styles required to work as a change agent?

In this chapter and the next we will answer these questions, review the key change models, and introduce the new Axes of Change model.[1]

What do we mean by *change* in the first place?
At the first and lowest level, *change is alteration.* When we change our mind, our feelings, our way of talking, our way of acting, our way of relating, we alter how we express and experience ourselves. Perhaps we grow up and mature. That's one form of change. Perhaps we give up old antiquated response patterns that no longer work and *learn* new ways for coping and mastering life—that's yet another form of change. Change is developmental change when it involves our identity and sense of self developing. Change is transformational if it involves altering our very sense of reality. We call that kind of change, a metamorphosis.

Change can be disruption, alternation, even a transformation. We can change the way we think and feel, the way we talk and act. We can change how we relate, love, and contribute.

What is change? Because we are never "the same," but always growing, developing, and evolving, *change is life.* To be alive is to change. Every moment we breathe in and out, we change. Our bodies are forever changing so that the composite make-up of our cells are completely renewed every seven years. In this, change is self-renewing growth that allows us to keep invigorating ourselves with new energy.

Change is also learning. That's because whenever we learn, we change. From the neuro-processing that occurs via neuro-transmitters and neuro-peptides to the bio-electric pulses that activates our nervous system, when we think and learn, our brain chemistry and energy literally changes the structure of our neurology and brain.

Some of the Current Models of Change
- How does *change* occur?
- What models are there of change?
- What facilitates change?
- If we act as change-agents, what do we know about the process of change that facilitate expertise in this area?

If coaching is about fostering directed purposeful change, what models do we have that can help us to productively conceptualize the change process? A key model of change comes from James Prochaska, John Norcross, and Carlo DiClimente. They developed a model to describe the processes and stages of change, the *Trans-Theoretical Model* (TTM). Prochaska, Norcross and DiClemente summarized the TTM in six stages:

1) Pre-contemplation

> In the pre-contemplation stage, a person doesn't even think that he or she has a problem and so resists any ideas or efforts at change. If the person thinks about possibly changing something, there will be little intention or commitment to change. Prior to contemplating a change, a person is only vaguely aware of any need for change.

2) Contemplation

> In this stage a person begins to consider changing something. Here there is an oscillation back and forth between wanting to change and wanting to keep things they way they are with no decision for a change.

3) Preparation for change

> In the third stage a person has become ready to change and so prepares for taking action in making the change.

4) Action or change

> In the fourth stage, a person actually makes a change in his or her thinking, feeling, or behaving to create a difference.

5) Maintenance

> In the maintenance stage a person builds a new lifestyle that integrates the change so that it becomes one's way of moving through the world.

6) Relapse — recycling through the change stages

> Given the ever present possibility of relapsing to former patterns, recognizing and preparing for lapses, as an inherent part of the process, helps a person to effectively negotiate such set-backs.

Richard Bolstad (2002) uses the Trans-Theoretical model as part of the theoretical foundation for the RESOLVE model which can be used to guide a coach in a coaching session. Tony Grant of Sydney University uses it in his coaching model, as do others in the field of coaching. The Trans-Theoretical Model, as a cognitive-behavioral model, maps the change process as one driven by cognitions and behaviors. While the stages in this model are presented in a linear fashion, the designers say that one needs to be aware that the stages will frequently have to be negotiated and re-negotiated, so they think of it as systemic.

Yet there are actually several problems with the Trans-Theoretical model. Don't you love that magical fourth step—*change.* This step is like the cartoon of the theoretician professor in front of a giant blackboard diagraming the cutting-edge formula of the secret of life. Rows upon rows of esoteric algebraic symbols span the blackboard. Then there's an arrow pointing to the space between two symbols that says, "And then a miracle happens."

Precisely because the fourth step (*action or change*) is what a change model should describe, we really have no clue of the change process itself. This leaves us in the dark as to how change occurs, what changes, and the role of the coach in the change process.

While Bolstad uses the Trans-Theoretical model, he goes beyond it by offering several unique facets of NLP as a change model. In doing so, he focuses on the actual steps that lead to successful change when working with a client as a person moves from present state to desired state. The RESOLVE model gives the coach specific tasks in facilitating the change process, namely, establishing rapport, creating a climate of safety, exploring the client's map with the client, creating a precise description of what to change, accessing resources to bring about the change, and verifying the change.

RESOLVE is the acronym for this model and the letters stand for the steps that facilitate change.
R — *Resourceful state:*
　　Get into your best states (confident, clear, flexible, compassion, loving).
E — *Establish rapport:*
　　Match and pace the client verbally, non-verbally, conceptually to create a sense of trust and safety.
S — *Specify outcome:*
　　Identify a clearly described outcome and reframe problems as skills.
O — *Open client's model:*
　　Probe the client's maps of beliefs, values, understandings, etc. Elicit problem strategy, frame client as "at cause," preframe specific change technique.
L — *Lead to change:*
　　Guide client through conversation or pattern to induce change.
V — *Verify change:*
　　How change actually occurred in the contexts where it's needed? Question to presuppose change, use client's convincer sort.
E — *Ecological check:*
　　Quality control the change by seeing if it is ecological to all of the relationships and systems.

The Levels of Change
Are there *levels* of change? Yes, of course. We can change a behavior—a way of acting, and we can change the thinking-feeling state that drives that behavior. Then we can change that mind-body state, and so on. We can even change the process of change.

When you think about it, the term *change* refers to nothing specifically, only to *the process* of altering something. Actually, the word "change" sounds like it refers to a thing (hence, a noun). Yet this noun-like word (or nominalization) is not a "person, place, or thing" and we can't put it in the refrigerator. Yes we can clean or change the refrigerator, because we are never "the same," we are always growing, developing, and evolving. Change describes a process, not a thing and so a verb more accurately maps *change*.

The term *change* is also a multi-ordinal term. That's a fancy way of saying that the word can be used reflexively on itself. If we ask, Can we *change* a change? we discover the reflexivity that's within the process. That's why we have to ask, "At what level are you speaking about change?" Or, "Change at what level?"

In studying learning and change, anthropologist Gregory Bateson created a model by which he mapped the levels of learning and/or change. He began with a situation of no alteration or change (Zero Learning) and then moved up the levels to as he detailed Learning Levels I to IV.

Bateson created this model as an anthropologist via his studies of numerous cultures with the expressed purpose of exploring them to create a workable description of how the system worked. From this Bateson used systems thinking and dynamics to describe a cultural system and frames to describe the structural framework. This led him to explore the information loops in a system and the layering effect of the loops. To describe the next level up in a system, Bateson used the term *meta*. From there he began describing the *meta-function* in schizophrenia, play, beauty, wisdom, culture, and much more.

Bateson identified what he called *the levels of learning / change*. Beginning with Zero Learning, he generated the first level of change (Learning I) where we change the Zero Learning and create the first level of change (Change I, expanded behaviors). Then, to the second level of change (Change II, new behaviors), where we change the change. When we step aside to change the change-of-change, we are at the third level (Learning III, new identity and beliefs). If we can later change Level III, we arrive at the fourth level (Change IV, new paradigms and directions).

In Bateson's levels of learning and change each higher level is more abstract than the level below it and each higher level governs or modulates the levels below it. To read the following, start at the bottom with Zero Learning / Change and move up the levels.

Levels of Learning

Level IV:	Change of Learning III
	Learning new and unprecedented things that creates revolutionary change
	Learnings that revolutionize our way and direction

Level III:	Change of Learning II
	Evolutionary change in one's self system
	Learning that changes direction and sense of self

Level II:	Change of Learning I
	Corrective change and discontinuous change
	Learning how learning works and changing the sequence of a strategy

Level I:	Change of Zero Learning
	Correction of errors, expansion of range of responses
	Learning new responses for expanding responses

Zero Learning:	A specificity of response not subject to alteration
	Pavlovian conditioning of responses, mechanical reflexes
	Learning as habitual, programmed for a singular response

When Robert Dilts (2003) reworked these levels of learning / change in his coaching model (*From Coach to Awakener*) he identified the kind of change that occurs at each level. This new set of words and descriptions resulted in the following list.

Learning IV:	*Revolutionary Change*
	Awakening to new world
	Transformative change

Learning III:	*Evolutionary Change*
	Shift from the old box of thinking and feeling to beyond
	Paradigm shift to new choices entirely

Learning II:	*Discontinuous Change*
	Shift to different behaviors and responses
	Shift to different box of behaviors

Learning I:	*Incremental Change*
	Corrections, Adaptations, Modifications
	Via flexibility and stretching within the box choices

| Learning 0: | *No Change* |
| | Repetitive behavior, Habits, Resistance |

What the *Axes of Change model* does is that it incorporates the best from the previous models of change as it incorporates the levels of change and then provides a coach flexible and adaptable steps for the conversational dance of growth and change. We will present this more fully in the next chapter.

Figure 9:1
Coaching within the Levels of Change

Bateson's Levels of Learning	Axis of Change	Kinds of Coaching
IV: *Revolutionary* Change	Internal/External Ref. MP *Creating Change* Inner and Outer Game Matching — Mis-Matching Same — Difference MP *Sustaining Change*	Transformative Coaching
III: *Evolutionary* New Direction	Probing frames and co-creating new frames The Inner and Outer Games	Developmental Coaching
II: *Discontinuous* New Self, Choices	Active—Reflective MP Readiness for change *Decision*	Developmental Coaching
I: *Incremental Change* New Behaviors	Toward/ Away From Push—Pull *Motivation*	Performance Coaching
0: *No Change* Habits, habitual responses	Toward/ Away From Push—Pull *Motivation*	Performance Coaching

Kinds of Coaching

Beginning with this description of change we extended and expanded it for the Meta-Coaching model to create the following list. Because all coaching is not the same, we can discern different *kinds* of coaching at different levels. In Meta-Coaching we have distinguish three different kinds of coaching: performance, developmental, and transformational. For these different kinds of change and kinds of coaching, we can now identify where they go in *the Axes of Change.*

Performance Coaching. At the lowest levels of learning, Levels I and II, we have performance coaching—coaching to the client's behaviors and skills. Coaching at this level is strictly concerned with the outer game of actions and activities. It's about refining and honing the client's skills. It's about using feedback and feed-forward to stretch and develop more flexibility and elegance in the skill set the client already has.

Developmental Coaching. At Level III, we move to developmental coaching. Here we work with exploring and facilitating the ideas and frames that allows a client to move to the next level of development in his or her experience. Developmental coaching involves facilitating how we move through various stages of development over our lifespan. In developmental coaching we work with the higher states of beliefs, values, understandings, and self identity. We facilitate the growth of the client moving through the psychological stages of development. In developmental coaching the client learns to step out of the matrix to engage in "out-of-the-box" thinking. The client then gets to create and expand to new ways of thinking, feeling, speaking, and acting.

Transformational Coaching. At Level IV, we move into transformative coaching. Here we focus on exploring and facilitating complete paradigm shifts in the client's thinking, feeling, acting, and relating. We facilitate paradigm shifts in the inner game that absolutely revolutionizes a client's life in the outer game. As such, transformative coaching can and does turn everything upside down and invite the client on an adventure of discovery. It is revolutionary change in purpose, meaning, and direction.

Summary
- Because coaching is all about facilitating and supporting change, *change that's generative for self-actualization is the domain of the coach.* In this, the coach is a change agent par excellence.

- Because all change is not the same, there are many kinds of change that we can discern. At the first level there's simple alteration of thinking and feeling; then there's performance improvement. After that comes change of one's self and finally transformational change regarding how we move through the world as governed by our paradigms.

- There are also numerous models of change. The most cutting edge models today recognize the levels of change and the cumulative effect of working at higher levels.

- When you are ready for the ultimate self-actualization change model, we introduce *The Axes of Change* model In the next chapter. It's a model that integrates the previous change models as it creates a unifying framework.[1]

End Notes:

1. For a far more extensive description of the Axes of Change, see the first volume of the Meta-Coaching series, *Coaching Change* (*Meta-Coaching,* Volume I).

Chapter 10

DANCING THROUGH

THE AXES OF CHANGE

- *How* does a coach facilitate and co-create change with a client?
- Knowing the levels of change and the structure of change, how do we explore and facilitate the processes?
- What are some of the internal processes that occur within the *change* process?

When I first observed that some models of change actually made "change" one of the steps in the change process, I knew that we needed to make "change" more specific. After all, a model of change ought to explain *how the change occurs,* the processes and variables involved, and the mechanisms that facilitate change. This is what the earlier models did not provide.

In response we began to probe *the change process* itself. We probed the nature of change and began to more thoroughly map it out. We did this by considering how thinking, feeling, and perceiving shifts as we make a change. This led us to explore the Meta-Programs model to determine precisely how our perceptual filters interface with an experience in terms of continuity and change. As a result, we gave birth to *the Axes of Change model.*

Meta-Programs are our *perceptual filters.* They are like the lenses or glasses that we wear and, through which, we see the world. Because of this, they operate as higher thinking patterns, the frames of mind that we bring to any experience as our assumptions.

A good example of *a meta-program* is the optimistic/pessimistic continuum as exemplified by the classic question, "Is the cup half full or half empty?" How do you generally see things? In terms of fullness or emptiness? In asking this question, *if* either side of the polarity (full/empty) dominates the way we think and perceive, then we might be a "glass half full kind of perceiver" or a "glass half empty kind of perceiver." In this, either the concept of *fullness* or *emptiness* becomes a perceptual frame that colors our subsequent perceptions.

What then is a *meta-program*? Meta-program distinctions refer to *the way we sort for information* and *what we pay attention to*. That's why we say that a meta-program is a perceptual filter or lens through which we view the world. Think of them as conceptual glasses. Or think of them as the mental software governing how we process incoming data. These "programmed" ways of thinking-feeling and acting govern the way we see the world and therefore the worlds that we see and cannot see. While there are more than 60 meta-programs, four seem especially critical when modeling the structure of generative change.[1]

The idea of using meta-program continua or axes to structure our understanding of change came from several sources. First, as Michael researched the literature on change and attempted several formats, searching for a way to put the cognitive-behavioral premises of Meta-Coaching together to as a description of the change process, the idea of using *meta-programs* seemed more and more appropriate given that no action or statement can cause change by itself. It depends entirely on *how a person thinks about* the action or statement.

When we felt that we were close to structuring and describing *change* using meta-programs, we began recalling several of our best and most successful coaching change interventions with clients and began modeling the natural way that change occurs when a coaching client successful experiences a desired transformation. At that point we began modeled *how* Michelle successfully worked with clients to facilitate change, and then compared that to how Michael worked with clients. Out of the synthesis of that research and modeling came *the Axes of Change model.*

We developed *the Axes of Change model* also to identify the specific steps of a person's energy as one moves through the stages of change. We had often talked about "following the energy" through the conversation or through a person's matrix of frames. At the time, however, we knew that "following the energy" was a phrase that lacked sufficient precision and so we set out to map the process. Michelle began focusing on how to describe *following of the energy* and began questioning how this might relate to a person's meta-programs. From this we began sketching the basic structure of the model.

In designing this model, we selected four central meta-program continua or axes, axes which governs how a person thinks-and-feels about things that lead to a change of motivation, action, implementation, and continuance. These four meta-program axes are axes of change in that they govern the *change process* itself. As we noted that the change process itself involves these four meta-program distinctions, we utilized them to build the model and then put the model at the heart of the Meta-Coaching training.[2]

What are these meta-program continua? The four meta-programs which we found that are intimately connected with learning and change involve the following facets of any experience of change, namely, motivation, decision, creation, and solidification.

1) Motivation: the motivating values for change.
> Change takes motivation. In change we move toward what we want and away from what we don't want. This gives us the push to avoid pain and the pull of dreams and visions to a more desirable and pleasurable reality.

2) Decision: the reflective action for change.
> Change doesn't occur until there's a decision. And we decide by reflecting, weighing, and then acting. Sometimes we prefer to first reflect and then act, at other times we act and then reflect. Our preferred style may be to take in information, reflect on it, and then take action to change what we're doing to something new.

3) Creation: implementing of the plans of change.
> Change involves creation and occurs twice. We change by designing and mapping a new plan and vision in our minds (the first creation), which we then implement as we act it out in actual behavior (the second creation).

4) Solidification: the reinforcing and testing of the change.
> To keep the change we have to reinforce it so that it solidifies into lifestyle. We do that by supporting and nurturing the changed behaviors, testing them, continuing to learn and refine the new way as we recycle through the continuous improvement loop.

Given that we can locate these four factors for self-actualizing change on four meta-program continua, we now present the four axes of change and the *Axis of Change model.*

Axis I: The Motivation Direction Meta-Program
The meta-programs of *Toward / Away From*

Questions:
- What do you want? What do you *really* want?
- What have you had enough of?
- What values or experiences are you motivated toward and what are you motivated to move away from?

This first axis is where we elicit the push-pull energy of a propulsion system that plays off of the energies of attraction / aversion and pleasure / pain. The poles on the continuum between *away from* and *toward* relate to how much energy we experience as we feel pulled or pushed toward a value or toward a dis-value. Here we awaken someone to a vision of new possibilities and potentials and/or we highlight the discomfort of staying where one is.

Valued Experiences	
Away From	**Toward**
Pains— Aversions	Pleasures — Attractions
The Push away from	The Pull Toward

Axis II: The Response Style Meta-Program
The meta-programs of *Reflective and Active*

Questions:
- How do you respond or act when faced with information or a request?
- Do you first reflect upon things?
- Is your first response to take action and then ask questions?

The poles on the continuum between *active* and *reflective* provide the oscillation between thinking something through to fully recognize the pros and cons of our decision, the advantages and disadvantages to just acting on something, seeing what happens, and then considering our decision.

Response Preference and Style	
Reflective	**Active**
Thinking, Feeling, Imagining, Analyzing	Acting, Doing, Taking Action
Inwardly focused in responding	Outwardly focused in responding
to data or challenge	

Axis III: The Reference Meta-Program
The meta-programs of *Internal / External* frame of reference

Questions:
- Where do you sense your locus of control—internally within yourself or externally in someone or something else?
- When it comes to the center of authority for you, do you mainly refer to your own internal frames, understandings, beliefs, experiences, and thoughts?
- Or, are you more aware that the source of authority is in the outside

world in experts, books, authorities, tradition, etc.?

The poles of the continuum between *internal* and *external* relate to our concept of authority, rightness, and legitimacy. Where is our reference point? Is it inside or out? Or is it a combination of both? Where is the source or locus of authority? How much flexibility do we have in moving back and forth?

Reference Focus

Internal	External
Internal maps and frames of the Game	External actions of the Game
Ideas, Thoughts, Words,	Sensory Awareness and Calibration
Representations in the Movie in our mind	Present on the outside
Strategy for how to do something	

Axis IV: The relationship meta-program
Matching for sameness and mis-matching for difference

Questions:
- What do you notice first, what's similar to what you already know or what's different?
- When testing for results do you default to noticing and appreciating what's working according to plan or what's not up to your desired outcome?
- How easily do you *count* even the first approximations of change and development?
- How easily do you jump into quality control to test the robustness of the performance?

Relationship Style

Matching for Sameness	Mis-Matching for Difference
Witnessing and noticing what fits,	Mis-matching for what differs,
Looking for matches between	determining strengths and weaknesses
new Game Plan and external actions	Monitoring and identifying what needs
	to be brought up to standard.

This meta-program distinction relates to how we relate or compare things. Do we compare things by matching and seeing how they are similar to something else? Or, do we mismatch things and compare them in terms of how they differ? Do we see people and events or do we hear ideas and suggests through the lens of *similarity*, "How is this similar to . . .?" or through the lens of *difference*, "How does this differ from . . .?"

Axes of Change Coaching Roles

Given the eight perspective and roles in *the Axes of Change model,* we now have eight *coaching states or roles* that we use as we dance with a client.

- What are the coaching states that we are called upon to access and use as we move through the change stages with a client?
- What states do we dance in and out of as we follow the energy and facilitate the desired transformations for the client in each axis?

Axis I: The Push-Pull Dance

This dance stirs up energy as it exposes consequences, awakens dreams and visions, and loosens the current frames. It covers the pre-contemplation and contemplation stages of change. For this we dance between the poles of *Awakener* and *Challenger.*

- *Awakener:* This is the coaching role of inspiring, standing in awe of the magnificence of a client, inviting new possibilities, seducing new possibilities, evoking dreams and wild imaginations, and doing anything that *awakens* within the client new visions.

- *Challenger:* This is the role of evoking current reality in its rawness and highlighting its pain and distress both now and in the future. The Challenger's role evokes consequential thinking about where current behavior will take one if one's course is not changed. In this role we confront, we get in the client's face, and we challenge to create a felt gap between what *is* and what can be.

Question: When do we shift from the Push-Pull dance and axis as Awakener and Challenge? Answer: When there is enough energy to explore one's Matrix to understand the current box within which the client is embedded. To that we ask:

- Is the person energized to explore?
- How's the motivation level to face reality as it is?

Axis II: The Decision Dance between Readiness and Leverage

This dance seeks to find and/or create the leverage point for change that leads to *the decision* to change. Here we seek to facilitate the client to identify the highest frames of intention, the key to his or her Matrix, and the structure of transformation for this client at this time. Does he or she have permission to change? Does he believe that change is a possibility for him? Does he believe he deserves it? It is to evoke the beginning of an attractor frame in the system.

- *Prober:* This is the role of exploring like a detective with total curiosity, persistence, and tenacity the current frames of reference that form and define things. We probe the existing Matrix to understand what it is, how it works, its structure, processes, and leverage point. We probe to understand the pros and cons of the decision to change, the advantages of changing and the disadvantages. Frequently, this invites blinding awareness of current reality. Oftentimes a painful awareness arises of *how* we have created a non-productive pattern in our lives. As we do, we will be wondering about what frame of mind could bring a complete transformation in the Matrix? In the role of Prober we search and research, we put the spotlight on the unstoried features of our experiences, and we tease out the higher frames of mind.

- *Provoker:* This is the role for teasing, provoking, and playing to get the client to turn up the push—pull energies to see just *how ready* the client is and if there's sufficient energy to actually make something happen, that is, to make a change. We provoke the commitment. As provoker we "challenge" as in the first axis, yet the push is different. We now push for probing inside for the frames of mind that make up the client's current position in order to face the facts of the decision, the pros and cons, and so move one on to a decision and commitment. Before, we pushed and challenge for motivational energy around our vision.

Question: When do we shift from the readiness—leverage axis to the next axis of creation? Answer: When there is an awareness of the problematic frame, when there's the discovery of the possibility of the leverage frame, when the person reaches a threshold, when there's a readiness to do the Inner Game work. Then we can ask:

- Do we know the frames that has created your current situation and state?
- Is the client clear about the pros and cons of the decision?
- Is the client ready to change those frames?
- Is the client committed to making the change?

Axis III: The Dance of Creation into the Inner and Outer Games

In this dance we move with the client to facilitate creation in two stages. First, we facilitate the creation of *the inner game* and then the creation of its performance into *the outer game*. This dance helps the client close the knowing-doing gap and put into practice the know-how of the new game that the client wants to play. Here we dance to co-generate with the client a self-organizing attractor frame in the form of a new inner game, or game plan, that will become self-generative. This is the experimenting stage for change.

- *Co-Creator:* This is the role of co-creating with the client the actual meanings of belief frames, decision frames, identity frames, etc. that make up a new game—*the inner game*. In this role we co-develop with the client the new game plan, the new strategies, and how-to steps that will create the transformation.

- ***Actualizer:*** The next role of coaching involves bringing the Inner Game out in terms of the client's *actions*. This is the step of making the actions *real* (i.e., *realizing,* actualizing) and experimenting to see how the actions work in real life. In this action stage of change, we externalize the internal changes.

Question: When is the inner—outer game over? Answer: When the client creates a new game—has a new map with new resources and rules for how to play that game and has specific actions to do to manifest the new behavior and performance in the outside world. When the client has successfully translated the actions to the outside world. Ask:
- Does the client have a new game plan?
- Does the client have an action plan?
- Is the client motivated and aligned with the new game?
- Is the client willing to be held accountable?
- Has the change occurred?

Axis IV: The Dance of Solidification through Reinforcement and Testing
In this final dance, we move with the client to solidify the new inner and outer game so that it not only is implemented in everyday life, but that it becomes more and more integrated in every aspect of the client's life. We do that by setting up a recursive process that facilitates continual improvement through continual learning and continual feedback for more and more refinement of the new actions. This describes the maintenance stages of change.
- ***Reinforcer:*** This is the role of providing reinforcements or rewards to the actions through supporting, celebrating, nurturing, validating, cheer-leading, and acknowledging. This role can be gentle and nurture or racus and "partying on." The reinforcing can occur through one's person, through a supportive community, through accountability structures, or through the person's own acknowledgments. In doing so, the behaviors become anchored and more solid.

- ***Tester:*** This is the role of testing to see how strong, robust, real, workable, and ecological the new behavior is. In testing, we feedback the changes and the results, we evaluate what's working well and how to make it work even better, we set up accountability structures, we look for problems, we trouble-shoot, and we cycle back to the co-creating stage. In this role we challenge the ideas and frames to make them realistic and tough and practical.

The *matching* and *mismatching* meta-programs deal with how we relate to information and experience. Do we sort for what's the same or what's different? With sufficient flexibility of consciousness we can match to pace and then mismatch to refine our awareness of distinctions or we can mismatch to identify the critical components and then match how that's important for success in a given area.

Actually, throughout the dance steps we match and mismatch, first with what we want and don't want, then with if we're ready or not, then what is and is not the leverage frame and then the inner and outer games. We match our desires, readiness, and frames, then we mismatch to test these things.

Question: When is the solidifying dance over? Answer: It's over when the client has so well integrated the new game that it has become a part of his or her way of being in the world. The change is now intuitive and automatic. Now the client owns and manages the change, and feels totally confident to keep the change. Ask:

- Does the client have access to the new behaviors and game at all times?
- Is the client continually learning and improving?
- Are there accountability structures in place?
- Does the client know how to reinforce, support, and nurture the change?
- Does the client feel confident of keeping the change?

Polarities Not Either/Or Choices
It's critical to understand that these meta-program distinctions are simply *ways of processing information*. They are simply choices of attention and focus. The information that we process may be *emotional* and involve what we call *values* (Toward/Away From). The information may involve our current awareness governing how we respond (Active/Reflective). The information may be about how and where we posit the source of authority (Internal/External Reference). And the information may be about how we compare things (Matching/Mis-Matching).

As ways of processing information, meta-programs create what and how we see. Neither choice is good or bad, moral or immoral. In different contexts and situations, one may be more useful and effective than the other. That's why we need both. So rather than think of them as either-or choices, we best understand meta-programs when we view them as the range of consciousness between the poles of a continuum.

When we frame these meta-programs as *polarities* (rather than problems to be solved), we recognize that resolution does *not* occur by getting rid of one side or the other. It comes by *balancing* both as we develop the flexibility to use both poles when appropriate. This describes *the flexibility of consciousness* that enables us to use both aversion *and* attraction, reflection *and* action, internal *and* external referencing, matching *and* mis-matching. This flexibility is also the foundation for the Coaching Conversation dance inasmuch as we will dance back and forth between these polar opposites.

Figure 10:1
The Four Continua of the Axis of Change Meta-Programs

Stage I: *Preparing For Change*

Axis I:

Aversions / Pains	Attractions / Pleasures
Push — Away From	Pull — Toward

Axis II:

Reflective: Think and Feel	Active: Do
Deciding, Weighing Pros and Cons	Committing to Change

Stage II: *Facilitating the Change*

Axis III:

Internal Reference	External Reference
Mapping, Matrix Building	External focus, Applying
The Inner Game	The Outer Game

Axis IV:

Matching for Sameness	Mis-Matching for Difference
Witnessing and noticing what fits,	Mis-matching for what differs,
Matches what works to	Identifies needs to deal with
reinforce and validate	and bring up to standard.

With this arrangement of these four continua or axes, we have four change processes to work with and eight states for eight coaching roles.

First process: *Motivation: our motivation direction for change.*

What are we moving toward?

What values, beliefs, experiences, benefits pull on us?

What do we want to avoid?

What experiences or dis-values do we dislike?

Second process: *Decision: our awarenesses that leverage change.*

What is our style as we become aware of our need to change?

Do we prefer to think, reflect, and analyze?

Do we prefer to jump in and just do it, just make the change?

Third process: *Creation: our preferred reference system in change.*

Do we prefer to map out the new way of thinking, feeling, and acting first?

Do we prefer to focus first on where and what to change?

Fourth process: *Solidification: Our way of making a change and keeping the change.*

Do we match any and every indication of the new behaviors and performance to validate and positively reinforce them?

Do we mis-match what isn't up to standard to monitor, refine, test, and feedback new insights?

The Change Process

These four steps describe the processes we go through when we change. First, we feel a pull toward or a push away from something. We want something more that we have or we want something to be different. Or we refuse to tolerate something, have had enough and want to move away from something, and so feel motivated to make the change.

Second, we move to understand what to change, perhaps why to change, what will happen if we don't, and to then make the decision to change. We reflect on our mental maps that need to be changed. What's inadequate or not serving us? With this we develop enough readiness as we get leverage with ourselves to make a change.

Third, with the motivation, readiness, and decision we then map out the rules and form of the new game and soon begin to play the new game. Finally, we nurture and support the changes, test them, refine tem, and establish continual learning as an ongoing process.

In coaching, we coach our clients through the states that correspond to each of the polarities in *the Axis of Change*. To expand and unleash new potentials, in Meta-Coaching, we coach to the unawakened side of the client's meta-programs. As we do, we dance back and forth moving the coaching conversation depending on where the client is in the change process.

If a client wants something more, or doesn't want any more of something, we explore both. Is there enough drive and motivation? What direction is the client oriented in? If the client has enough motivation to change, then we dance to explore his or her readiness for change and the current belief frames. Has the client reflected on making the change sufficiently? Has the client acted on the new vision? Where is the leverage for the client to make the change? Does the client have a new game plan? How well developed is it? Does it work? Has the client tried it out? Altogether we have four dances and eight dance steps:

- Toward / Away From

The Push—Pull Motivation Dance

- Active / Reflective
  The Decision Readiness—Leverage Dance
- Internal / External
  The Inner—Outer Game Dance
- Match / Mis-Match
  The Reinforcement — Solidification Dance

Hidden Meta-Programs

While we have identified four key meta-programs, there are also some other meta-programs within this change model. Yet because we will work with them within each of the four axes or continua, they are not major dance steps, but minor ones.

Central to the change process is the information size meta-programs of *Global—Specific*. This meta-program refers to the size of data or information that we deal with. Do we want the big picture or specific and precise details?

Size of information refers to our degree of detail in specifics or generality in global description. We move up and down the levels of specificity to abstraction. With sufficient flexibility of consciousness we move from details to meta-awareness and frames and back from meta-frames to detailing. When we put this together we have what we call *meta-detailing*.[3]

Meta-detailing refers to the critical ability of bringing a meta-frame idea, principle, or concept down to the practical everyday details which makes them practically real. Meta-detailing facilitates the ability to actually *implement* what we know in our heads. Here, for example, the coach may ask, "What is one thing that you can do today to begin to make this goal real in your life?"

We do all of this in our push—pull dance moves as we move up and down the levels of specificity regarding our goals and intentions. We do this in the readiness—leverage moves as we develop and activate both our neurology (the active meta-program of readiness) and our semantics (the reflective meta-program of leverage frames). We move up and down the levels from global to specific also in the inner—outer game dance steps as we bring our inner frames down into our activities in the outer game.

Coach's Central Dance as Explorer and Facilitator

The coach who initiates the conversation with a client operates primarily and essentially as an explorer and facilitator. That's what a coach most essentially does. A coach *explores* and, in the exploration of the client's maps and frames and matrix, the coach *facilitates* the development and activation of that matrix of frames. From the heart of these exploring and facilitating skills the coach now does eight things (awakens, inspires, and challenges, provokes and probes, co-creates, constructs, actualizes, reinforces and tests). The coach does these dance steps along *the Axes of Change* in stages. Although there are four axes, there are only two overall stages.

The first stage covers the first two axes. Here the coach seeks to build up sufficient energy in the client for the transformation and to provoke enough readiness in the client to make the change.

- What does the client want?
- What has the client had enough of?
- What pulls and pushes on the client?
- What are the old frames that have to change?
- How ready is the client to do the work of changing?

In the second stage covers the last two axes. Here the coach shifts from discovering the old matrix of frames to co-creating a new inner game of frames and the transformation in frames (reframing) to create the new reality (the inner game of our frames). This allows the coach and client to dance into translating or actualizing the inner to the outer game, the game of performance. As a coach we cannot move on to the second stage (the inner—outer game dance) until there's sufficient neuro-semantic energy and awareness. We then shift to making the change, actualizing it, supporting and reinforcing the change, and then monitoring and testing the performance so that it is continually refined.

Stage I: Building up of the transformational energy. In the process of creating transformational energy in a coaching conversations, stage one is designed to evoke within the client a self-organizing attractor which uses both the push and pull energies and the propulsion to a desired future. The dance moves between *pulling* the client forward toward his or her desired goals and values and *pushing* away from those things that are painful and intolerable.

This creates a push—pull propulsion system of motivation within the client. The coaching conversation at this point centers on creating a well-formed outcome of exciting and compelling goals and intensifying the client's awareness of the price to be paid if he or she doesn't act. This push—pull dance aims to widen the gap between the present state of current reality and the preferred vision of future of possibilities.

The second dance oscillates between building up readiness to change power and finding and/or creating the leverage for that change. *Readiness* has to do with finding out and facilitating the client's way to become fully ready for change.

- You say you want this, *how much* do you want this?
- Are you ready to do whatever it takes?
- How committed are you?

- How much are you willing to commit? To give?
- How long will you persevere?
- Do you have the ego-strength to face whatever will come?
- Are you resilient? Courageous? Optimistic?

Leverage has to do with entering, exploring, and finding or calling forth both the focal point that interferes with change and which creates the fear of change.
- What do you need to believe to experience that?
- What do you need to decide?
- What stops you?
- What frame of mind would you be in once you take action?

From these four states and roles and the meta-program distinctions that the presuppose, we move to stage two of the change process.

Stage II: Creating the frames for the inner game and manifesting them in the outer game. Once the leverage point of the highest frames have been identified, the matter moves to creating, enhancing, and articulating them. This builds up the rules of the game—*the inner game* of our frames. These are our internal references that gives us permission, power, and articulation to play a new game. Here the coach explores and facilitates to generate the new game plan, the strategies, and know-how to pull it off. Once the change begins externally, the coach becomes a reinforcer of every step in the right direction, no matter how small, a cheerleader of the change that we manifest in our actions, and after that a monitor and tester to quality control the new changes.

Stage II is where the inner reality hits the road of actual performance. Here we mind-to-muscle the great ideas that forge and navigate a new reality.

The Eight Coaching Roles in the Dance

With these axes of change we now have eight coaching roles. In the coaching conversation dance these are the activities and roles which the coach plays. These eight roles correspond to the four axis and the eight meta-program distinctions in *the Axes of Change*. To summarize them, these roles involve the following:
- In *the Push—Pull dance* from attractor values and aversion dis-values:
  1) Awakener
  2) Challenger

- In *the Active—Reflective dance* from readiness to leverage:
  3) Provoker
  4) Prober

- In *the Internal—External reference dance* that actualizes the outer game

from the inner game of frames:
5) Co-Creator
6) Actualizer

- In *the Match—Mis-Match dance* that supports and solidifies the new changes:
7) Reinforcer
8) Tester

In the *Awakener* and *Challenger* roles we seek to facilitate an awakening in the client to the own inner passions and visions about life. We challenge to not put up with average or mediocre, but to become the best they can be. From one side of the continuum we are inspiring, seducing, inviting, and stimulating to the other side where we are pushing, demanding, angering, and frustrating.

In the *Provoker* and *Prober* roles we seek to facilitate sufficient energy and realism that the client reaches a threshold and breakthrough to a new level of existence. The provoker role is a fun and respectful one that honors that which is unique, special, and sacred in the person so much that we won't let them get by with playing it safe or failing to live up to his or her potential. As a coach, we often believe in the client far more than he or she does. In provoking we test, amplify, and bring the readiness to a threshold.

In the prober role we are co-creating with the client the very ideas, beliefs, decisions, stories, etc. that get us to thinking outside-of-the-box and exploding into a new world of possibilities. This probing similarly pushes until something new, something more than the sum of the parts emerge.

In the *Co-Creator* and *Actualizer* roles we seek to facilitate both the inner and outer games. In the first we work with the client to co-create the best kind of frames that will set all of the navigational rules of the game. Next comes the actualization—making the action plan real in action and behavior.

In the *Reinforcer and Tester* roles we work to provide nurturing support for the new fragile changes, giving positive validating that reinforces it, thereby solidifying the changes. Then we begin testing what the client is actually doing, monitoring it, and feedbacking back new learnings and insights to serve as attractor frames in the inner game so that they now become self-organizing in the client's mind-body-emotion system.

The Coaching Conversation Dance

In the *Coaching Conversations* in the second half of this book we will use these eight distinctions to highlight the structure of the conversation dances. We will do this after each coach—client interaction. For the coach, this also provides a way to think about how to *follow the energy of the conversation*.

1ˢᵗ *The Push-Pull Game.*

The coaching dance typically starts here where the coach plays the roles of *challenger* and *awakener*. We base the first two steps on the *toward /away from* meta-program distinction which sets up the motivation, focus, and direction of change.

Coaching these two poles on this continuum give us the push—pull dance. This lets us explore and facilitate both the *approaching* and *avoiding* energies and motivations in clients. We can activate or create the dual propulsion feeling of attractions or aversions. We begin by evoking either *awakening* vision or the *felt-need gap*.

*   What do you want?
*   What do you not want?
*   What is your current situation?
*   How do you feel about that?
*   How far are you from what you want?
*   What will getting what you want do for you?

In the push—pull dance we both lead and follow the energy of the client's approach or avoidance. To do this we first detect the client's natural style and default mode, and match it. With those who move *toward,* we only have to awaken, invite, attract, and seduce—the feminine energy. With those who move *away from* we challenge, probe, and get in their face—the masculine energy.

As we play off our masculine—feminine energies we move between nurturing, caring, loving, supporting, and seducing and challenging, provoking, pushing, scaring, and threatening.

How do we know we're ready to move on from this stage? Our intention in the first dance is to build up enough motivational energy in the client for the change to take place. We are ready to move on to the next dance when we have calibrated and confirmed from the client that they have sufficient self-motivation for the transformation.

2ⁿᵈ *The Readiness—Leverage Dance.*

The next steps in the dance come from the Active—Reflective meta-program distinction which relates to how a person responds to information, activity, or the call for a change. Here the coach steps into the roles of *provoker* and *prober*.

On this continuum, we question and explore a client's current maps to understand his or her values, perceptions, meanings, and matrices. We do this for several purposes. First, we want to find out if the client is really *ready* to change, if the client knows *what to* change, and how many vested interests the client has in maintaining the status quo. For the coach, the twin tasks are to provoke readiness for making changes and to probe to find the leverage point for the change. Readiness involves *action* and finding leverage involves *reflection*.

In provoking readiness, we provoke, tease, and play. Here we step into the role of a catalyst and provoker as we playfully seduce the client with the possibilities that a change will make for a bright future. Simultaneously we test the person's readiness and ego-strength in facing the challenges that will come, for operating from the person's inner strengths and resources, for staying positive and determined, and for persevering.

With readiness to change we explore with the client his or her matrices of frames. In doing this, we are able to dance into finding or creating the leverage point of change. How does this occur? It occurs as we enter into and explore the client's current matrix. This invites the client to discover the current frames and games that make up his or her reality.

How do we know that we're ready to move to the next dance? This occurs when the client has detected precisely where the change needs to take place in his or her matrix of frames and has made a decision to change. As the coach conversation dances around these issues, the energy is now ready for mapping out a new game and making it happen.

3rd *The Inner—Outer Game Dance.*

On this axis we dance between the meta-programs of internal and external reference. The coach has two tasks as he or she dances back and forth along this continuum, the roles of *co-creator* and *actualizer*.

One task is to co-create the inner game by dancing with the client to co-create the highest frames of meaning to facilitate the change. The tease and play here moves to a more reflective mode as the client searches for the just right frame of mind that will make all the difference in the world and that will lead the change.

In co-creating new belief and value frames, we co-construct a matrix of beliefs and decisions that will suffice for the rules of the new game. The inner game governs and drives the outer game, it is the place where we usually win and lose the games that we play in life.

The other task involves translating our inner game to the outer behaviors that we need in order to produce high level peak performances. Here we focus on closing the knowing-doing gap. Here we seek to practice and refine in practice what we preach. Here also we identify the necessary how-to information that will take our performance to the next level of excellence.

How long do we stay here? This dance continues until the client has actualized his or her desired outcome in the needed frame of mind and behavior that achieves the desired goal.

4th The Solidification Dance.

In positively reinforcing the new behaviors that indicate the change, a change of new skills or a change in refining skills, we support and nurture the changes so that they last. Continually using feedback, testing, and feed forwarding of new responses, we support and celebrate with the client until the changes are made real, and the client is able to sustain them. This involves monitoring, observing, checking, holding accountable, checking ecology, inquiring about its fittingness, giving feedback, learning what's working well, and testing its robustness.

Summary

- If coaches are to operate as experts in *change* and *change technology,* they need to have some powerful and effective models for their coaching conversations.

- As a coach, we not only explore and facilitate the client's motivation for change, but understanding of current reality and what needs to change, the readiness for change, and the mapping out of a new game plan for a new outer game.

- The *Axes of Change* model, as a new and cutting-edge model that's grounded in the work of Bateson and others, enables us to dance through the various roles in coaching a client through the experience of change and even transformation.

- Where we start with a client depends on where the client is when we meet. *The Axes of Change model* provides a sense of where we are with a client in the change process. This means we may start with Axis 2, 3, or 4.

End Notes:
1: You can explore the realm of Meta-Programs in the book, *Figuring Out People* (1997/ 2006).

2: *Meta-Coaching* is the particular name of the coach training that we do. It's a Cognitive-Behavioral model of coaching within the field of Neuro-Semantics. For more about this see the websites: www.neurosemantics.com and www.equilibrio.com.au.

3. For more about the magic and genius of *meta-detailing* see *Sub-Modalities Going Meta* (2005) previously entitled, *The Structure of Excellence*. Meta-detailing is truly one of the prerequisites of mastery or genius.

PART II:

COACHING

CONVERSATION

PATTERNS

Chapter 11

THE OUTCOME

CONVERSATION

"You see things and you say Why;
but I dream of things that never were and I say, Why Not?"
George Bernard Shaw

- What does it mean to coach someone toward his or her dreams?
- How is a coaching conversation about desired outcomes able to co-create with a client a new destiny?
- What are the prerequisites for a powerful and transformative outcome conversation?
- How can we ensure that talking about desired outcomes will translate into life actions?
- What's the difference between an outcome conversation and merely talking about "positive thinking?"

The Theoretical Framework
Coaching conversations deal with *outcomes* precisely because clients sign up for coaching because they *want* something. They want something new, something different, or something more. People come for coaching to change things. They come to transform things, to make things different. They want a better quality of life. They want more fulfillment, they want more balance, they want to accomplish their life dreams.

All of these are future outcomes. All of them look forward to a client's future time-line and invite a coaching conversation about outcomes, goals, hopes, dreams and the resources for getting there. Actually, the success or failure of a coaching partnership rests on the *Outcome Conversation*. This is first conversation at the beginning of the coaching process unleashes a natural spring of self-motivation and passion. By its own velocity, it propels a client to take action and make the commitment to follow through the rough and winding roads that inevitably occur during the journey.

In the role of both *Awakener* and *Challenger* the coach "pushes" the client away from where he or she is currently and "pulls" the client into a compelling future. This Outcome Conversation sets frames that contracts with a client as to what the coaching is about, how to evaluate its effectiveness, and what to celebrate when the coaching comes to an end.

Outcome Questions
- Where are you now?
- How do you find this unpleasant or undesirable?
- What does it do to you or in you?
- How much aversion or stress does that create for you?
- Where do you want to go?
- How can you get there?
- What, if anything, stops you or might stop you?
- What, if anything, is in your way as an interference?
- What resources do you need in order to move to your preferred destination?
- When you get there, what does that do for you?
- What does it look like, sound like, and feel like?
- Do you know what to do to begin the process?
- What's the first step, the second, and the ones after that?
- Do you know anyone who has achieved this outcome?

The Structure of Well-Formed Outcomes
There is a structure for forming desired outcomes in such a way that they are well-formed, dynamic, and transformative. This pattern was developed by looking at the subjective experience of "goal setting" and identifying the core variables that comprise an effective strategy. This is critical because most goal setting is ill-formed and poorly designed. As one of the most fundamental NLP patterns, this pattern remedies that.[1] It is also at the heart of all successful coaching.
- What makes a goal or outcome *well-formed* from a design standpoint?
- What are the prerequisites for constructing and setting goals that will signal our mind-body-emotion system in to actualize our desired outcomes?

For a goal to be well-formed in design, the outcome must meet the following criteria:

1) Positively represented.

> State what you want, rather than what you do *not* want. Represent what you will be *doing* and *thinking* when you reach your goal. Create a movie in your mind of life beyond the challenge or problem.

2) Empirical.

> State in sensory-based terms in the here-and-now so that your internal movie will be close and immediate. Benchmark the specifics in empirical see-feel-hear actions and behaviors that can be video-taped.

3) Specific contexts.

> Describe the contexts of the outcome, when, where, with whom, how often, etc. In what context or contexts do you want this goal?

4) Actions steps.

> Represent the outcome in terms of processes, the specific steps and stages, including the behaviors which will move you to achieve your goal. Use verbs rather than nouns and nominalizations to map the action steps.

5) Person centered.

> Describe the processes and behaviors that within your own control so that you can initiate and maintain the specific action steps. This puts the goal within your zone of control.

6) Resources.

> Describe the resources you will need to achieve your outcome, and how you will specifically experience those resources.

7) Evidence procedure benchmarks.

> How will you know when you get your goal? What evidence procedure will let you know when you achieve your outcome? What will inform you that you have succeeded? What benchmarks will you set for to measure the success?

8) Compelling.

> Describe the outcome and the processes in language that you find compelling. Do the actual words and language of your goal excite passion within you?

9) Ecologically balanced.

> Describe your outcome in a way that you recognize as balanced and ecological for all the contexts and relationships in your life. Is the goal empowering and enhancing for all of your contexts? Is the goal realistic?

10) Forecasted in time.

> Locate the goal on your time-line so that the action steps and pathway fits into your sense of the future.

A Weight-Loss Example

In the following transcript of a coaching conversation, Sue explores her goal of losing weight.

Coach: If we were to enter a coaching partnership, want would you want to accomplish, Sue?

> *Sue:* I *don't* want to be fat. I'm sick and tired of *not* looking good in my clothes and of people thinking that I'm fat.

Coach: So that's what you *don't* want, and if you *don't* have that, what will you be experiencing. [*Getting the goal stated in the positive.*]

> *Sue:* I would be slim and fit. I'd be feeling more energy, more aliveness, and I'd be exercising regularly.

What would be "slim" for you? How would I know that you are slim when you reach that goal? [*Asking for empirical evidence.*]

> I will be slim when I weigh 55 kilograms and can easily slip into my size 8 jeans. Then I could jog or swim without running out of air.

That sounds good. And when and where would you like to experience this? [*Asking for specific contexts.*]

> When I go to the beach in my bikini to jog or swim. I want to be able to go there and just feel comfortable and not self-conscious.

Do you know what you need to do to make this happen? What could you do that would turn this into a reality for you? [*Asking for the specific action steps involved in reaching the outcome.*]

> I know that if I were to do three cardio-vascular workouts each week, and watch my diet, that would do it.

Can you do that? Are you dependent on others or external situations to make that happen? [*Applying the criterion of person centered, within one's own power for initiative and maintenance.*]

> Sure. I just need to decide to do it and then get off my rear end and make it happen.

What resources do you have or do you need to access in order to make this happen? [*Searching for the resources that will create the bridge from present state to desired state.*]

> Resources? Well, I already have a gym membership that I can renew, I already have nutritional supplements, I have the ability to learn more about healthy eating, to make a decision; is that what you mean?

Yes, excellent. And how will you know when you have your outcome? What will you see or hear or feel? [*Asking about evidence procedure.*]

> That's simple. I will see the scales saying, "55 kilograms" when I step onto the scales. And I will have the experience of going to the beach 3 times a week.

As you think about this, does it feel compelling to you? Does it excite you and captivate your attention? [*Inquiring about the compellingness of the goal, its degree of attraction.*]

> It didn't when we started to talk about it, but it does now. As I think about it I have a sense of feeling so proud and excited about losing the weight and looking good.

Is this balanced and ecological in all the contexts of your life? Do you have any concerns that it will cause problems or distress anywhere? [*Checking for the ecology of the outcome.*]

> Oh no. My boyfriend will love this, and I'll have more energy for work. It's so healthy that it is very balanced.

When do you plan to reach this goal? What is realistic on your time-line? [*Checking on whether the goal is forecasted on the person's sense of the future.*]

> If I start now here in February, I think that I can reach this goal without any problems by the first of June.

Meta-Analysis: When Sue began her goal was ill-formed, it was fluffy, vague, and only described in terms of what she did *not* want. Through the questions, she was coached to form a specific well-formed outcome that excited her, that she bought into and owned, and that invited her to make a decision about as she put it into her time-line.

Embracing the Process

How do we begin the process of co-creating with a client an outcome that's designed with all of these qualities? We first gauge the distance and difference between our current present circumstance and state and the desired outcome state. Gauging the difference invites us to begin asking the central questions about our desired destiny.

The well-formed outcome pattern gives us a clear way to think more about moving away from the aversions that now exist (or that will arise if we do not alter the course of our present state) and toward our desired outcome. The questions of this pattern allow us to elicit and coach a client to customize the key components of a well designed strategy and action plan. Doing this enables a client to construct a roadmap for moving to that desired state. Simultaneously, the questions also elicit many of the resource states that will help facilitate the actualizing of the goal.

This pattern not only hands the responsibility for achieving outcomes over to the client, it also facilitates the ownership process. In a coaching context, this pattern also becomes valuable as a reference tool for measuring the progress of the coaching relationship intermittently and at the completion of the coaching.

This pattern allows us to do several important things in coaching:

- We facilitate a greater sense of responsibility and ownership within a client for his or her own plans and life.
- We set up milestones for measuring and confirming progress and success.
- We set up a directional frame for coaching.
- We set up a process that gives us and the client a leverage for change.

Figure 11:1

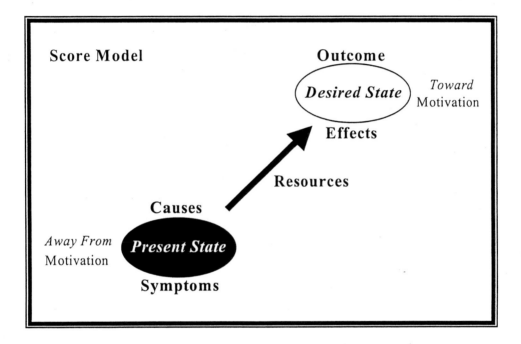

Questions for Well-Formed Outcome Conversation

1) State the outcome in positive terms.
        Where are you now? (Present State)
        Where do you want to be? (Desired State)
        What do you want in that desired state?
        What do you want to positively achieve or experience?
        What are you going toward?

2) Specify the outcome in sensory based terms.
        What will you see, hear, feel, etc., when you have it?
        What steps or stages are involved in reaching this outcome?

Have you used all of your senses in this description?

3) Identify the contexts of this desired outcome.

Where, when, how, with whom, etc. will you get this outcome?

In what context or contexts is this outcome appropriate?

What are the most fitting and appropriate contexts for this outcome?

4) Identify the steps and stages involved in reaching this outcome.

What are the steps involved in reaching this goal?

What are the stages involved?

Is this goal chunk down into small enough bits so that you feel that each piece is action-abl—something you can actually *do*?

Does the size of this outcome seem overwhelming to you at all?

5) Frame it so it is self-initiated and maintained.

Is the outcome something that you can initiate yourself and maintain?

Do you have it within your power and ability to reach this goal?

Is it within your control?

Can you initiate the actions to get started?

Can you maintain those actions or is it dependent upon what someone else needs to do?

6) Identify the resources needed to achieve this outcome.

What resources will you need in order to get this outcome?

Who will you have to become?

Who else has achieved this outcome?

Have you ever had or done this before?

Do you know anyone who has?

What prevents you from moving toward it and attaining it now?

7) Specify evidence and procedure.

How will you know that your outcome has been realized?

What will let you know that you have attained that desired state?

How do you know when to exit the strategy?

When will you feel satisfied with your achievement and ready to celebrate the success?

8) Make sure the outcome is compelling and motivating.

Is the outcome compelling?

Does it pull on you?

Will it get you up out of bed in the morning?

How much do you want this?

How much do you feel this as compelling from 0 to 10?

How much do you want to feel the motivation of this goal?

What do you need to do to make it more sparkling for you?
What would make this really sparkle?

9) Quality control the outcome for balance and ecology.

Is the desired outcome ecological?
What will you gain through it?
What will you lose?
Is it achievable?
Does it respect your health, relationships, etc.?
Are there any parts of you that object to actualizing this desired outcome?

10) Put the outcome on your time-line and try it on.

As you imagine a time and place in your future when this will become real to you . . . allow yourself to go there now . . . in your mind . . . and be there . . . fully experiencing it and enjoying it . . . that's right, and as you do just notice what it's like when you have reached this goal. Notice how it feels, what things look like, sound like, what your world is like, how you are moving through it . . . and enjoy this . . . checking it out on the inside to see if this is what you want . . . and being aware of how you might want to edit it and make sure that it really fits . . .

An Outcome Conversation

The conversation that follows is a bit wobbly compared to the earlier one with Sue's goal for becoming slim and energetic. Like Sue, it begins with some fluff and vagueness, but then it seems to go all over the place. That's because the coach is following the energy of the client rather than asking the client to fit his model. Yet if you look for the criteria of a well-formed outcome, you will see how the conversation is well structured. We include it here because most outcome conversations will be more like this—unwielding at times as it seems to go all over the place.

Coach: What would you like to accomplish in our coaching session today? What are some of the critical variables for your success that you want more choice around? [*Invitation to identify an outcome for the coaching session and frame for an outcome orientation.*]

> *Client:* I feel like I've run out of options with my work. I'm worn out. All I'm doing is the same thing over and over. It's so repetitious. [*Client identifies some of the away from values that describes his push motivation.*]

Coach: That sounds like a problem, something that is *not* working well. So since you are feeling that your work is too repetitious and wearing you out, what *do* you want? What would put some zest or passion or life back into your work? [*Awakening by pacing and validation, eliciting what the client actually wants.*]

> *Client:* I really don't know. I feel so stuck in it and have tried so many things. I'm really tired of it. I've been down this road so many times that I feel I'm now in a deep rut. [*Client still doesn't provide what he wants, just more of what he doesn't want.*]

So . . . given this, what do you want? [*Asking the question again.*]

> I want to get out of the rut, to become unstuck.

Sounds good to me. What will that be like? How will you know that you are no longer in the rut and no longer stuck in a repetitious job? [*Challenge by validation and continual exploration into what solution he wants to create for himself.*]

> I guess when I have more interesting things to do. When what I'm working on really matters.

What you're working on right now doesn't matter to you? Is that what you're saying? [*Challenging by questioning to understand where the client is and seeking clarification.*]

> Well, it matters, kind of . . . It has to be done. But it's just the details, it's not the really important stuff. [*Client more fully describes his Push—Pull motivation for change.*]

And the important stuff is what? [*Probing.*]

> It's getting beyond all the finer contractual points that I'm working on now, it's doing the negotiating with the corporate clients and setting up the deals in the first place.

How much of your work involves doing that? Didn't we discuss the negotiations that you were working on with that new client a month or so ago? [*Probing to explore and checking with a previous understanding of things.*]

> Yes, that was the fun part. Now I'm ironing out the contractual details, and spending lots of time going over and over the same papers.

You said that this is a necessary part of it all, "the details," is that how you think about it? [*Inviting a step back to look at his experience as a thinking pattern.*]

> Well, sure. It's the details that have to get done.

Why? [*The "why" of intention and importance, a meta-question exploring his value frames.*]

> Why? Because this is where the new business comes from. Without this there wouldn't be any work order at all.

So it is important? [*Awakening through confirmation question.*]
    Sure.

And how much do you feel this as important? [*Attempt to awaken through probing question about incorporation of the frame in the body as a feeling.*]
    Not very much. [*Important information about what's missing.*]

On a scale of 0-to-10 with 0 meaning "not at all" and 10 signifying "absolutely important," how important do you feel it in your body right now? [*Gauging question that exploration motivation to change.*]
    A one, maybe a two.

And would you like to feel it as more important? Would that help you to not only get through this part of the job, but to feel good about it, to feel motivated? Would that address your feelings of it being just "the details" and boringly repetition? [*Awakening the importance of feeling the importance. Helps identify outcome for the coaching*]
    Yeah. . . . it would some.

But not a lot?
    No, not really.

So what's missing? What would enable you to *feel alive* in doing this, to feel *highly motivated,* to be *completely focused* in doing this? [*Awakening with a resource question probing the client's frames about what's missing and what's desired.*]
    Hmmmm . . . I really don't know.

Pretend that you do for a moment and just notice what comes to mind, and just let the words flow as you listen to yourself. [*Awakening using a hypothetical question to open space for the client to discover what he really wants.*]
    If I knew it was important to the client and to my boss. . . . Yeah, if I
    knew they actually appreciated all of the man-hours I'm putting into it.

How are you feeling as you say that? [*Exploration into the effect that this awareness.*]
    Good. Yeah, really good.

Their validation and recognition of what you're doing is important to you? [*Awakening question into the importance of recognition.*]
    Umm hmmm.

I want you to step back from this for just a moment and if you rise up in your mind and reality test this, what do you think? Do they recognize what you're doing? Do they not? How much importance do they give to the details that you're ironing out? [*Question to reality test things and to facilitate the client exploring his own matrix of frames.*]

     Yeah, they know it's important.

To what degree? How much do they know that? [*Probing through a gauging question that presupposes feelings are always matters of degree.*]

     On a 0-to-10 scale? Oh, I would say maybe a 7 or 8.

That's sounds pretty high. Yet I have the feeling that you typically forget that, or don't allow that to be a part of your awareness, when you are ironing out those details. [*Validation and more reality testing to posit a possible needed resource, i.e., remembering and counting.*]

     True. I seldom do that.

Would that help if you did? [Nodding yes.] So be with that awareness for a moment . . . that's right. Let a movie play in your mind so that you see your client and your boss recognizing and knowing and acknowledging the importance of what you're doing. How does that feel? [*Invitation to access state and to try on the new frames.*]

     Good. [*Client experiencing more readiness to change and possible a leverage point of change.*]

How good?

     It's a 7 for me.

Imagine playing this movie in your mind at work tomorrow and the rest of this week—how does that affect things? Does that transform how you go about your work? [*Inviting a future pacing of the resource and use of a presuppositional question about transformation.*]

     Yeah. It does. I'm surprised actually. I always thought I needed them to give me more strokes and validation, but I'm now realizing that I can do that myself. I don't even really need their approval, although I like that, more than that, I need my approval. [*The beginning of constructing a new inner and outer game.*]

Intellectually you have recognized it as important, and *intellectually* you have known that they recognize your contribution, but you have not been *feeling* it as important in your body, yet when you take a moment to do that—it makes a big difference? [*Summarizing and highlighting one missing resource for a new game at work.*]

     Right. [Pause] . . . Yes, that is right.

Do you have permission inside yourself to recognize and acknowledge the importance of your own work or do you only have permission for that if someone else validates it? That is, how well can you do your own self-validation for what's important? [*Probing to explore if there's a permission frame for self-validation.*]

> Hmmmmmm. It's interesting that you bring that up. I've always needed approval. My motivation has always gone up and down depending on what other's say or don't say.

Is that literally true? That is *always* the case?   Have you ever taken on a project, hobby, sport, or anything because *you* wanted to do it and then found satisfaction in it because of what it meant to you regardless whether others validated it or not? [*Shifting into the provoker role to challenge and reality test the "allness" of the client's statement.*]

> No, actually there are some exceptions. I do have some things that I do whether I get approval or not. Like my music. I write and play my guitar regardless.

And how do you do that? What keeps you interested, fascinated, engaged, and motivated?   [*Co-creating by exploring the resource using a frame-by-implication question which assumes the client already knows how to keep himself motivated.*]

> I just love it. [*Client responds as if it's a simple matter.*]

Because . . .? [*Exploring the supporting frames.*]

> Because it's important to me.

And how do you know that? [*More co-creating that provokes the client to create the resource frames that he needs.*]

> How do I know? I know because I feel good playing and creating new melodies.

What are you paying attention to when you are doing that? What's the focus of your attention then? [*The probing for co-creation continues.*]

> It's on the rhythm, the smoothness of my playing, it's on making the pieces so familiar that my competence is unconscious. [*Client begins to specify the details of his strategy.*]

Hmmmmm. So here is something very repetitious and yet the way you focus your attention on these elements keeps your interest and energy and motivation because it means something to you, it means something above and beyond just the rhythm and smoothness. [*Summary of resources and further exploration for an even higher frame.*]

> Right.

So where are you now? Have you made any discoveries in this that can translate to your work? [*Starting the translation from inner game to outer game by inviting the client to summarize learnings, decisions, the processing.*]

> I'm going to shift the focus of my work to making music with "the details" so that I seek to please myself with it rather than needing external approval. I've learned that it is not the "repetition" that is boring, but the attitude I took toward it and that there are several things that are interesting in ironing out the details that I can focus on. [*He begins describing the new inner and outer game to play.*]

And that would put you in charge of your experience rather than make it dependent on outside sources of validation? [*Inviting confirmation.*]

> Right.

So your goal is? [*Open-ended discovery question.*]

> To learn to enjoy how to "make music" with my contractual work and to become more skilled in giving myself approval.

Is that goal compelling? Is it a big enough goal to pull you toward it when you wake up in the morning? [*Awakening and checking on the well-formed nature of his goal.*]

> Yes, I think so.

How much do you feel it as compelling and exciting? [*Gauging.*]

> About 5.

And how compelling would you like it to feel? [*Awakening by a question that explores a motivation goal.*]

> About an 8 or even a 9.

So as you think about your internal movie of that goal, what can you do to your images and your sound track so that it becomes bigger, brighter, more focused, and so on? [*Awakening by using a resource question.*]

> I just put myself playing my guitar into the picture of being at work and hearing some of my favorite tunes . . . [*Client details out the solution.*]

And you're glowing! [Yeah.] That's great! And you can let those feelings grow and double and fill up your movie . . . can you not? . . . How will you measure this goal so that you can gauge your success at becoming more internally motivated? [*Confirmation and cheerleading, with final induction.*]

> Hmmmm . . . maybe I could rate my motivation at the beginning and ending of each work day.

Meta-Debriefing

This conversation began, as do so many, with the client mostly aware of what he did *not* want rather than what he wanted. This is typical. When things aren't going as we want them, it's not unusual for us to become focused on what we don't want and don't like. We focus on the problem. Yet a *problem-focus* mindset is not equipped to find solutions. In a problem-focused conversation, complaints about how difficult things are can pull coach and client down into mental and emotional quicksand. You know you're in the quicksand when complaints dominate and when the Blame Game is in full play.

The first thing in a coaching Outcome Conversation is to shift attention from the problem to what a person wants—his or her Vision. To do that the coach will awaken and challenge by probing, teasing, and seducing—it's the *Pull* step of the *Push—Pull dance.*

- What do you want?
- What do you *really* want?
- What will get you up in the morning?
- What will make you feel fully alive, fully vibrate, fully in charge of your own life?
- What would be an ideal day for you?

After we use the coaching Outcome Conversation to identify *the what* that a client wants, we then shift upward to exploring *the why*, "Why is that outcome important and valuable?" This means asking *the why* question which is part of the *awakening pull* step of the dance.

- Why is that important to you?
- Why do you want that?
- Why would you care about experiencing or having that?

In this conversation, we explored the *why* with the client regarding "the details" of the contract. We found that it was important, but had the sense that it was "not very much." So we then asked a gauging question to scale the intensity of the feeling of importance. Later, when we found another *what*—the validation and recognition of the leaders, that turned out to be very important, a 7 or 8 on a scale of 10. All this was dancing around *Readiness.* Is the client ready to change?

For this client, it was important, yet it was not *felt* as important. There's a difference and it's a critical difference. So we explored that by asking if the client remembered it, counted it, kept it as part of his consciousness. He did not. That signaled us to offer a suggestion about letting it count more. So we invited the client to create a more vivid movie in his mind about it. That helped a lot. It created for him a surprising realization and led to an awareness of "the need for approval." This part of the conversation moved back and forth between *readiness* and finding a *leverage* frame to create the change.

We then asked about exceptions to his always needing the approval of others. Discovering those exceptions enabled us to coach him to use his own inner resource for himself in the context of his career. This he was willing and able to do.

In coaching Outcome Conversations, we begin with a precise and clear definition of *the what*, then of *the why*, and then move to focusing on *the how*. That invites the practical step-by-step identification of the resources for getting to one's outcome. This is where the person's know-how resources, strategies, motivation, intentions, sense of self, access to the right states, etc. all come together to provide a pathway and action plan to the outcome. This is the *inner to outer game* dance.

- In terms of *the coaching conversation dance*, what occurred in this Outcome Conversation?
- How did the coach and client *dance* around *the Axes of Change*?

There was, of course, the push and pull dance toward what the client wanted and didn't want. The readiness to leverage dance occurred in the gauging of the importance of work and inquiring what would enable her to feel alive and motivated. The *as if frame* helped to begin define the leverage frame—the desire for validation and recognition. Since that was already occurring, but not registered, the leverage point occurred as the client recognized and registered the validation. Then as he tried on that frame, he noticed how it began to transform things.

> **The Coaching Dance**
>
> - Toward/Away From: The Push—Pull Dance: *Challenger* and *Awakener*.
> - Active/Reflective: The Readiness—Leverage of Decision Dance: *Provoker* and *Probe*.
> - Internal/External: The Inner—Outer Game Dance: *Co-creator /Actualizer*.
> - Match/Mismatch: the Solidification Dance—*Reinforcer / Tester*.

In creating a new inner game, the coach searched for exceptions to needing approval and the client found it in his guitar playing. When this was then related to work, he found it a sufficient resource for activating a new outer game of motivation for handling the details of his work.

Summary

- Typically Outcome Conversations are the first conversation in coaching as well as an ongoing conversation that makes the coaching immensely practical, pragmatic, strategic, and performance focused.

- Outcome Conversations focus first and foremost on the outer games that a client wants to play. "What do you want to do, experience, achieve, have, or be which is vitally important to you?"

- Yet a full conversation about outcome isn't complete without moving into the inner game of our frames of mind that support and empower the outer game. That's why we ask about intentions, motivations, and agendas. *Why* do you want that outcome? *What* will do that do for you? *How* is that significant?

End Notes:

1. For more about the Well-Formed Outcome pattern as well as hundreds of other NLP or Neuro-Semantics patterns, see *The Source Book of Magic*, Volumes I and II.

Chapter 12

THE RESOURCE

CONVERSATION

- Is it possible to elicit and create mind-body-and-emotion *resources* via a coaching conversation?
- What does a Resource Conversation sound like? How is it structured?
- Can we presuppose potential resources in clients and then call those resources into being with our questions?
- If we can do that, how does the process work? What skills do we need to do that elegantly?
- How do we engage in a Resource Conversation so that it creates the kinds of transformations that a client desires?

The Theoretical Framework
Coaching as a paradigm begins with several assumptions about people and human nature, assumptions that set it apart from the traditional psychological models. Based on some of the basic premises of the Human Potential Movement, Coaching begins from the following ideas:

- People are basically healthy, not pathological.
- People have an innate urge for growth and development.
- People will naturally self-actualize once they feel safe, secure, validated, and respected.
- People have all that they need to follow and actualize their dreams.
- People operate from positive intentions, seeking to fulfill their values and visions.
- People get off track through limiting beliefs and erroneous ideas.
- People have sufficient resources to solve their problems.
- People make the best choice when given a menu of choices and the freedom to choose.
- People mostly need guidance and some facilitation in order to access

their resources and make their dreams happen.
- People naturally want to solve problems and love to stretch to meet new challenges.
- People will naturally assume responsibility and ownership and become proactive in living if given a chance.

What's at the center of these assumptions? At the core is our belief that as human beings we don't need to be "fixed," cured, or psychoanalyzed. And why not? Because *we already have the ingredients for success within us.* Having capacities for intelligence and creativity, we only need to tap into these capacities to unleash and facilitate their development. We have far more potential and resources than we have utilized or dared to believe that we have. We have incredible resources for learning, for discovery, and creating new and better maps.

Coaching a *Resource Conversation* plays off of these premises as it invites clients into a new way of thinking about life's everyday challenges. In a Resource Conversation, we coach clients to focus preeminently on finding and creating solutions. Doing this shifts the client's focus away from problems, regrets, resentments, complaints, excuses, pains, and the things that go wrong or could go wrong. Instead of a problem-centered focus, the conversations orbits around the spheres of resources and creatively considers new possibilities.

We coach to tap into the natural inner resources and to recover the natural creativity inherent in us all. We coach to explore with the client those "sparkling moments" where there are unmined resources which remain ready to be discovered and exploited for living life with more passion and authenticity.

For the coach, there are numerous coaching skills presupposed in this approach. What are they? This approach assumes that *the coach has the ability to see and call forth solutions in the midst of problems.* For this the coach has to be able to elicit states, validate the best, reinforce first approximations by cheer-leading, be present to the client, believe in the client's potentials, hold a vision of what's possible, and stand in awe of those possibilities.

Resources in the Power Matrix
We're using the term "resource," but what precisely is a resource? What do we mean as we use the term resource? The term *resource* refers to reserve supplies, support, available means, and abilities for meeting and handling a situation. What serves as human *resources* in the context of success or effectiveness in a given area are our thoughts, emotions, ideas, actions, speech, and potentials. These are the *sources* into which we can tap. When we tap into them and take

ownership of these innate powers, we feel resourceful. In the Matrix model, we describe these sources as the content of the *Power Matrix*.

What enables us to get back to the *sources* of our power—to our ability to take effective action?

- Our basic human powers for *responding* to life and to the world which include our powers of *mind* (mental powers, ideational power, symbol power), our powers of *emotion* (emotional powers, emotional intelligence), our powers of *speech* (linguistic powers, powers to encode our ideas in symbols of all sorts), and our powers of *action* (behavioral power that allows us to take effective action to make things happen).

- Our sense of *empowerment* comes from detecting, acknowledging, owning, honoring, and celebrating these powers. Doing this endows us with the sense that *we can do something in response* to the things that life throws at us, that we are not doomed in a fatalistic way to the throws and fortunes of life.

- Our sense of *learned optimism* (in contrast to learned helplessness) empowers us to even use our power of stubbornness to stubbornly refuse to act helpless or as a victim.

- Our sense of being active, taking the initiate, developing proactivity as a way of thinking, feeling, speaking, and acting.

- Our sense of having multiple intelligences which supports our creativity and possibility.

- Our ability to *approach* life with an open, curious, playful, respectful, and intelligent orientation.

The richer and fuller we map our Power matrix, the richer our sense of resources for not only coping with life, but mastering it. This opens up numerous resource states so that we live with a new *modus operandi* in the world: one of possibility, excitement and passion (desire), willingness to experiment, trust of self to recover (resilience), the ability to learn, appreciate, and discover better ways.

The principle of resourcefulness can be expressed in numerous ways. Each of these experiences highlight the importance of developing our personal resources.

- It takes personal resourcefulness to move from our current state to our desired states.

- Often we are defeated from the beginning because we start from some unresourceful state. To actualize our goals and dreams necessitates starting from a resourceful place.

- It's critical to always access a powerful and dynamic resourceful state before initiating any action plan.

- We are much more than our states, yet we are dependent on our states for the nature and quality of our experiences.
- The quality of our life can be no better than the quality of our states.

Resource Questions

In the previous chapter, we explored resources when we began looking for exceptions to "the need for approval." Once we found those examples, we "thickened the plot of that story" by simply asking lots of questions about that resourceful state of mind and emotion.[1]   This is what makes the Resource Conversation so easy. All you have to do is use your curiosity to ask scores of questions about that experience or imagined resourceful state of mind-body-and-emotion.

- What resources do you need to pull off this goal?
- How resourceful do you feel right now?
- How much more resourceful do you predict that you'll be in one week, one month, one year?
- What will you be doing to increase your resourcefulness?
- Is there anything interfering with your best resourcefulness? If so, what?
- What are the factors that bring out your resources?
- In what dimension do you need more resourcefulness? In the mental, emotional, verbal, or behavioral dimension?
- What are your best resources when you play to your strengths?
- What are some of your resources that are yet untapped and unused?
- Is there anything to stop you from playing to them?
- What one resource could you develop that would transform this situation?
- Has there ever been a time when the problem didn't occur?
- What was that like?
- How did you pull that off?
- Has there ever been a time when you had that resource? What was that like?
- What would it be like *if* you did step into that state of mind or body or emotion and fully experience it?
- Do you know anyone who can do that? If you could step into that person's experience, what is it that allows them to experience that resourceful state?
- What belief (decision, memory) do you need to release in order to become resourceful?

A Resource Conversation

Coach: So I understand that you want to work on handling criticism more effectively? [*Awakening a vision.*]

   Client: Yes, I've never been able to handle criticism very well. I've always been really sensitive to it. I guess I just take things too personally. And I know that it has really holds me back, I don't try some things because of it and I don't put myself out there at times when I really want to because I know that I'll be criticized and that I'll just feel terrible or even explode if I do. [*Feeling the Push away from.*]

Coach: You say you *always* have been sensitive to criticism and have *never* handled it well? Is that absolutely true? You have *never once* taken another's comments or views in stride knowing that it's just the other's views? . . . And you *always* do this with everyone, with children and people whose opinion you don't care about? [*Probing to awaken an exception in order to gain leverage.*]
     Client: Well, no. There have been times. I'm not *that* bad.

Good. Can you tell me about some time when you took what you call "criticism" effectively, handled it, and did not personalize it? Have there been times when you did that and felt good about it? [*Further exploration of exceptions to co-create a new inner game.*]

     Well, when I know that I'm right about something, and like when my
     husband tells me that I messed something up and I know that I did not,
     I don't take that personal. I just tell him what I think.

That's great! That seems to me to demonstrate several resources that you can use for handling criticism well at work. First, the ability to know your own mind, what you think and feel about something; and then the ability to stand up for yourself and just say so. [*Cheerleading the exception, expanding on how-to responses to co-create the inner game.*]

     Well, that's easy with Jim. But I can't do that at work. My immediate
     supervisor, Robert, doesn't have the gentleness or compassion that Jim
     has. He likes being in control and has to be right, and besides, I think
     he loves to make others wrong. [*Constructs the problem as outside her
     control.*]

Robert sounds like the perfect person to practice your skills for "taking criticism effectively," but before we get to him and to applying the skills, let's make sure that you have all the skills, models, and resources that you need to do so with power and elegance. How does that sound? [*Actualizes by preframing Robert as a person to "practice" the new skills with, refocuses on skills and awakens client to that possibility.*]

     That would be wonderful. That's what I want. [*Feels the pull to s
     better vision.*]

Good, then *how* are *you* able to do it with Jim? What are the inner resources for how you're thinking, feeling, speaking, behaving, and relating that allows you to pull that off? [*Co-creating a solution focus, probing how current resources

work, building up inner game mapping, inviting client to own the resources.]
> How do I do it? Well, I just do. I don't know how. It feels safe with Jim. He doesn't make me feel wrong. *[Client still mapping things so that the solution is in the hands of others.]*

So he never disagrees with you? *[Exception question.]*
> Oh yes, he disagrees!

And how do you respond when he disagrees after you have spoken up to assert what you're thinking and perceiving? How do you do that? *[Co-creating questions that presuppose the client has the resources.]*
> Well, I just ask questions, or find how what he means and then tell him what I think. *[Demonstrating the inner game.]*

Is his disagreement "criticism?" *[Probing question that explores how she codes the experience linguistically.]*
> No, of course not.

Yet he is disagreeing with you, isn't he? And doesn't he communicate to you that he thinks you have it wrong? *[Probing the exceptions to identify the difference that makes the difference.]*
> Well . . . yes, kind of . . . but it's not like that. It's not criticism, it's just us as a couple communicating and figuring things out. *[Identifying the resources that fuel her inner game]*

Now there's a resource! *[Co-creating through cheerleading.]*
> What do you mean?·

That's one of the most resourceful frames to put on things that I know of, that is, to *re-define* a certain kind of communication as "not criticism, but communicating and figuring things out." What if you used that frame of mind as your basic attitude toward Robert? How much would that alter things? *[Co-creating by supporting client's frame and transferring it to the problem area.]*
> I never thought of that as a "resource." But, yes, if I took that attitude toward Robert, it would be different . . . well, for me, but not for him. He still wants to control things and he will still get his kicks for trying to put me down and making me wrong.

And for you, how will *you* think-and-feel if you view things as "just communication and figuring things out" even though you know that Robert has those limiting ideas? *[Co-creating by applying resource question.]*
> Well, I'd handle it a lot better, that's for sure. *[Beginning to map out the new inner game to outer game.]*

What other resources would you need in order to take whatever Robert dishes out and *not* personalize it, *not* let it mean anything about you as a person, and just let it be *his stuff*... and able to keep communicating and figuring things out? [*Co-creating by probing for resources.*]

> I would need to feel safe. Protected. That his words can't get to me or upset me. That's what usually happens, he pushes my buttons and then I can't speak, so I feel helpless, which I hate and then it gets inside and bothers me for a long time. [*Question invites the construction of the inner game, then she slips back to a problem-focus.*]

It sounds like the key resource for you then would be to feel safe? [Nodding, yes.] So how well acquainted are you with that feeling? If you were to *feel safe*, as you do with Jim, and *feel safe* in yourself fully and completely in the way that you want to—how would you feel? What would that be like for you? [*Asking a hypothetical question to invite further development of this resource for her new inner game.*]

> I'd be feeling secure in myself... And... I'd be... I don't know... it will be strange. I've nevere been like that.

Then instead of trying to "know" it consciously, since you know that feeling, just *step back into that state* that you have with Jim... that's right... and breathe as you breathe when you *feel safe*. Good. And put your body and posture into that *feeling safe* feeling. And now just allow your entire mind-body-emotion system to adjust itself so that you *feel safe* even more fully. There you go. Do you like that? [*Co-creating through induction for the new inner game.*]

> Yes. It's great.

So just being with that... now listen to your voice, the voice you use when you are in the feeling safe state... and notice how calm and collected your thoughts ... Good. And now imagine having all of this when you encounter Robert so that it is with this state that you hear his seductions to recruit you to play his game... and you can *feel totally safe*, can you not... and notice how this state transforms things for you... transforms your responses.... How is that? [*New Game Induction.*]

> That is great.

Did you imagine handling what you might call his "criticisms" and doing so effectively? [*Preframing the ease and naturalness.*]

> Yes.

And?

> Well, it's like I can imagine doing that now. Before now, I could not even imagine it.

And now you can? [*Actualizing by testing the inner game mapping.*]
    Yes.

And somehow you *feel safe* while "just communicating and figuring things out?" That's the new inner game that you will play? [*Testing her decision to play this new game.*]
    Yes.

Do you have a sense that what he says and does "out there" does not have to get inside you? [*More reality testing of the new inner game.*]
    Yes. It's like there's a barrier now, a boundary or a wall . . . and that I can stay on this side of it and not take in any of his stuff. [*Indication that client now has constructed a new map.*]

What frame of mind, like something you could believe about yourself, about communication, or a value of how this is important, could you create that would support this new attitude? For example, suppose you had the belief frame, "Whatever others say to me or even about me is theirs, it is not mine." [*Inviting a meta-level frame to support the new inner game.*]
    Yes, that would work. And also, that I have the right to my own thoughts and opinions. [*Beginning to take ownership.*]

That would support feeling safe and standing up for yourself and just communicating to figure things out? [*question to invite confirmation.*]
    Yes, that would.

Do you need anything else as a resource? [*More testing.*]
    I can't think of anything else.

Let's set a task for this next week, okay? How about accessing this state every day, say 3 to 5 times, and creatively imagine using it to encounter Robert or anyone else who might "criticize" you? Would you be willing to do that? [*Tasking to actualize the change and integrate it into life.*]
    Sure.

Meta-Debriefing
The challenge in coaching a Resource Conversation is to not get seduced by the *content* of the client's story and to avoid any and all advice giving. Coaching is not about giving advice, fixing, doing therapy, or consulting. It's about eliciting from the client the inner resources so that the person can take full responsibility and ownership of his or her own discoveries and decisions. It is in that way that we facilitate another person to become inwardly empowered.

In this conversation, the coach had to spend a little time identifying what the client meant and defined as "criticism" and "never" able to handle it. The questions coached her to provide a crisper and cleaner definition and highlighted that there were exceptions which were then used to call forth the resources hidden in those exceptions. All of this explored and facilitated the client in finding the *leverage point and frame* for creating the new *inner game*.

At first the client was tempted in this conversation to focus on the problem and to go into an unresourceful state. At that point, the coach kept refocusing on solutions and resources by engaging in *pulling* and seducing her toward the vision of what she wanted. This had the beneficial effect of interrupting the problem focus and state.

There was also a lot of *cheer-leading* in this Resource Conversation as the coach confirmed, validated, and highlighted the client's strengths. Cheer-leading in this ways enables a client to begin to develop a more extensive map about skills and resources that have not yet been mapped. It's part of both the *pulling dance* and the *readiness dance*. Here they found some sparkling moments of excellence that had not been storied. By asking questions about them (i.e., when, where, how, etc.), the coach facilitated the client to tell a new story and to thereby *story* those sparkling moments and make them part of the person's life story.[1] This is part of co-creating with the client the new *leverage frames* for the *inner game*.

This Resource Conversation concluded with *an induction*. Inviting a person to access a state of mind-body-or-emotion is an important coaching skill. As a trance phenomenon, an induction allows a client to turn inward in a highly focused way and to access the resources so that they become a *felt* reality or experience, and not just something talked about. As such, this works as part of how to install new behaviors and responses. This allows the client to formalize and solidify the new *inner game* and to practice it in her imagination.

In terms then of *the coaching conversation dance*, we saw each of the meta-program axes of change activated in this Resource Conversation. We saw the coach and the client *dance* around *the Axes of Change*:
- Toward/Away From: The Push—Pull Dance: *Challenger / Awakener.*
- Active/Reflective: The Readiness—Leverage of Decision Dance: *Prober / Provoker.*
- Internal/External: The Inner—Outer Game Dance: *Co-Creator / Actualizer.*
- Match/Mismatch: the Solidification Dance—*Reinforcer / Tester.*

Summary

- Because coaching is about finding, accessing, building, applying, and installing *resources,* coaching inevitably engages in Resource Conversations. It is present in all coaching conversations.
- To facilitate the engagement of a Resource Conversation, a meta-coach will resist the seduction of *content* in order to work at the meta-level of *structure.* The meta-coach will also need to be able to hear, recognize, and call forth inner resources that the client presents, but does not notice.
- The test of an effective Resource Conversation is that the client walks away feeling empowered, in charge of his or her own life, and more alive with the vitality to take on the presenting challenges of life.

End Notes

1. This comes from Narrative Therapy, a powerful cognitive-behavioral model that looks at life and events through the lens of "a story." As such, there are events that are like sparkling moments have not been storied, but which when storied, become powerful resources. There are also stories told or given that create pain, dis-empowerment, and conflict. These need to be de-storied, or torn apart, by identifying who told that story, is it enhancing, and do you want it to be a frame within which to live your life?

Chapter 13

MATRIX
CONVERSATIONS

If the Matrix is the key,
What is the key to the Matrix?

"Words are the most powerful drug
used by mankind."
Rudyard Kipling

• Is it possible to explore our Matrix of frames and to wake up to the matrix of meanings that govern our sense of reality?
• How can we engage in a conversation with a coaching client about his or her Matrix without it becoming philosophical or psychological?
• What is it like to have a Matrix Conversation? How is it structured?
• What is the value and purpose of Matrix Conversations? How does that fit into the coaching relationship?
• Can we have a Matrix Conversation that sounds conversational and down-to-earth?

The Theoretical Framework
The idea that we live inside of a matrix of frames is derived from the Meta-States model. And the Meta-States model is build around the simple idea that we not only experience states, but also *states about our states.* This means that there is more to our "mind" than just what's immediately "on our mind." There are higher thoughts. We have thoughts embedded in other thoughts—thoughts that are outside our awareness. We have frames within frames that make up the mental contexts of our ideas. This is the matrix of our mind-body-emotion system. With our higher level awareness we can become aware of our awareness. We can move up into the frames of our mind. This is the difference between awareness and emotion at the primary state level and those at meta-state levels.[1]

In *primary states* we are aware, yet our awareness is mostly about things "out there" in the external world, the "real" world in which we live, work, and play. We are aware of see-hear-feel objects: our boss, the paycheck, the tone of voice that our lover uses, the house we live in, the car we drive, John's temper, the stranger who came up on us by surprise, our friends, the business we want to create, the project we want to finish, our exercise program, how we relate to our loved one, etc.

In *meta-states,* we shift our awareness from the outside world to the inside world. Our awareness *reflects back* onto ourselves. We become aware of our thoughts, our feelings, our experiences, our hopes and dreams, our fears and angers, our dreads and shames, our visions and loves. In this process our most human quality emerges, namely, our *self-reflexive consciousness.*　It is the reflective nature of our awareness that creates layer upon layer upon layer of awareness. And from the layering, we create *worlds* within our minds.

In *primary states,* our thoughts and emotions come and go. We experience our awareness like a "stream of consciousness" always flowing, moving, changing, altering. Thoughts, memories, imaginations, fears, emotions, loves, and desires come and go, they pop into the court of our mind like thought-balls ever alluring us, seducing us, distracting us. This is the "mind" that we try to control by commands when we want to concentrate and focus.
　　"Stop thinking about the pressure of that assignment . . ."
　　"Don't worry about making a fool of yourself!"

In *meta-states,* there is a greater stability to our thoughts and emotions. As a higher frame of thought-and-emotion about the lower, we carry them with us. We keep them with us. That's why they seem solid and real. They make up our *attitude*—our way of looking at the world, our frame of mind. Learn anything (and especially over-learn something) and the thoughts-and-emotions about that learning become so familiar, so established that they become our mental disposition. That awareness then becomes the mental context or atmosphere in which we live. It is in this way that we create our matrix.

In the beginning, we were born without a matrix of frames. Then as we slowly became conscious, we began differentiating ourselves from mother and family. We began to adopt their frames and use them to build our own matrix. All this happened unconsciously. We didn't even know we were doing it. Our mind was simply hungry for creating a structure that could make sense of things and so we adopted ways of thinking-and-feeling about things as our *frame of reference.* What we didn't know (what most people as adults still do not know) is that the slow absorption of mental and emotional frames became the matrix that today makes up their mental schema or "model of the world."

We absorb our first matrix from the frames of meaning and then we begin creating many of our own unique frames. Most of it we construct haphazardly —bits and pieces from school, from television, from conversations, from parties, from traumas, from novels, from music, from a thousand sources. These comprise the maps (our beliefs, understandings) that we now use to navigate the world. We use them to navigate work and career, handling people, relationships, managing our own states, negotiating, finding love, making money, etc. Some of them work well; many of them do not.

The *matrix* describes how our mind-body-emotion system works as a whole and creates our felt sense of "reality." We don't deal with reality directly, but indirectly through our matrix of frames upon frames upon frames. And we have sub-matrices within our overall matrix. We have a matrix of frames that we use to create and maintain meaning and to set intentions.

As an overall view of the *Matrix model*, there are seven matrices with one unnumbered matrix (which is the grounding matrix).

   The process matrices of the Matrix:

      0) *State:* The grounding matrix of our mind-body-emotion state where everything in the entire matrix comes together to express itself.

      1) *Meaning:* The spiraling matrix of meaning-making at multiple levels that defines and interprets things.

      2) *Intention:* Our purposes, desires, outcomes, aims, and "spirit" behind our meanings.

   The content matrices of the Matrix:

      3) *Self*: Our sense of self, self-definition, identity, and multiple thoughts-and-feelings about worth, value, dignity, confidence, etc.

      4) *Power or Resource*: Our sense of efficacy to take action, to cope, and to master to the world, our powers and resources.

      5) *Others or Relationship*: Our internal audience of friends and enemies, lovers, mentors, proteges, associates, our social panorama, all of our thoughts-and-feelings about people, human nature, and social emotions.

      6) *Time*: Our sense of events past, present, and future, our sense of mortality, origin, destiny, scheduling, etc.

      7) *World*: Our mappings about all of the worlds "out there" that we can visit and navigate.

We have a *Self matrix* that we never leave home without that gives us an internal map and structure for how to *be* a self, to define ourselves, to operate from a concept of self, and to feel esteem or contempt. We have a *Power matrix* that defines our sense of our resources for dealing with things. We have an *Others matrix* that contain all of our representations and frames about people, relationships, and human nature. We carry this with us everywhere we go as our map for navigating society and the social panorama. We have a *Time matrix* that helps us map and format things that have happened, that are happening, and that will happen. We finally have a *World matrix* of all our maps for all of the worlds we do and can live in from the world of business, to the world of politics, or physics, or television, etc.

For the most part, our unique matrix is invisible. We don't see it, hear it, or smell it as a matrix of frames. It is so much a part of us in our muscles and bones, in our eyes as our lenses, we see the world through it. That's why we don't see it. Like our glasses, after we put it on, we forget it. It drops out of consciousness and we just assume it as our reality.

It is "real" in one way. It is real *inside*. It is neurologically real inside of our mind-body system and it is the world that we are forever trying to *real-ize* and actualize in our actions. Yet it is not "real"—it is constructed. No one else can see it. No one else can feel it or even recognize its existence. We only detect it when one begins manifesting it through speech and behavior.

When you meet a someone who lives in a very different matrix to you, you may scratch your head and wonder,

- "Where in the world is he coming from?"
- "What planet did she grow up on?"
- "There's something wrong with that boy! I don't know what, but he doesn't think right."

Why Matrix Conversations?

Coaching always involves conversations about a client's inner and outer games. Clients engage us in the coaching relationship usually because they want to improve their outer game of performance in business, career, health, relationship, etc. Sometimes, the rare client will come ready to work on his or her inner game of frames. More typically, we begin with the outer game about managing people, starting a new business, writing a book, and so forth and then we backtrack to the frames of mind that drive or interfere with the outer game.

We engage in matrix conversations to explore the matrix, to more deeply and thoroughly understand a client and to facilitate the client's self-understanding. After all, it all makes sense. Everything everybody does makes sense. *How* it makes sense—well, that's another question. That is the question we explore in Matrix Conversations. Doing that involves inviting a client to go inside and use the very meta-awareness by which he or she created the matrix (self-reflexive awareness) to explore, detect, understanding, and transform the matrix.

This explains why people need coaches. Left on our own, we are likely to get lost in the labyrinth of our matrix. Using our reflexivity to explore our own mind, we get into loops, go round in circles, spiral downward into nasty vicious spins that make matters worse, we create fire-breathing dragons that can sabotage from the inside.   Many philosophers and psychologists who encountered this infinite regress of our self-reflexive consciousness drew the over-hasty conclusion that it's better left alone, assuming that we cannot master the spiraling reflexivity of our mind.

Yet we can. It's only a matter of learning *how* to do it. It's a matter of being coached to "run our own brain" more effectively—another reason for Matrix Conversations. With an experienced meta-coach who can serve as a guide through the canyons of the mind, we can learn how to turn on the light and treat our frames with the respect and honor they deserve. We can learn to handle the counter-intuitive and paradoxical nature of mind and we can learn how to construct powerfully wonderful frames that enhance and bless.

From Matrix Conversations, we can also recreate robust matrices of self, power, time, other, and world as well as meaning and intention so that we experiences a complete transformation. It shifts us so that we begin living as it were in a new world—inside of a new canopy of consciousness. Then, by installing and sustaining new and higher frames of mind—our attitude changes, our ability to translate what's in our mind into everyday action becomes a congruent dynamic, and we feel more resourceful, curious, playful, loving, and optimist than we have ever imagined possible.

Meta-Questioning that Teases out Higher Frames

All meta-levels in our mind are made up of the same "stuff" that governs the primary level: thoughts, feelings, and physiology. We *use* our see-hear-feel representations and words to build up meanings at the meta-levels to create the mental matrices. The following set of questions in various categories offer lots of ways to explore and elicit these higher level structures. As you use these, remember the different categories are *not* different things—just other ways of expressing the same thing, the meta-frame.

It is not trivial that "meaning" consists of the ideas that we "hold in the mind" whether as beliefs, values, identities, understandings or any of the 26 categories that follows. Every frame contains within it *every one of these categories.* Confused?

If this seems confusing, welcome to the club. It confuses most of us because we have been tricked by language itself. It happened when these higher levels, or "logical levels" we described using noun-like words. By nominalizing these categories as "beliefs," "values," "meanings," etc. we mis-cue our minds-bodies and begin assuming that they are actual "things." We think of them as different things. Yet they are not. All of these words are only expressions of *mental processes—the framings* that we do to create our neuro-semantic reality or matrix.

Think of the following questions as 26 ways to dance around the *diamond of consciousness* and to explore the many *facets of awareness.* These are *facets of focus* that give us multiple ways into the matrix of our mind.[2]

Matrix Questions

In entering and exploring the matrix of frames that governs our feelings and our sense of reality, we explore the thoughts-and-feelings that we have used to set the frames for other thoughts-and-feelings. The matrix is created from our self-reflexive consciousness out of the stuff of our primary states—thoughts, feelings, and sets of physiologies. It's the mixture and the structure that makes the difference.

The trick in exploring the matrix is that the very words and language that seems so precise at the primary level seems like an Alice-in-Wonderland world at the meta-levels. There's a fluidity and relativity to how each of us experience the semantics (meanings) of our words. Consequently, we often have to use lots of synonyms and come at the same idea or concept from numerous perspectives. That's the purpose of these terms and questions. Each term refers to yet another way to think about a particular *level* or *frame.*

1. **Meanings:** The ideas that we hold in mind.
        What does this mean to you?
        What else does it mean to you?
        How much meaning does it hold for you?
        Do you know how you came to attribute this meaning?
        How well does this meaning serve you?

2. **Beliefs:** The ideas that we affirm, validate, and confirm (also **convictions**).
        What do you believe about that?
        How much do you value that belief?
        Do you have any beliefs about that belief?
        How have you confirmed that belief?
        How strong is that confirmation?
        What other convictions do you have about this?

3. **Frames:** The ideas that we use to set frame of reference, structures of context in our mind.
        What's your frame of reference for this?
        How do you frame this?
        How else could you frame it?
        What's the most empowering frame you've heard from others about this?

4. **Generalizations:** The ideas that we draw as summary conclusions about things, "ideas" we have about other ideas.

What do you think about that?
What do you feel about that?
What comes to mind when you entertain that thought?
What conclusions have you drawn about this?
How have you generalized from this experience?

5. Realizations: The ideas we develop as new insights, understandings, and even eureka experience.

How does it feel to realize this?
When you realize this, what do you think?
Now that you know, what do you want to do?
Now that you're aware of this, what comes to mind?

6. Permissions: The ideas that we allow and permit which open up new possibilities from old taboos.

Do you have permission to think or feel this?
Who took permission away from you?
What happens when you give yourself permission to experience this?
Would you like to have internal permission for this?
Does the old prohibition or taboo against it serve you well?
As you give yourself permission and notice what happens, how well does that settle?
How many more times will you need to give yourself permission?

7. Feelings: The emotional ideas and feeling judgments that we bring to other ideas.

What do you feel about this?
What specific emotion do you associate with this idea or experience?
Framing it with this feeling, does this empower you as a person?
Does this feeling map things in a way that enhances your life?

8. Appreciation: The ideas of appreciation or value that we use to frame other ideas.

What do you appreciate about this? About yourself in this experience?
What could you appreciate about this emotion or experience?
If you could stay totally resourceful *and* have this experience, what value would that hold for you?
How much appreciation would you like to have about this?

9. Value / Importance: The ideas that we value, treat as important and significant, esteem.

How is that important to you?
What do you believe about that value?
Why is that important or valuable to you?
When you get that value from it, what's even more important than that?

10. Interest: The ideas of fascination, curiosity, interest, etc. that we bring to other ideas.

What's the most fascinating thing about this experience or idea?
What could you become curious about in this if you allowed yourself?
How do you best like to put yourself into something (inter -est)?

11. Decision / Choice / Will: The ideas that we separate and "cut off" (cision) from other ideas or choices so that we say *Yes* to some and *No* to others.

>What decision or decisions drive this?
>So what will you do?
>What would you like to do?
>What are you saying to yourself in terms of choosing or deciding?

12. Intention / Want / Desire / Strategy: The ideas you have about your motive, intent, desire, wants.

>What is your purpose in this?
>What is your intent in this? And what is an even higher intention than that?
>When you have that in just the way you like it, what do you get from that?
>Why is that valuable to you?
>What's your strategy for making that happen?

13. Outcome / Goal: The ideas we have about goals, outcomes, desired ends.

>How do you want to see this turn out?
>What is your preferred desired outcome from this?
>What consequences do you hope will come from this?
>What is the outcome of this outcome?

14. Expectation / Anticipation: The ideas we have about what we anticipate will happen.

>What are you expecting?
>Where did you learn to expect that?
>How legitimate is that expectation?
>What is the quality and nature of that expectation? Is it rigid or flexible?
>Does that expectation keep you open and curious or demanding and controlling?

15. Connection: The ideas we have about our connection with other ideas, experiences, and people.

>How connected are you to this idea, feeling, or experience?
>What does your connection to this do for you?
>Is this connection linked up to your self-definition or identity?

16. Causation: The ideas we have about cause, influence, contributing factors, what makes things happen, etc.

>What makes you feel this way? Think this way? Experience this?
>Does it have to make you have these thoughts and feelings?
>Who says? What's the rule that makes this so?
>Does it always work this way?
>When has it not caused this? What other exceptions are you aware of?
>What are the mechanisms that make it work this way?

17. Culture: The ideas we have about our cultural identity, definition of reality, and cultural ideas.

>Is this part of your cultural heritage?
>What cultural context did you learn this?

What do you think about these cultural values and beliefs?
How well do they serve you?
If you were to pass on a new cultural legacy, what would it be?

18. Presupposition / Assumption / Implication: The ideas that we use as higher frames that reflect our assumptive world and understandings.
What's implied in that statement? How does it make sense?
What are you assuming that enables you to think or feel this way?
How many presuppositions are you running with in order to believe this?
Where did these assumptions come from? Are they from your upbringing?
Are they in the structure of language itself?

19. History / Memory / Referent: The ideas that we bring with us about previous experiences and use as our "referential index" for making-meaning.
Does this remind you of anything?
What comes to mind when you surrender to these thoughts or feelings?
What previous examples or experiences have you had that relate to this?
How does your personal history play into this?

20. Rules / Demands / Shoulds / Musts / Authorize: The ideas that we use that set up the Rules of the Games that we play out in our lives, the modal operators that generate our *modus operandi* in the world.
You should, must, and have to do this? Why? Who says?
What creates the demandingness in your statement or feeling?
Who or what is the authority beyond and above this experience that demands this?
What if you don't? What then? What will happen then?

21. Definition / Language / Class / Categorizes: The ideas that we have that set the frames and categories for our minds.
What does this word or term mean to you?
How do you define it?
What emotional associates have you connected with this term?
How would it feel if you knew that this term was just some sounds and didn't have to be so semantically loaded?
What other definitions could you give to this to make it more useful as a map?
How does this term classify things? What does it mean in terms of the categories that it suggests?

22. Understanding / Know / Knowledge: The ideas you have that "stand" "under" you as the mental support for your world.
What do you understand about that?
What background knowledge are you accessing that creates your understanding about this?
What do you "know" about this? How do you "know" that?
What kind of knowledge is this?
In what modality is this knowledge?
What kind of intelligence is this? (Use Gardner's Seven Intelligences).

23. Identity / Identify / Self / Self-definition: The ideas we build up about our "self," the ideas we use in self-defining.

> Does this affect your self-definition or identity?
> How does it affect the way you think about yourself?
> What does this say about how you perceive yourself?
> Are you identifying yourself with this thought, feeling, or emotion?
> Does that enhance your life or empower you as a person? Do you really need to do this?

24. Paradigm / Model / Map / Schema: The ideas we have that come together as more complex mappings about things.

> What paradigm (model, schema) drives and informs this?
> What paradigm are you relying on in your understandings?
> How valid or useful is this map?
> Would you like to map it in another way?

25. Metaphor / Symbol / Poem / Story: The ideas that we form through stories, analogies, and non-linguistic forms.

> What is this like?
> If this was a color, what color would it be?
> If this was an animal, what animal would it be?
> What would this sound like if you put it to music?
> If you made up a poem or story about this, what would you say?
> How have you been storied? Who storied you? What is the story?
> Would you like to create a new narrative for yourself, for this experience?
> What would a new narrative sound like?

26. Principle / Concept / Abstraction: The ideas that we treat as guidelines, laws, settled conclusions.

> What is the guiding principle that you hold about this experience?
> What concept or conceptual understanding governs this?
> How does this principle or abstraction work in everyday life?
> Do you have a good relationship with this concept?
> If you were to remap this abstraction, how would you change it?

A Matrix Conversation

When I (MH) worked with Brenda O'Reilly (not actual name), she wanted to focus our conversation on some health issues. For several months she had been experiencing symptoms of fatigue, anxiety, and disorientation and didn't understand where they were coming from or what they were about.

Coach: What are things like in your body? [*Exploring to identify the client's current situation and state.*]

> *Brenda?:* It's mostly fatigue—a tiredness that I feel when I wake up in the morning that doesn't go away. [*Identifying what she wants to move away from, the push.*]

Coach: How intense is this feeling of fatigue? [*Challenging to gauge the energy of the push.*]

It's about a 7.

So pretty strong? [Yeah.] And what's the most disturbing or unpleasant thing about it for you? [*Challenging to bring more attention to the push or away from energy.*]

The lack of energy, how it drains me of the *"ump!"* to just get up and go and make things happen. That's the most disturbing part.

Is there a certain part of your body where you mostly experience this or is it pervasive throughout your body? [*Challenging how pervasive the push is.*]

It's mostly like in my chest area and then it radiates outward to the rest of my body.

Are you sensing that right now? [Yeah.] And when you do, how unpleasant is it right now. ["It is a 6."] And are there any words that go with this feeling? [*Probing.*]

Just an "Aggggghhh." It's a groan, a moan-like sound that a tired person would make, it sounds tiring, in fact, and debilitating.

And any other words or ideas? [*Probing.*]

Oh, ideas! Yeah, lots of them. Like, "What wrong with me? Make I've got some fatal disease and am going to die." Then I say to myself, "This is awful. I hate this. This isn't me."

That sounds very unpleasant and not the way you want to live. When you step back from these things, is any of that true or accurate? [*Supporting the client by pacing, then probing and testing.*]

No, I've been to the doctor and she says that there's no physical cause, my blood tests check out just fine and she can't find anything wrong with me. She says it's about stress or frustration or unfinished emotional business or something.

Does that ring true for you at all? [*Probing the client's mind and maps about that.*]

Actually it does. I've been under a lot of stress lately, so many pressures at work, and then there is my relationship with my boyfriend.

So you are up against a lot of stresses which could be amplifying this? When you step back from that, what seems like the most critical and emotionally important thing in all of this? [*Supporting and probing.*]

My relationship. Things haven't been going well there. It seems that everything we try to do just irritates both of us; Jim gets on my nerves a lot with all of his advice. It's, like, first of all he doesn't understand,

and then he goes in lecturing, which I hate.

Hmmmm. And so how do you respond? [*Probing.*]

>I argue with him at first, then when I see that it's going nowhere, I clam up. That infuriates him even more. We haven't had any fun in a long time.

After all of that happens, then how do you respond to the responses that you make? Do you like responding that way? Where does your mind and emotions go then? [*Probing.*]

>Round and round. I wonder if we should split, then I'm afraid of losing him; then I wish he would get out of my life, then I'm ashamed for feeling so angry at him.

Ah, the loop! The downward spiral loop that just gets worse and worse? [*Pacing and giving words to the client's experience.*]

>Exactly.

So if you were past all of this, how would you prefer to feel about Jim, respond to him, think about your relationship, etc.? [*Co-creating through using a hypothetic "as if" question to invite and frame the constructing of a new inner game.*]

>I would rather feel calm and relaxed so that we could talk things through calmly and feel supported by him instead of attacked. I want to feel loved by him. [*A clearer vision of what she wants.*]

What do you believe about yourself in relating to men in general, or to Jim in particular? That is, what do you believe about working through conflicts and misunderstandings. Just say whatever comes to mind, not what you want to believe or "should" believe, but what do you believe? [*Probing the matrix of frames about men, conflict, and relationships.*]

>I believe that we shouldn't disagree and that if we do, maybe there's something wrong in us being together . . . That maybe we are wrong for each other. [*Leverage, Readiness*]

Hmmm. And as you hear yourself say that, what do you believe about those beliefs? [*Probing to find leverage frames.*]

>I want to change them.

Yes, I can imagine that you would. And you may want to set that as one of your goals. But, just for a minute, let's assume that these are your governing beliefs, what beliefs do you have that support you believing them? [*Confirming and probing further into the client's matrix.*]

>Well . . . that conflict is bad, that we should always get along and never

disagree. . . . I can't believe I'm saying that. [*Feeling the leverage to change.*]

That's good. Your sense of shock means that you are just flushing out the higher frames that govern and support the lower belief frames. Yes, before we can quality control them, and reality-test them, we have to flush them out. You're doing good! [*Validating by cheerleading, then* a*wakening, probing, and co-creating.*]

> I guess I also believe that I can't handle conflict, that conflict will destroy a couple and make life a living hell. . . . Where is this stuff coming from?

Good. Now as you step back from that—as you've been doing, and really listen to this, do you buy these ideas, *intellectually*? [*Question to get more leverage and develop more readiness to change.*]

> No, I don't.

Yet these are the higher frames in your matrix of frames that's determining your feelings and actions. [Right!] And these are the frames that creating the stress and anxiety . . .

> . . . and sense of threat. That's why I feel so much fear. [*Demonstration of good ego-strength to look at what is.*]

Fear? [*Probing for further leverage.*]

> Yes, fear that my whole life is going to cave in. [*Discovery of a leverage frame.*]

For a moment I want you to stay with these feelings, and gauge how intense they are for you. [*Testing the energy in this frame.*]

> About a 9.

Breathe these feelings in . . . that's right . . . and notice if you need to take counsel from them. Do they serve you well? Do they offer you any ideas or insights that help you handle things and as you keep whatever is valuable, then just release whatever is not. Breathe out . . . fully . . . and expel them . . . just let them go . . . There you go. Now breathe them in again, and how intense are they now? [*Co-creating questions that invite the client to quality control her feelings to get even more change leverage.*]

> Only a 4. I'm feeling much calmer.

As you keep breathing in and out, taking very deep and long breaths, let your thoughts come together to identify what you would prefer to feel . . . and what would you like to feel that would empower you to handle the stresses in an effective way and to be more in control of your own life? [*Question to co-create new inner game.*]

> I want to be more accepting, to feel more calm in myself knowing that I don't have to give so much meaning or power to conflict or disagreement, that I can be lighter. I want to feel more humor, more playfulness. That's it.

Have you ever been playful and humorous? [*Co-creating by inviting the client to find memories of existing resources.*]

> Of course.

Then has there ever been a time when you were really playful in a resourceful way . . . then just go back there now . . . see what you saw when you were there, hear what you heard, hear you own laughter and giggling . . . and let that feeling grow and expand . . . and set that as your frame of mind when you think about conflicting and see Jim giving you so much advice, like Mickey Mouse, really informing you about things . . . [laughter] and know that arguing about really serious things like toilet paper and time schedules that make the world go around and that's why we get together, to argue with our loved ones [laughter] . . . and how does it feel when you feel all of this about your relationship with Jim? [*Induction to co-create a new game and provoking the client to access the needed resources.*]

> I lighten up. I relax. It really helps me to be more calm and mentally collected.

How does it affect your energy level?

> Hmmmmm. That's amazing, I feel more energy, the fatigue is down to a 4.

And are there some other resources like humor, calmness, and lightening up that would put new energy and meaning into your life and body? What if you made it a goal this week to make a list of ten other resources that invigorate you, that put new energy in your mind and body, that allow you to experience more calmness? [*Tasking the client for the Inner and outer games.*]

> I'd like to do that.

Meta-Debriefing

If you go back over this Matrix Conversation with Brenda you will find that it is mostly made up of questions and invitations to explore her own matrix. In Meta-Coaching we refer to this as "pure coaching." That is, when we just ask questions and facilitate an exploration, we are not teaching, training, consulting, doing therapy, or giving advice, we are coaching to enable the client to unleash his or her resources.

We invited Brenda to use her *Step Back skill* repeatedly throughout this conversation. We use it for several things—for quality controlling, checking ecology, reality testing, and trying on new frames. We used it to dance between the *Push—Pull* also. Inviting a person to *step back* from our experience, and especially from that person's thinking, emoting, and framing, invites an expansion of awareness. It invites the person to move up the levels of the mind and as one does, that matrix as a system changes. To support the step back, we invited Brenda to use her breath, to breathe in and out with an emotion or an awareness, and to just be with it, to just notice it without judgment. This facilitated her ability to co-create new frames for a new relationship game.

Did you notice that within this conversation the Outcome and the Resource Conversations were used? And while there are questions for precision that ground the person back into her everyday experiences, most of the questions are meta-questions—questions designed to move up into the matrices of frames that create her reality. These serve both to probe for the *leverage* point and frame and to begin to create the new inner game frames.

Did you catch *the coaching conversation dance* as it occurred in this Matrix Conversation? Did you identify how the coach and client *danced* around the four meta-program axes of change?
- The Push—Pull Dance where the client moved back and forth between the vision to move toward. The coach spent a good bit of time in the challenger role, gauging and building up the unpleasant problems of her current state to highlight what to move away from.
- The Readiness—Leverage of Decision Dance wherein the client reflected upon her current frames and ideas and then began to feel active about changing, doing something different, not tolerating her current situation.
- The Inner—Outer Game Dance where the client internally designed a new game with sufficient supporting frames and then began trying on what the game will feel like and sound like in the external context.
- The Solidification Dance of matching anything that fits with actualizing the new game and mismatching to test everything that doesn't measure up—*Reinforcer / Tester*.

Summary
- Coaching to any person's matrix of frames is the *inner game*. This is where we go in and find the "rules of the game" that govern any particular experience.
- A Matrix Conversation, by its very nature, has the power to change a game completely. By moving inside to the key leverage places of framing and meaning, a meta-coach is able to more quickly and efficiently bring transformation to an entire mind-body system. It is in this way that "change" can become even fun and enjoyable.

- We have hundreds of meta-questions that enable us to hold a Matrix Conversation. The trick lies in realizing that there are no "logical levels" but only *psycho-logical* facets of the experience.
- Matrix Conversations moves up and beyond what's in conscious awareness to the larger mind that's outside of awareness. It takes us to the frameworks that we have grown up in and built—usually unconsciously. In that, the Matrix Conversation can be very trancy, that is, hypnotic.

End Notes

1. The basis of the Matrix and Meta-States are the following books: *Meta-States* (2000, 2nd edition), *The Matrix Model* (2003 2nd edition), and *Secrets of Personal Mastery* (1999).

2. We have written much more about "logical levels and logical types" in *NLP: Going Meta* (2002) and on the website: www.neurosemantics.com. In *Meta-Coaching*, we will describe the fluidity of the logical layering of frames in relation to these meta-questions and how to use them for an effective and probing conversation that gets to the heart of a person's matrix.

Chapter 14

THE POSSIBILITY

CONVERSATION

"We cannot solve the problem
with the kind of thinking that created the problem."
Albert Einstein

- Is it right or legitimate, or even useful, to use *imagination* in exploring outcomes, resources, or matrix?
- Should we engage in conversations of pretend, magic, miracles, and possibilities? Will that not set us up for illusion, disappointment, and disillusionment?
- Are hypothetical explorations really practical?
- Can we think in possibility terms *and* still be realistic, and practical?
- What is the value and purpose of thinking in terms of possibilities?
- Are Possibility Conversations just for the artistic types, for those engaged in creative ventures, or is it for practical business also?
- How can pretending, imagining miracles in the middle of the night, and acting "as if" actually nudge our behavior to new levels of achievement? How does that work?

The Theoretical Framework
The coaching relationship is pre-eminently practical and pragmatic. That's one of the reasons Coaching, as a movement, has exploded in the 1990s and early twenty-first century. Beginning with professional athletes who simply wanted to refine and hone their skills, and obtain a cutting-edge advantage above their superstar competitors, they began hiring personal coaches to obtain peak performance in their skills.

It wasn't long before business executives and CEOs recognized that an executive coach could do the same thing for them in terms of leadership, speaking, creativity, and negotiating. From there politicians, movie stars, managers, business owners, entrepreneurs, and many others began looking for a personal or executive coach who could bring their skills and performance to new levels of expertise.

This pragmatism of coaching puts a premium on skills and tools and de-emphasizes theory. The mantra was, *"If it works, use it."* Only now has the field of coaching begun to settle down to think about its theoretical framework and the governing premises that make it work.

- Given this focused emphasis on practicality, where do the states and processes that we associate with the impractical (i.e., imagination, possibility, and pretending) come in?
- Can we use these as central coaching tools?
- If so, how can we use these as coaching tools?
- How can we structure a coaching conversation around possibility thinking using hypothetical questions?

That answer is simple. When we think in terms of possibilities, in terms of imagining wild options, we temporarily step "out of the box" of our assumptions and limitations. Frequently, it is such "out of the box" thinking that allows us to try on new possibilities, and to move forward, to more exquisite levels of performance. It's for these reasons that Possibility Conversations are central to the adventure of coaching.

Pretending Our Way to Reality
Given the nature of our constructed matrix of frames that create our inner game of reality, is it really any surprise that we can use imagination to create new ideas, new products, new services, new possibilities that add value to others?

Actually, this has always been the way the human race has progressed. Somehow, and in some way, creative men and women get an idea in their heads and begin playing around with it. Eventually they begin experimenting with the idea. They begin experimenting, trying things out, exploring, and testing. Eventually we dubbed this as "science," and turned it into a discipline. Those who succeed at creating new models, products, systems, services, etc. are designated "creators" and "inventors."

If it works this way with the onward progress of human knowledge and technology, then certainly it works just as well for progress in coaching people for higher levels of performance and expertise in how they live, relate to others, and manage themselves. It works for improving both our inner and outer games.

This also highlights the difference between coaching and therapy. Coaching focuses on people progressing to the next level. It focuses on developing and actualizing our best. In a word, it is about generative and transformational change. Coaching focuses on stepping up to the next level to make things better. By way of contrast, the tradition of psychology has focused on remedial change, on fixing things. Freud began by looking at problems, hysteria, and mental disorders. He assumed that people were broken and needed to be fixed. This is the domain of psychiatry.

Traditional psychology continued that focus until the 1950s when the cognitive sciences began to develop. Then, along with the Human Potential Movement (i.e., Maslow, Rogers, Assagioli, May, *et. al*), numerous therapists began studying *healthy* humans rather than sick ones. Prior to that time, psychologists studied those with mental illness, personality disorders, and sociopathic behaviors. In a way, that's like a car engineer studying the cars in a junk yard to come up with ideas for designing next year's car.

Coaching follows the lead of the cognitive sciences, the neuro-sciences, systems and cybernetics, Human Potential Movement, solution-focused therapy, Ericksonian hypnosis, etc. It starts from the assumption that people are *not* broken. People only need to be given a chance in the right context and atmosphere and they will move toward growth, development, choice, and the best states.

This is where possibility thinking comes in.
- What's possible for human beings in terms of advancing the way we think, feel, speak, behave, relate, and create?
- If we don't use the past to determine our future, how can we open up new vistas of possibility for accelerating our learning, transformation, state management, and relationships?
- If we pretend that we have all the resources and are seeking the do the best with what we have, what can we discover in the best humans, the most developed members of the human race, and the most self-actualized of individuals that gives hope for everybody else?
- If we modeled the thinking, feeling, states, beliefs, behaviors, etc. of the best, of geniuses in creativity, in relationships, in leadership, etc., what then becomes possible in these fields?
- What possibilities would you like to feed your mind that will give yourself a chance for peak performances?

The Magic of Possibility Thinking

As we enter the twenty-first century, we have plenty of examples and evidence of the power of using possibility as a frame for generating new potentials. We have seen it in sports. Every year Olympic athletes break records that were once considered beyond human possibility. In 1954 Roger Banister broke the four minute mile, a record that had stood for decades. With that event suddenly dozens of top-class mile runners were breaking that barrier. Nearly 200 runners crashed through the barrier within the next decade. Today, a four-minute mile runner isn't even in the running for a world-class performance. That barrier, as with so many barriers, was mostly a barrier in the mind.

Because possibility thinking frees us from the old constraints and invites us to use our creative imaginations to look for solutions, we are more likely to find such solutions. To presume that it can't be done forecloses the subject before we begin. Manned flight, home computers, and ten thousand other inventions were foreclosed on by the majority of scientists before one dared to imagine and to entertain the wild idea, "What if we could?"

Possibility thinking is one of those mechanisms that allow us to explore our matrix and beyond. It enables us to step aside, in our mind, from the very matrix that structures our thinking so that we give ourselves a chance. When we try on *the "As if . . ." frame,* it loosens the hold of the matrix on our thinking-and-feeling . . . and momentarily allows us to step out into the void and unknown of yet unmapped possibilities.

In the coaching of Possibility Conversations, we use these frames.
- If you could actualize your dream of creating that new business, what would be the first thing you would do?
- If you woke up in the morning, and a miracle happened over night, so that you no longer have those old feelings or constraints, what would be different? How would you even know that a miracle happened while you were sleeping?
- What would be the most important resource for solving this problem if you could solve it?

What do such questions provoke or engage inside us? Do they not invite us to entertain and map out new possibilities? Do they not loosen up the old constraints and enable us to look reality in the face and come back to see what actually exists instead of the world as colored by our fears, apprehensions, and "knowledge of what's not possible?"

Of course, it's scary to turn loose of our trusted frames that have defined reality. What if it doesn't work? What if we fall on our face? What if someone laughs? What if we do succeed?

No wonder that it takes courage to engage in a *Possibility Conversation* with a coach and to be led beyond familiar maps and out into the unknown. What if we can't find our way back? What if we get lost in the unknown? What if we become unrealistic and foolish? Ahhhh, the dragons roar in the back of our mind and that carry on when we threaten to step outside our familiar Matrix. This is where trust in the coaching relationship provides the security and safety to experiment, to explore, to be a little outrageous, and to inject lots of courage for the risk it takes to welcome in new possibilities.

Possibility Questions

Is this desired outcome possible for you?

Is it possible for anyone?

What do you say that you *can't* do which is not a *physiological* can't, but a *psychological* can't?

What would it be like if it were possible?

What is the probability that you'll be able to achieve this outcome within the next month, year, or decade?

What limitations or constraints play into this objective?

Do you know anyone for whom this is possible? What makes it possible for that person?

What are the critical variables? How did they develop them?

What is the language that is part of your internal conversation?

To what extent do you use the language of possibility or that of impossibility?

Do you know how to tell if your *can't* is a *physiological* or a *psychological* can't?

Would you like for this outcome to be possible for you?

If you woke up in the morning after a middle-of-the-night miracle, how would you know that you were living in the day after the miracle? What would be different?

How would you know? What would others notice?

In the coaching context, Possibility Conversations occur around numerous challenges and conflicts that we often map as "impossible," and then feel helpless about.

Time Management:

I don't have enough time in the day to do everything.

Feeling Overwhelmed:

I will never get all the things of this project completed.

We have tried everything in our relationship and, not only does nothing work, but every attempt only increases the problems.

General Unhappiness:

I've reached all the external signs of success, yet I'm still not happy; those less successful than I seem much happier. What's going on?

Limited Thinking:

I want to write a book, but I don't think I could do it *and* maintain my current style of life.

A Possibility Conversation

Coach: How are things better or different since our last session on your wealth building plan? How did you go with the assignment? [*Testing results of tasking assignment.*]

> *Client:* Actually, the week has not gone well. I didn't do the tasking that you gave me to do. And that's because I've really have struggled since our last session with serious questions of whether it's really right to set such high goals for financial success in my life.

Coach: This sounds really significant and perhaps at the heart of things. What do you mean about if it is "really right" to set such high goals? [*Pacing to confirm the client's thinking and feeling, exploration question for probing.*]

> *Client:* Just that, Is it right?

Coach: You mean as in "morally" right? [*Probing with a confirmation question.*]

> Yes, exactly. What if it isn't? What if I shouldn't be doing that?

Help me understand your perspective. How could it be morally wrong to aim high and set the goals that you have set? Are you intending to hurt anyone in the process, take advantage of the less informed, steal or do something illegal? [*Probing to understand the client's model of the world.*]

> No, no. Nothing like that. Of course not. . . . But what if things are supposed to be more equal in the world, and my seeking for such high goals creates a mis-balance in the world? [*Expressing what he is moving away from.*]

Is that what you actually believe? [*Probing through testing.*]

> Well, no. I'm just asking.

Then, I'm wondering what's the real question behind this question? What are you really struggling with that is actually driving this question and these fears? [*Probing to find out what lies behind and above the question.*]

> Hmmmm. Well, I guess it is, Do I deserve to have so much? What if it's not for me?

So, is that what you believe? Do you believe that some people are . . . what? . . . *destined* to such high goals and dreams and some, namely you, are not? Is that what you believe? [*Presenting the belief in a more bold form and provoking the client.*]

> Well, no, not really.

Somehow I have the feeling that there's something else, something else eating at you . . . perhaps really far back in your mind . . . something you're not conscious of, but which you could become aware of . . . if you allowed yourself to go there and ask these probing questions of yourself. Are you willing to do that? [Yes.]   Good, then be with these questions, and if you knew the answer, what would you say? [*Challenging the client's frame by inviting awareness and using a hypothetical frame.*]

> [Long pause. . .] I'd say I'm afraid of trying and failing. I'd say that the fear of failure is holding me back. I'd say that I don't want to be embarrassed in front of my friends, and that I don't want it to create any stress or strain with my wife. I'd say that I'm very scared of making a mistake, of doing something wrong. [*The client presents his thoughts tentatively, "I would say . . ." as he tries on these thoughts in the back of his mind.*]

How does that now feel that you are facing those dragons, looking them in the face, and look! . . . You are still here! They didn't get you! I know it took a lot of courage to do that . . . how do you now feel? [*Provoking the client to a bolder courage to face his matrix.*]

> It's strange. It's almost like a relief. It's like that there's something about just saying it out loud that changes it. . . . It's like saying it gives me some distance from it and makes it less serious. In fact, some of it now seems pretty silly and ridiculous. How can just saying it make that much of a difference? [*An "Aha!" experience for the client of the power of a witnessing awareness.*]

That's great. So you feel relieved and that perhaps those ideas—when they were in the dark—exercised a power of fear over you? So where are you now? Is it wrong to want to set high goals, obtain financial independence and success, and choose your own lifestyle, and contribute back to the world in the ways you've decided that you want to? [*Cheerleading, and then returning to the subject and testing the new resources and co-creating the inner game.*]

> [Laughing] No, not at all. It's like none of that seemed possible as long as it was way in the back of my mind, but now it's almost as if I've expelled that way of thinking.

So do you think you can complete your tasking this week? Are you willing to finish your Action Plan for your career and financial success? Is there anything stopping you now? [*Testing to see if the client can take the necessary actions for his outer game.*]

> I don't think so.

So what about your feelings of failing, of making a mistake, of being embarrassed, of putting stress and strain on your wife Linda? Are you able to handle those things? [*More testing.*]

> I think so.

You don't sound fully convinced or congruent about it yet. Are you? [*Testing.*]
> No, not fully.

So what's the possibility that you can overcome these fears and handle failing, making a mistake, etc.? What resources do you need so that it becomes a possibility for you? [*Inviting the client's creating of more resources to use, Tester and Actualizer.*]
> I'm not sure. When I think about it, I feel stuck about coming up with an answer.

Let's say that tonight, when you go to bed, that tonight something very special happens when you're sound asleep. Did you ever pretend as a child? [Nods yes.] Then I want you to pretend that during your sleep in the middle of the night a miracle happens so that, in the day after, you have the ability to powerfully and profoundly handle these things, to handle them with grace and elegance. Would you like to experience a miracle like that? [*Awakening and co-creating with the client new possibilities.*]
> Yes, I would.

So just pretend, because you are just using your imagination . . . and what if you did wake up so totally resourceful in yourself that there was absolutely no fear of mistakes or failure, but a robust and vigorous courage to take on the world. Would you like to imagine that? . . . Good. . . . Now if this did happen, how would you know on the day after the miracle? [*More awakening and co-creating as inducing a possibility state.*]
> Well, I'd feel different. I'd stand taller and breath fuller and I'd feel more confident in myself that I can make things happen.

Show me. How would you be standing? Breathing? Moving? . . . That looks good. And how would you be thinking? [*Testing and actualizing via state induction.*]
> I'd be thinking about things to do, strategies for making things happen. I'd be telling myself that mistakes are just part of the process for learning, that there's no growth without mistakes.

Now you're sounding more convincing and congruent.
> I feel more confident too!

Do you feel confident about handling those challenges? [Yes.] Do you feel more congruent about setting some bigger goals for yourself, fully confident that you can make them happen and that you have the right to do so? [*Testing.*]
> Yes.

Meta-Debriefing

The Possibility Conversation is most appropriate when a client feels stuck, locked into a limited kind of thinking, or unable to generate creative ideas. In this case study, the conversation began with the limited thinking that feared setting high goals for financial success as if it was morally wrong. The coach and client began dancing with that *Away From*. Yet that wasn't really the issue. Behind, or above, that feeling frame were several layers of belief frames that were really running the show. The abstract ideology about wealth was a red herring. The real dragon was the fear of failure, embarrassment, and conflict. Those were the frames that had to be flushed out and addressed.

The coach here used the know-nothing questions to bring out more of the information, and then challenged each one, "Is that what you really believe?" In some ways, this was a fierce conversation as the coach kept driving to the heart of the matter. And when the client expressed it, there was an anti-climax. It was all over. The dragon went "Poof!" as it evaporated.

Yet the coach wasn't satisfied and so kept testing. He kept testing to see if the person was fully and completely and vigorously ready to pursue his goals. The *Readiness* dance for finding a new *Leverage* point and frame wasn't strong enough. That's when the coach used "the miracle question" to facilitate the creation of sufficiently powerful frames for a new *inner game*. From there the coach inquired about the differences and used those differences to coach the client to experience and their own as his own. That helped to flesh-out and give birth to the *outer game* of performance.

In a Possibility Coaching Conversation we explore the edges of a client's map with a client. When we do, we can expect dragons to show up. Why? Because we are at the edge of the person's map of reality. And what lies beyond? "Beyond there be dragons" wrote the old map-makers when they got to the edge of their maps. Similarly, we often have a similar feeling psychologically when we get to the edge of our worlds. And yet "beyond there" can also be other things—new possibilities, incredible opportunities, wonderful resources, and whole new worlds for exploration.

Did you catch *the coaching conversation dance* as it occurred in this Possibility Conversation? Did you identify how did the coach and client *dance* around the four axes of change?

- The Push—Pull Dance where the coach challenged and awakened the client and the client oscillated back and forth between the vision to move toward into financial planning and wealth and the negative feelings that doing so would endanger him in terms of failure, embarrassment, stress, and conflict—things he definitely wanted to move away from.

- The Readiness—Leverage Dance wherein the coach probed the client to reflect upon his current frames about the price for moving forward in creating wealth and the fears that held him back from doing that. The primary level reason was just an excuse and not the real sabotage. The meta-sabotage was fear. That made accessing resources for handling the potential dangers the leverage point.
- The Inner—Outer Game Dance where the coach co-created with the client a new game with sufficient resources for moving forward on his wealth building action plan. The coach tested to see if the new game was in the client's body and breathing.
- The Solidification Dance of matching and mismatching —*Reinforcer / Tester.*

Summary
- Because coaching is all about *possibilities*, within every coaching conversation there is going to be an explorative dialogue about possibilities.
- We can "pretend our way to reality" by using language to create new vivid mental movies that provide us a map to new possible realities in our work, relationships, and health.
- Coaching for possibility thinking enables us to step out of the mental boxes that we get ourselves into so that we can try on a different kind of thinking—different from the thinking that sometimes locks us up in fears, dreads, and anxieties.

End Notes
1. *The Miracle Question* originated with Steve de Shazar. In the field of Brief Psychotherapy, de Shazar introduced the Miracle Question as a frame of reference for talking about new possibilities. For the Neuro-Semantic pattern that utilizes this question, see *Secrets of Personal Mastery* or *Source Book of Magic, Volume II.*

Chapter 15

THE FIERCE
CONVERSATION

*"Powerful questions are provocative queries
that put a halt to evasion and confusion.
By asking powerful questions,
we invite a client to clarity, action, and discovery
at a whole new level."*
Laura Whitworth
Co-Active Coaching

- What is a "fierce" conversation and how does it relate to coaching?
- Does *fierce* mean threatening, confrontative, critical or does it refer to something else?
- If we fiercely pursue a subject to its core truth, won't we offend and threaten the coaching relationship?
- What's the purpose of a fierce conversation?
- What does a Fierce Coaching Conversation sound like?
- What is the structure of a fierce conversation?

The Theoretical Framework
The conversations that really matter, that really get to the heart of things, and that lead to transformation are not the easy or shallow ones. Anybody can have those; most people do. These conversations are, in fact, all too common. They are the conversations that don't make that much of a difference. They are only nice chats. These also are *not* the conversations that coach a person to greater excellence or expertise or that unleash potentials. The conversations that matter are more fierce.

By *fierce* we mean robust, vigorous, energetic, focused, intense, indepth, probing, caring, and committed to the truth and to the person—no matter what.

For most people, a fierce conversation only happens once or twice in a lifetime. It happens when something suddenly is on the line and someone calls up the courage to speak up, to care enough to no longer be silent, and to chance rejection.

For people who are forever growing and stretching themselves to new goals, new expressions of creating and becoming, who are committed to their personal excellence and development—fierce conversations are much more frequent, perhaps even a regular staple in life. They love them. They hunger for them. They want to be challenged, held accountable, and invited to go where they have not gone before.

We take the phrase *fierce conversations* from Susan Scott's book by that title.[1] As an executive and corporate consultant/coach, she describes a fierce conversation as one where people have the courage to interrogate reality, come out from behind ourselves to be present and real, and to participate as if the conversation absolutely matters. The intensity and strength of a fierce conversation is such that it expresses each person's passionate eagerness to live life fully and to not miss the magical moments where transformation could occur.

- If that's a fierce conversation, then what does it do?
- How does it work?
- What does it evoke or create in the participants?
- What is the benefit of such?
- How do we set it up?

In a fierce conversation we use our own "reality" or authenticity to pursue the truth of our lives. That is, as we come out from behind ourselves (as both the coach and the client) we set out to search for the truth of how we feel, what we want, what we're truly thinking, the frames that truly govern our Matrix, and how to accurately describe the heart of a subject. The implication is that it takes real and truthful people to explore the truth of a situation and to fiercely pursue the truth.

The Fierce Pursuit of Truth

Regarding the word "truth," we are not using it as an absolute term. After all, "truth" is not a sensory-based term and so does not refer to anything that we can see, hear, or feel. "Truth," as a term, does not refer to a thing, but a *concept*. "Truth," linguistically, is what we call a "nominalization," a verb turned into a noun so that it seems like an externally real "thing." It is not. There is no actual *thing* we are referencing in our use of "truth." The actual verb takes us back to the word "real" or "actual."

- What is really, actually, or truly present?
- "Truth" refers to a concept, an understanding, a set of assumptions.

When we say that something is "true," we mean that we hold it as existing or accurate within some domain of understanding. When we ask, "What is the truth about X?" we are asking,

> Given the premises and assumptions of Y (the background knowledge and presuppositions) what is *true* to this domain?
> What is "true" about gravity?
> What is the truth about gaining and losing weight?
> What is the truth about getting a raise in this company?

Fierce Questions

To explore "truth," we need a whole series of questions:

- Who is it true for? When is it true? Where is it true?
- Under what circumstances and conditions?
- In what way is it true for him or her?
- What is the evidence?
- How does the person know to view it as true?
- True according to what set of understandings?

Consider a statement like this from a lady about her boss:

> "When he cuts me off in the middle of a sentence like that, it is so disrespectful. I hate it when he does that, it makes me feel like a little kid being disciplined."

In a typical argument, he will deny this. He will say, "That is not true." Yet if she is authentic and true to her current thinking and feeling, then it is *true for her, it is her truth*. To explore this truth, to understand it, and to discover how it can be transformed, we begin a fierce conversation at the intensity of the heat of these feelings.

A coach initiating a fierce conversation: "It sounds like this means a lot to you and that this threatens the core of how you are relating on your joint projects." [*Probing through mirroring, validation, and seeking confirmation about the accuracy of this reflection.*]

> *Jill:* That's right. It cuts at my very heart, and I can't stand it any longer.

Tell me, is this something that you've experienced very often with men, or in communicating, or is this an entirely new experience and really foreign to you?

> Actually, it's all too familiar. I have gotten this kind of rejection and disrespect all my life. That's why I won't put up with it at work, especially from my boss. The job is not that important.

It doesn't sound pleasant at all. So help me to understand this experience, how does this process work? I mean how can Phil cutting you off carry that much meaning? Is it that he disrespects women in general, or does he have something against you, and is showing this contempt to hurt your feelings?

> [Pause . . . as she thinks.] No, I think it's that, I just hate being cut off. . . . It's disrespectful. Why does he have to do that?

So does Phil do this with other people?

> Oh yes, all the time. He is so impatient and demanding. He just jumps in and cuts people off, Wham! As if nobody's opinion counts but his.

That's fascinating. It sounds like he is impatient or eager or overly excited, or never took "Listening 101," or something that shows some lack of good management skills, or over-excelled in Time Management! And yet I'm wondering, . . . if you'll let me explore this a bit further . . . ["Yes, sure."] Do you need to frame *his inadequate behavior* in terms of you, and personalize it in the way you've described. What do you think? Do you have to personalize it so that it makes you feel so bad?

> No, that's just the point [sniffling], I am so weak this way, so sensitive to disrespect. It pushes my buttons and then I get stressed out. If only I could speak up and let him have a piece of my mind!

Hmmmmm. I bet that would surprise him! I wonder how much of your mind you'd like to give him?

> [Laughing] No, no, it's not about him . . . it's me.

And it must be everybody else too, if he's cutting them off, and not listening to what they have to say. I guess they all feel disrespected and insulted and violated too. They *have to*, don't they?

> [Long pause.] . . . No, I don't think so. I never thought about that before. Some of them, like Linda, she just lets it go, she never seems to mind. I don't know how she does that.

Could it be that she has different frames about it, frames that interpret his behavior as *his* problem, whereas you have frames that somehow take his behaviors, suck them in like a vacuum cleaner, and make them about *you*, or acts of violence against you?

> Yes. I do that.

What are your frames? How do you do this? How can some behavior "out there" in the world, and behaviors that you don't even appreciate or accept, do you? What frames do you have that cause you to see them through the lense of insult or contempt?

> I don't know. I never thought of it that way. . . . I suppose I am really hearing my dad who did that all the time when I was growing up.

So it sounds like, and correct me if I'm wrong, that you've taken that experience and created a belief frame that "to be cut off is to be disrespected," is that right? [Nodding yes.] And well, so what? What if someone has such a limiting behavior, do you *have to* believe that it equals disrespect?

No, I guess I don't have to. But it's so easy to see it that way.

Yes, that's the truth of your feelings, the truth within that frame of reference. Inside that frame, that is true for you, isn't it?

Yes.

And do you *want* it to be true for you, or would you prefer to create a more empowering belief so that you're not so reactive to the limiting behaviors of others?

I'd like that.

Conversing in the Crucible

In fierce conversations, we go for the heart of a matter. We relentless pursue an experience to understand it and to create space for transformation. Yet doing so we hold the clients emotions and intense inner experience in the crucible of our commitment to his or her development and we do so with compassion and gentleness, all the while firmly not letting it go. Doing this creates a coaching *containment* for the client—a place where it is safe to explore.

Holding the clients' truth, emotion, frames, awareness, and experience as in a crucible allows us to have fierce conversations that get to the heart of things. Yet to do this takes moral courage, clarity about what we're working with and dealing with (which we'll get to in a moment), and skill for how to converse with a firm gentleness or gentle firmness.

What we're dealing with is *human stuff*, just human stuff—thoughts, emotions, sensations in the body, physiology, ideas, beliefs, memories, and imaginations. And yet all of that stuff is just *frames*. There's nothing more. That's why there's nothing to fear. There's no aliens or demons inside. There's just strong, intense thoughts and emotions. And because it is all *human*, we can fully accept and embrace it and explore it, can we not?

There is another premise that's critical for conversing in the crucible. It is the frame that *the person is never the problem*. The problem is only and always the *frames* that the person is operating in and sometimes (but much less often) the experience is a problem. But not the person. The person is doing the best he or she can given those experiences within those frames. When the frames change, the experience will be transformed.

We engage in fierce conversations by chasing down (or up) the frames to flush them out. And here's the incredible magic that's involved in this: We can't change what we're not aware of. No wonder awareness is the first step in making changes. In fact, there are times when the mere process of becoming aware of our frames *changes* them. Some changes occur automatically and organically with awareness. When that happens, we say,

> Oh that's what I've been doing! Oh, that's where that comes from. That's ridiculous! No more of that!

It is the support of the coach, holding the higher frames of change, transformation, possibility, opportunity, generating better responses, becoming more skilled, etc. that enables the person to stay in the crucible while facing the inner dragons.[2] In the process, the client learns how to do the same for him or herself.

In this, there are several challenges in having a fierce conversation. These include: staying focused, being in the moment with the client, asking clear and powerful questions, holding the higher frames, holding the client's purposes and outcomes, and modeling the authenticity that we want to evoke.

An Example of a Fierce Conversation

The following comes from Nathaniel Brandon's book, *The Psychology of Romantic Love.* Here is an example of a probing dialogue that gets to the heart of things and that invites a person to step into a new reality.[3] This example comes in the context of Brandon discussing the importance of being real, open, honest with self, and giving up all of the masks and defenses that protect our ego. He used his own experience to invite a young woman to reflect more fully upon her own reality. It was a call to a fierce conversation. The only caveat about this example is that Brandon used his intuitive "mind-reading"[4] of her motives and feelings rather than sensory-based referents for his assumptions.

> I recall an incident when I was lecturing to a college audience on the psychology of romantic love. Afterwards, a group of students crowded around with questions. Among them was a young woman who began by complimenting me on my talk and then went on to say, quite bitterly, how much she wished "men" would understand the principles I had been discussing

> As she went on talking, I became aware of an impulse to withdraw from her, to turn away. At the same time, I was intrigued by my reaction because I was in a very good mood that evening and feeling very benevolently disposed toward the whole world. She was delivering a monologue to the effect that men did not appreciate intelligence in women and I stopped her by saying,

>> "Listen, I'd like to share something with you. Right now I'm feeling an impulse to break off talking with you. I am feeling

an impulse to avoid you. And I think I know how its happening. I would like to tell you about it, if you're interested." [*Honestly sharing his thoughts and feelings about the current situation and challenging her experience.*]

Take aback, she nodded, and I went on.
"As you began to talk, I received three messages from you. First, I received the impression that you liked me and wanted me to like you, wanted me to respond to you positively. [*Awakening her to a vision.*]
Second, and at the same time, I got the message that you were already convinced I could not possibly like you or be interested in anything you had to say. [*A challenge.*]
Third, and again at the same time, I got the message that you were angry at me for rejecting you. And I had not yet opened my mouth to say a word to you." [*Mirroring and reflecting his experience of her.*]

She became thoughtful, and then smiled sadly in recognition, and acknowledged the truth of my description. I said,
"What's fortunate for you right now is that I'm willing to explain myself. But if you're talking to some young man, and sending out these messages, very likely he's just going to walk away. And, watching his disappearing back, you're going to tell yourself the problem is that men don't appreciate intelligent women. And you're going to be blind to your own role in creating the very situation over which you are suffering." (p. 127) [*Inviting her to creating some new frames for a new inner game.*]

Types of Fierce Conversation Questions
Given that a fierce conversation addresses *the reality or truth* of our lives, there are numerous subjects that we can broker that will invite such a conversation.

Existential Fierceness
Perhaps the most basic questions that get to the heart of matters are the questions about *how* we are living our life. These relate to our direction, meaning, purpose, essence, and style.

For the self-coaching experience of having our own fierce conversations, we ask the following. Then when we are coaching a client, we can use the same questions.
*   Where am I going?
*   Why am I going there? Why is that "why" important?

- So what, what does that give me?
- Who is going with me? Why that person? What do I get from this companion? What am I giving to this person?
- How am I going to get there? What is my plan? Do I even have a plan?
- How strategic am I in living my life?
- Will this enable me to reach my full potential?
- Am I willing to realize my full potential?
- Am I fully extending myself in using my capabilities?
- Is there value and fulfillment in my work today?
- Do I feel the value and passion in my relationships today?
- What unmet needs am I moved and positioned to meet?

Focused Strategic Fierceness

Another set of questions enable us to take any subject or topic and to begin exploring its reality and our truth in relation to it. In this we will explore the following features:

1) *Today's Reality:*

> What is the currently reality or state?
> What are the threats and opportunities before me at this moment?

2) *Impact.*

> What is the impact of this reality today and what will be the impact into our tomorrows and future?

3) *Key Variables:*

> What makes this reality as it is, what are the causes, contributing factors, and key variables?
> What factors go into the mix?
> What is your influence on it?
> How does your thinking, feeling, speaking, and acting contribute to it?

4) *Preferred Future:*

> What is your desired state and outcome?
> What do you want instead?
> What does that look like, sound like, and feel like?

5) *Resources:*

> What resources do you need to move from present state to your desired state?
> What resources of mind and emotion?
> What skills and capabilities?
> What learnings?
> What relationships?

6) *Action Steps:*

       What is the first step in the journey to the preferred future?
       What are the first steps this month, this year?
       What actions will put you in the pathway to that future?

Focused Business Dialogues

One of the problems in business is the "CEO Shelter Syndrome." This refers to the fact that the higher up a person moves in an organization, the less he or she encounters the business' reality in its brute facts. The people who actually do the business are those closest to the customers and typically lower in the organization. Raw factual sensory-based feedback is cut off from the executives. Those at the top are typically shielded from the raw data on the floor, he or she is only fed data that has been filtered through front-line supervisors, managers, and junior executives. By the time the information reaches the CEO, it is watered-down, sanitized with hushed tones, spinned for political correctness, and unintentionally falsified by not wanting to deliver bad news to the boss.

The classic "Yes Men" surrounding the chief executive abound in many organizations. The result is that the reality of the business, of sales, of accounting, of skating on the cutting-edge, etc. is often highly compromised. Yet it is the raw and bloody "truth" of the actual marketplace that we need to understand, make decisions about, lead, innovate, and anticipate future trends.

It is at this place that an executive coach with no agenda to promote, or expertise in the business' actual content, can powerfully enable an executive to get to the truth. This power of having the courage to ask dumb questions, and to naively "not-know," becomes a powerful tool in facilitating new discoveries.

Kinds of Fierce Conversations and Questions

Honing in on a focused issue that's current:

       What is the issue that you most need to resolve in this business?
       What is currently going on? How long has this been going on?
       How bad are things?
       How is this issue currently impacting you and your staff?
       What results are currently being produced for you by this situation?
       How is this issue currently impacting others?
       What results are currently being produced for them by this situation?
       What is this costing you?

Using emotions as signals of the hidden reality:

       When you consider the impact on yourself and others here, what are
       your emotions? What do you feel?

What do others feel? How do you know this?

What are some of the things people are saying and doing that doesn't make sense?

If nothing changes, what's likely to happen? How do you feel about that?

What's at stake for you relative to this issue?

What's at stake for others?

When you consider these possible outcomes, what do you feel?

Honing in to discover the key variables:

What are the key variables in this problem?

Who are all the key players that contribute to the current state of affairs?

What is your contribution to this issue?

How have you contributed?

Focusing in on a preferred future:

When this issue is resolved, what difference will that make?

What results will you enjoy?

When this issue is resolved, what results will others enjoy?

When you imagine this resolution, what are your emotions?

When you consider these outcomes, what do you feel?

Honing in on action steps:

What is the most potent step you could take to move this issue toward resolution?

What will attempt to get in your way, and how will you get past it?

When will you take this step?

Honing in on the meanings involved in the issue and solution:

What does it mean to you that you're having these problems and challenges?

What does it mean to your staff and employees?

How does this fit in with your vision state and mission?

What are the words that you and others use about this?

Are these the words that wake you up in the morning and excite you?

What words do wake you up and make you alive?

What are the semantically-loaded words that you would like to have said about this business and company?

Why are you here? So what? What do you actually do for your customers that matters to them?

What is your ideal relationship with one another as you provide those products and services? So it matter?

What is the contribution that you wish you could make by running this company?

A Fierce Conversation Example

This conversation occurred in the context of a training for trainers. A highly intelligent and passionate man in his mid-forties had given a presentation and demonstrated a process. When he received feedback for the strengths and weaknesses of his presentation skills, he found himself surprisingly defensive, out-of-sorts, and generally confused. Later he asked for some coaching to discover what happened within him and how to handle feedback with more grace and elegance.

Coach: What did you find the most challenging or even disconcerting about the experience? [*Exploring and probing.*]

> *Client*: That everybody seemed to know something that I didn't, and that I didn't get it even after asking about it again and again.

Coach: I guess that put you in a strange place—mentally and emotionally, especially considering your general quickness and intelligence. To almost always get things, even before someone finishes speaking, and then to have the experience of another asking over and over and feeling like you were the only one in the dark . . . [*Validating and pacing.*]

> *Client:* It was terrible. I hated that. I felt tongue-tied and as it went on, I felt disoriented. It was like everybody was in on a private joke. I even wondered if it was all a set-up and you were trying some new process for testing us [laughing]. [*Description of the unacceptable experience he wanted to move away from, the Push.*]

What do you now think it was all about? What does it mean to you now as you have had some time to step back from it and think about it? [*Inviting a co-creation by eliciting new insights.*]

> I'm still not clear as to exactly what it was about, what the feedback was, what to do differently.

If you were to summarize what you think you heard from the group regarding the feedback, what would you guess they were trying to say? [*Co-creating through the use of a suppositional question to invite possible learning to awaken new frames.*]

> It's about how I come across. Beyond that I really don't know . . . [*A vague description of his learnings.*]

Would it be alright if I gave you some of the key words from the group and you tell me what you remember about them in terms of the feedback? ["Okay."] The group commented that the way you jump in, and respond to questions cutting off the speaker, and the way you grimace when you disagree, comes across as "arrogant," as "discounting the person asking questions," and that you seem to come from a place of "superiority." Do you remember those comments? [*Feedback and challenging the behaviors that are problematic.*]

> Yes, but I don't buy them at all. I don't want to mind-read, but I think there was some jealousy going on.

That very well could be. But for the sake of this exploration, let's assume that there's something of value in those comments. After all, you got them from five individuals and the rest of the group concurred with them. If we assume for a moment that there's something valid in them, what would it be? [*Challenging through validating and using a hypothetical question to probe.*]

> I just don't even want to go there. It seems so negative and that it undermines myself as a trainer. I'm just better than to go there.

That's interesting, how are you "better than to go there?" [*Provoking and probing.*]

> If I give any validity to such comments it undermines my own self-value and self-esteem and I'm done enough of that in my past. I just don't want to do that anymore. [*Identifying the things he moves away from, the Push.*]

Larry, this is fascinating because it's something that I don't understand at all, so I hope it's okay for me to keep asking about this. [A slight nod for "yes."] What I don't understand is how your sense of yourself, your value and worth as a human being has any relationship to exploring the comments that you received as feedback. How are these things related? Can you help me to understand this? [*Getting permission to explore and then probing into the current frames.*]

> Well [sighing] ... I'd think you'd understand this. If you even consider the validity of arrogance or those other things, you are agreeing with the criticism and acknowledging it. That's why I won't go there. I won't give them that satisfaction.

Okay ... [pause] ... Now I want you to take a deep breath ... that's the way. Good. And just in your mind listen to what you just said to me ... and listen to the tone to your sighing. ... Now, see if you can step into my shoes, my presence, so that you can turn and see you saying that. [*Inviting to experience his outer game from another's perspective.*]

> Well, I was just feeling frustrated with this. It seems like it's more of the same . . .

So Larry, you are feeling what? Angry? Defensive? [*Probing.*]

> Yes. Of course.

And what else?

Just angry and frustrated. I can't believe that this has started up again and that everyone is against me.

What has started up again? [*Prober*]
The criticism of who I am. The disrespect for what I've done.

Okay, be with that feeling. . . . Now what has triggered it? What have I said or done and with what tone or look have I set this off? [*Prober.*]
It's like . . . [tears gathering in eyes] . . . it's like how my dad used to take me apart.

And when he "took your apart," what did you feel? [*Probing for history and emotional frames of mind.*]
Judged. Unacceptable. A reject.

So to cope with that you . . . did what? [*Probing his coping frames.*]
I would not let him see any weakness or vulnerability. I had to be tough, strong. I couldn't show any tenderness.

And you did that by . . . ?
By being smart, perfect, flawless.

So any flaw, any imperfection, any lack of smarts means . . . what?
Being vulnerable . . . being exposed, judged, disliked, rejected.

And that's what you felt during the feedback session and now—just a moment ago?
[Crying] Yes.

Do you know that your self-esteem and value as a person is separate from and independent of what you do, your skills, abilities, talents, and performance? [*Inquiring about and inviting a distinctions to co-create a new frame about self and invitation to co-create a new game.*]
Yes I know that intellectually. [Sniffing and crying] [*Feeling the leverage to create a new game.*]

Do you know that *emotionally* and *experientially* in yourself as a valuable and loved and precious human being? ["No, I don't."] Would you like to? Would you like to feel that so fully and completely that being open and vulnerable as a human being would feel natural and easy? [*Awakening a vision.*]
Yes. That's what I really need.

You have a young child, don't you?
Yes, she's five and a half years.

Do you remember when she was born? When you first picked her up and held her, rocked her, kissed her? [Yes] And do you remember how you valued and loved her unconditionally—just because she is precious, and wonderful, and lovely . . . and not based on her skills, talents, or performance? [Yes] . . . Are you feeling that now? [Nodding yes] . . . how much do you feel that? [*Co-Creator*]

> A lot . . . like a ten!

Great! *Feel* that fully [At that point, I touched his shoulder to set an anchor] . . . there you go, and feel this about you as a person. Your value, your worth, your preciousness, your loveability—above and beyond anything you do or achieve. [More tears] . . . Is that good? [Nodding yes] . . . then be with these feelings of esteem and value and worth ... let them grow and expand to fill you completely and imagine receiving some feedback about some mistake, flaw, area for improvement but only at the rate and speed that you can *feel this* [touches the shoulder] and hold this feeling solid inside. . . . How's that? [*Induction of resource state he has for daughter to create a new inner game of unconditional self-esteem.*]

> Great. And yes, I'm going to keep it for the rest of my life! And no you can't take it away from me! And yes, with this I see how I've come across with that false ego, that need to be superior. It seems ridiculous now.

Meta-Debriefing

Did you catch *the coaching conversation dance* as it occurred in this Fierce Conversation? Did you identify how did the coach and client *danced* around the four meta-program axes of change?

- The Push—Pull Dance where the coach challenged and awakened the client to move back and forth between the vision of a strong sense of self, of not personalizing, of treating feedback as just feedback, and moving away from feelings insulted, put-down, violated, picked on, etc.

- The Readiness—Leverage of Decision Dance wherein the coach probed and provoked the client to slowly explore and reflect upon his current frames that create such intense feelings. These frames, apparently set early in life in his interactions with his dad, now recruited him to see insult in almost any feedback. And the leverage for change was in these frames. In this example a lot of time was spent building up the readiness to reflect on those frames.

- The Inner—Outer Game Dance where the client already had the new game *intellectually*, but did not feel them or use them. The induction was that of a resource he already had. The induction simply led him to apply that resource of awe and esteem for his daughter to himself.

- The Solidification Dance of matching approximations of the new action plan and later mismatching what doesn't measure up—*Reinforcer / Tester.* Larry did this mostly on his own in his last comment, knowing the Neuro-Semantic patterns for doing this.

Summary

- By definition, a *fierce* conversation refers to *getting to the heart of things.* It's a robust conversation because it is straightforward, honest, and transcends the kind of overly polite encounters which we typically engage in.
- The power of a fierce conversation lies in its invitation to be authentic at a higher level. The transformational experience of a fierce conversation occurs when we come out from behind our roles and masks, our defenses and cover-ups and just be ourselves.
- It takes a lot of love and care to create the safety, respect, and security necessary to conduct a fierce conversation.

End Notes:

1. Susan Scott, *Fierce Conversations.*

2. See the book *Dragon Slaying: From Dragons to Princes* (2000, 2nd edition).

3. While I (MH) had read Brandon's books many years ago, I came across them again while researching for *Games Great Lovers Play* and so have included this as an illustration here.

4. *Mind-Reading* is a linguistic distinction in the Meta-Model that indicates a lack of a well-formed structure in communication. See *Communication Magic.*

Chapter 16

NARRATIVE

CONVERSATION

"A coach gets inside a client's story and plots
in order to question and explore
how the story can best evolve and develop."
Frederic Hudson
The Handbook of Coaching

"Narrative is the Guardian of time."
Paul Ricoeur

- What's the role between coaching and narrative?
- Is it possible to coach a client's narrative? If so, how?
- What questions and processes enable us to facilitate a Narrative Conversation?
- Why? Why hold a Narrative Conversation?
- What is its value and purpose?
- How is it structured?

The Theoretical Framework

To say that we are *narrative beings* is to recognize the degree to which our minds are full of stories. It is from these stories that our goals and motivations, our understandings and decisions, our beliefs and our emotions arise. *Narrative,* as we're using the term and concept here, provides a key structure or paradigm which we use for thinking about our lives and framing our meanings and actions. From the database of our experiences, we draw conclusions about ourselves, others, and life. In this way we create the frames that make up our inner game and which drive the outer games that we play or prohibit us from playing.

Narrative Conversions refers to working with the *narrative* that a client has created and coded regarding the events of his or her life. We engage in this conversation about the plots and dramas that we act out as well as about the themes that we want to invest energy in and those that we want to withdraw energy from.

Narrative gives us the ability to succinctly summarize the "times" of our life. How do we do this? We narrate our *story* as we present a script, a plot, and/or a theme. In this way narrative encodes our life in a particular linguistic form, a *story*. I emphasize "a particular linguistic form" because story and narrative hardly seem like linguistics, they are just . . . well, *stories*. Yet stories are the made-up stuff of our own personal P.R., myths, gossip, hopes, fantasies, fears, etc. Stories are also more alive than an analysis or a psychological description. A story runs and jumps and stands on its head. No wonder stories, and various kinds of narrative, can so completely and powerfully entrance us. With the entrancement, narrative sets up meta-level belief frames that can keep us in distress or pleasure, can expand or limits our choices, can label and define who we are, and set a plot that either imprisons or frees.

Stories are powerful in many ways. On one hand, they can be extremely succinct. If you were to put the story of your life in one word, what would that word be? I got this idea many years ago from a young man who told me that he could summarize the story of his life in one word, "Bum." Another said his was the story of "Always trying, never succeeding." As you can imagine, both had lots of examples in the database of their history frame to support those words. Both treated their stories as if they were the truth, "That's the way it is."

Using a single-word or such short phrase can generalize the meaning of the times of our life and create a very limited map. What these two needed was a *new narrative*—a new story to lead to a new way to do life. Yet we often get stuck because we literally do not know of anything else that we could possibly say about our experiences than what we have said. Multitudes of ugly and hurtful meanings encoded in a story can imprison us in a matrix.

In the next chapter we will use the configuration of a time-line to think about "time" as a path. This metaphor enables us to go *above* time, to think *about* the times of our life, and to recode the happenings that occurred to us *in* time. Sometimes we will want to go to a time prior to an unpleasant experience and sometimes we will want to work from within the womb of those times. Sometimes we will want to de-frame and unload all of the semantic meanings attached to events so that we can create a new story—a new narrative.

Our use of language can create boxes that limit us or can free us from such boxes. This is the "magic" of language. White and Epston (1990) in *Narrative*

Means to Therapeutic Ends present a change model called *Narrative Therapy.*[1] It's based on most of the same premises as that which governs coaching: the client's has the resources and is the expert of his or her own life, the coach facilitates the process for the client's own self-management, etc.

The Narrative model gives us a powerful coaching format. Since the Narrative model packages our experiences as *a story,* a story that we live, story is part of our Matrix of frames. As a way to think about transformational change, stories direct us to think about *structure.* Stories enable us to examine the themes and plots of our lives, which empowering us to identify those that need to be de-storied.

Sometimes the problem just that—we are living in, and continually rehearsing, a story that interferes with releasing our potentials. Do you have any stories like that? Do you have any stories that you tell yourself or others that undermines your resourcefulness?

If so, then the "problem" is precisely that. It's the re-telling and re-living of a story which has long outlived its usefulness. In de-storying, we invite a person to *stop* telling him or herself a story that blinds him or her to possibilities and potentials. We may even question it enough to start pulling it apart. In that way, can we allure them to *re-story* themselves with another plot and theme.

- How about you—do you like your story?
- Who storied you?
- How empowering is the story?
- Does it bring out your best?
- Would you like to de-story or re-story yourself?
- What are the themes and plots that make up the story?
- What dramas are implied within the story?
- What events have been used to build up that story?
- What stories work well and what stories undermine living with passion?

The structure of "time," as a narrative frame, gives continuity to the events of our lives. It enables us to feel that life is going somewhere and is meaningful. Stories hold the events of our lives together as a larger frame. The plots we invent in our stories can re-configure new themes and directions.

Because stories give us a narrative form that holds our life together, they operate as *"the guardian of our time"* (Riceour). Narrative encodes the events that we select from the database of thousands of events and fit it into a large format. This solidifies and crystalizes our sense of our life thereby making it more difficult to change. When we create a narrative, we impose a structure on a set of events that enables us to group them together in various ways. It provides us rules for eliminating other stories as having no relevance in our mind. So it is the very structure of narrative that gives us a process for creating a new story via a conversation to facilitate new stories.

Transforming Time Via New Sentences

Because our sense of self, and our belief frames about what things are and what they mean, arise from our use of narrative time and since narrative operates as a large-level linguistic structure that guards and structures "time" (the events we have experienced), our narratives are tellingly insightful. Would you like to discover some of your operational linguistic narratives? To explore this, respond to the questions and sentence stems that follow. Generate five to ten sentence completions for the sentence stems.

- If my life was a story, it has been a story of . . .
- Up until now, I have lived the story of . . . (being a victim, a failure, having bad luck, stress, rejection, ease, success, liked by lots of people, etc.).
- The stories that I have used to narrate some of the things that I've experienced are . . .
- Those who have cheered on this story are . . .
- The plot of the narrative of my main story is . . . [Has it been a tragedy, a drama, a soap-operate, the lone ranger, survival island, etc.?]
- From this day on, the story that I choose to live is . . . The new theme will be . . .

One of the most useful change processes within Narrative Therapy[1] is *externalizing*. The opposite of this is *internalizing*. When we internalize, we take an event inside and identify with it. We use it to define and identify who we are. We *invest* our mind and heart into it. Depending on the content, this can create genius states and it can equally create limitation states and states of self-sabotage.

Problems begin when we create a story from our experiences, problems, and emotions. Taking the events as the raw data, we tell a story about it. We invent a story that ends up asserting something about ourselves, something like, "I am X ..." (the experience). "I am a failure," "Because I am unemployed, I am a failure." "I am stuck in this bureaucracy and can do nothing about it." This identification of our concept of self with an experience brings the experience *inside* and sets the implied frame, "That's all I am. I am nothing more than that." This initiates the lie that we then begin to live.

In externalizing the story we de-construct that old narrative. We pull apart the old identification, and we separate self as a person from our behaviors, events, words, and emotions. So, to a someone who may think of himself as "a hotheaded angry person," we might say,

"The *Mads* have had a long history in sneaking up and tempting you to give way to them, haven't they? How do you feel about *the Mads* getting that much power over you? Are you ready to stand up to *the Mads* and blow the whistle on their strategies?"

To a couple who have fought and argued with each other, we might externalize the problem by saying,

"Yes, *Misunderstanding* has lured both of you into treating each other as if you were enemies, but no longer. Now that you have turned the light on *Misunderstanding,* you have caught many of its tricks. Isn't that great? I wonder how many more of its tricks you'll spot this next week?"

To externalize a problem and de-story an old narrative, think of a problem that you have experienced frequently (i.e., an emotion, behavior, circumstance, linguistic label) and externalize it. What re-occurring event keeps appearing in your life which seems to have control over you? Procrastination, perfectionism, self-criticism, judgment of others, feeling disgruntled and out of sorts, feeling unsatisfied about the direction of your life? Pick one.

There was an eight year old boy who was in the habit of wetting his bed. When his mother introduced to me (MH) in a counseling session as her "little bed wetter" I immediately recognized it as a story being internalized to make up the boy's identity. That's when I used a classic example of externalizing from Narrative Therapy with the boy.

"Do you wet your bed intentionally?" I asked. [*Probing to understand and provoking a bit.*]

"No." he said curtly and embarrassed.

"You don't?" I said in a surprised and delighted way, very animatedly. [*Playfully validating him.*]

"Well, no."

"Really! This is great! You don't do that on purpose just to irritate your mom here and make her do extra laundry and have her bring you to see me? You don't do it for those reasons?" [*Cheerleading and teasing to co-create some better frames.*]

"No, of course not!" he said more emphatically.

"Then it sneaks up on you, right? It sneaks up and tricks you to wet the bed. It tries to get you in trouble and make you feel bad, right? [*Inviting a new story and frames for a new inner game.*]

"Well, yeah . . . I guess so."

"Well, you are tricked by it, aren't you? You're not doing it on purpose or cooperating with *Sneaky Pee,* are you?" [*Provoking and teasing.*]

"(Laughing) *Sneaky Pee?* . . . No."

"So have you ever stood up to *Sneaky Pee* and refused to let him get you in trouble? Have you ever used your stubbornness so that *Sneaky Pee* didn't get the best of you?" [*Externalizing the problem as if a kid trying to get him in trouble.*]

Well, as a matter of fact, he had stood up to *Sneaky Pee.* On several occasions, he had not wet his bed. So I began exploring those *un-storied events.* I got him to tell me about them, to as it were narrate them. And as he did I engaged in lots of vigorous cheer-leading to reinforce his successes. With that he began to feel more and more pride about his resistance. And that, in turn, led me to create a collaboration with him, "Let's figure out some sneaky ways we can do it to this *Sneaky Pee*!" I said. He agreed.

When we create identifications, we turn *dynamic processes* which are more accurately coded as verbs into nouns. This creates nominalizations which sounds like real things, "Bed Wetter." Since we naturally do this anyway, in *externalizing* we run with it, exaggerate it and play with it in such a way that we can tell a whole new story about the events we have come through. This allows us to create a new narrative.

> "While *Sneaky Pee* usually gets you in trouble, you have stood up to him before, and I think it's time to let him stop bullying you around. What do you think? Would you like to come up with a plan to let him have it?"

Finding the un-storied narrative and creating new stories gives us a powerful coaching tool. We can now probe and search for *counter-examples* and *exceptions* to the dominate story and build new frames from them. In Narrative Therapy these are viewed as special and unique outcomes or "sparkling moments," by framing them in this way, coach and client can then begin a search for those hidden, unstoried *sparkling moments* where a client felt something, thought something, had an *"Aha!"* moment, an insight, etc. This awakens a new vision, a new game. It enables us to plant small seeds of resourceful ideas that can grow into a new narrative. Asking *the how question* frequently brings this out. After identifying a counter-example, we ask, "How did you do that?"

- How did you not fall into self-pity, but just kept at it?
- How did you resist not losing your cool, and listened to your boss anyway?
- How did you not discount yourself in that instance?
- How did you prevent things from getting even worse with all of that

happening?

What I find fascinating about narrative is how our questions can link sequences of behaviors and responses together. By questions we can link past, present, and future together to create a new narrative with a new drama and set of actions. Asking questions which presuppose enhancing responses enable us to assist people in re-narrating their life story.

- *How long* have you cared about improving yourself and making a significant contribution?
- *Have you had any times* when you felt that way?
- *Why* would you choose to prefer to live your life that way?

The first question identifies the resource, the second question invites the person to access historical events, the third encourages them to justify, explanation, and build up semantic reasons for it. Such questioning encourages people to "thicken the plot" of their preferred life's plot (Freedman and Combs, 1996).

Questions for Re-Narrating Your Story
1) Discovery questions:
What story have you lived in up until now?
Who storied you with that narrative account?
Is that story part of your cultural story, racial story, religious story, family story, etc.?
How much of the story did you personally buy or create?
What is it like for you when you tell about the theme of your life and listen to your narrative story?
What kind of narrating do you do?
Do you tell a story of victimhood or survival, of failing or winning, of connecting or disconnecting, of being loved or rejected, etc.?

2) Quality Control Questions:
As you step back from the story and evaluate its usefulness, productivity, value, emotional enjoyment, and so on, what comes to mind for you?
Would you recommend living in that story to anyone else?
How well has this narrative served you?
What doesn't work very well or feel very well about that story?
How has the story affected the quality of your life?
What story would you prefer to tell?

3) Questions for inventing a new story:
Just for fun, make up a wild and woolly story. Use your pretender to its fullest capacity as you do and turn loose!
What positive and bright "sparkling moments" have you experienced

that has not fit into your dominant story?

What would be an outcome completely at odds with your current problem-saturated story?

Would you like those outcomes to become your dominant story?

If that had happened in your history, how would that have played out?

What story would you have wished to have lived?

Who do you admire and appreciate and what story do they tell themselves about their self, others, the world, etc.?

4) Questions for re-storying your life and career:

As you continue to use your imagination, what it is like when you fully and completely step into the new re-storied version and experience it fully in all of the sensory systems?

How can you enrich this new story with even more details so that it becomes more vivid to you?

What audiences can you find to "perform" this story before?

Now imagine moving out into tomorrow living out that story. . .

Do you like that?

Narrative Conversation

Coach: Ray, what is your goal for this session? [*Awakening by setting a frame for outcome focus.*]

Client: I don't like the way things are going my department. Too much stress, too much politics, too much undermining of each other. It didn't used to be this way. It started when Robert was promoted to manager, that's when it all began. [*Expressing his complaints and the things he wants to move away from.*]

That doesn't sound good at all. So what can I help you with? What would you like for yourself from this session that will help you handle that? [*Awakening through pacing to validate, then setting a solution focus exploration inviting Ray to take ownership.*]

I don't know. That's the problem. I've tried everything I know and last month I thought things were looking better, but then things have gone downhill since.

So are you pretty disappointed by all of this? ["Yes. Very disappointed!"] So I'm wondering what it is like, that is, if somebody made a movie out of this, what kind of a storyline would it be? A soap opera, melodrama, war story, winning by intimidation, what? [*Probing and pacing; questioning inviting the beginning of the narrative approach.*]

It would be a political soap opera full of petty gossip and . . . oh, I have it, it would be *Robert and the Peter Principle.*

And what do you mean by that? [*Probing for frames of meaning.*]

> Well, you know, it's the story of a little man with a big ego, Robert who gets promoted to the level of his incompetence and then goof-ball things happen that turn work partly into a soap opera and partly into a slack-stick comedy of stupid mistakes. [*Chuckling in a slightly sarcastic tone.*]

And what part do you play in this story? What's your character? [*Narrative type of questions for exploring the situation. Probing for client's self identity.*]

> Oh. . . . let's see, I am the straight guy who suffers the blunts of all the jokes, the serious one who gets stressed out and uptight.

Who designated you to play this role? . . . [pause] . . . Is this a role that you have often played in life? [*Probing for client's self identity.*]

> Actually, come to think of it, yes. I have always been serious and a little perfectionist; that's why I'm good at what I do. That's why I hate all the small-minded politics that interrupts our work.

So if you were to step back from this story for a moment, what is your story—the story that you're inside and that's playing out? [*Probing to invite meta-awareness of the overriding story of his life.*]

> Hmmmm. I think it is *Troy,* or maybe *Judas,* and I'm the fall guy, the one who gets tricked or deceived.

And that's certainly not the story you signed up for! [*Pacing and challenging by inducing a stronger move away from state.*]

> No, not at all! I would never have signed up for this!

Yet, it sounds like you know the plot of this story all too well? ["Yeah."] So what's all that about? [*Provoking for more energy.*]

> What do you mean? It's about incompetence and people playing games and not being truthful, that's what it's about.

Yes, it's about that *and* if you didn't sign up for to play this role, then what frame of minds about all these things—work, business, the tasks you do, or the relationship to politics at work—recruits you to get involved in this kind of plot? [*Probing for leverage frame.*]

> I donno . . . It just seems to happen to me.

Then let me ask it this way, what frames of mind do you need— resourceful and powerful frames of mind—so that you would not get sucked into that story? What would you need to be thinking or feeling so that this would no longer be a problem for you? [*Hypothetical question inviting the co-creation of resources and vision of a desired outcome.*]

I would have to *not* care about their silly games and I'd have to be able to block all of that out and just focus on my own work. [*Starting to build the new inner game.*]

Great! There's two resources. If you didn't care about their silly games, what would you care about? And how is it that you now *care* about their silly games, I thought you didn't like the politicking that goes on? [*Validating the discovery of some resources and provoking a seeming incongruency.*]

Well, I don't. But they get to me. They push my buttons and get me involved in their silly games.

And how do they do that? What are the hooks or cues that they use to recruit you? What are your buttons? [*Probing and exploring.*]

My buttons? They get me by sneaking around and talking about each other. And they create a drama out of it . . . yes, that's it, they make it sound like everything is a big deal when it's just their stupid egos.

So what resources do you need so that when they do that, you don't buy it, it doesn't get you, it doesn't push your buttons? How do you need to unplug your buttons so that you don't enter the story any longer? [*Co-creating questions probing for more resources for the new inner game.*]

I think I mostly need to think and feel that I don't have to please them, that I can just ignore them, and that I don't have to give them any energy.

That's sounds great. Can you do that? Have you ever done that in your entire life?

Well, sure.

That's not convincing, I don't think you ever have stood your ground and refused to be recruited by the non-sense of others! I think you're doomed to always have to play the games and roles that others set for you and that you don't have enough stubbornness in you to pull that off? [*Provoking and teasing, done in a light hearted, playful tone.*]

Of course I can. And I will. All I have to do is decide that I've had enough, and that's it. And I can tell you that I've had enough of their nonsense.

You sound pretty sure of yourself. But have you really reached threshold? Maybe you need, what? Five more years of this until the stress gives you a heart attack . . . [*Validation to confirm and provoking to strengthen the feeling of Ray's resolve.*]

NO! I've had enough.

But will you remember this feeling and the resources and actually *use* them tomorrow when you're back at work? How will you look or sound or what will you do to play a new role and start a new story? [*Testing the resolve by future pacing the new game so that it becomes the outer game.*]

> Yes, I know precisely what I'll do. I will calm myself with some deep breathing so that I can keep stepping back and recognizing that it's not my story, but theirs, and to remind myself that I don't need to please them.

That sounds great. If you do that, what will be the theme or plot of your new story? [*Cheerleading and inviting consolidating the new game.*]

> It will be *The Pathway to Success through Focus*. And it will be an adventure story, a hero story. I think I'll have some *Rocky* music playing in my mind to pump me up.

Meta-Debriefing

Did you catch *the coaching conversation dance* as it occurred in this Narrative Conversation? Did you identify how did the coach and client *danced* around the four meta-program axes of change?

- The Push—Pull Dance where the coach challenged the client to begin moving away from all of the things he disliked about his work situation: the stress, politics, and incompetence. The dance continued as the coach kept awakening him to identify or create a vision of a more desirable outcome. He seemed to describe life and the story has happening to him as if he played no role in it.
- The Readiness—Leverage of Decision Dance occurred when the coach began exploring and probing Ray to recognize what recruits him, and how he gets recruited into the story. Slowly he began to reflect on the frames and the story that he plays that corresponded to the other story. In getting leverage for change, the coach pushed and probed, teased and provoked so that Ray could get to a threshold point and make up his mind about what to do.
- The Inner—Outer Game Dance took place very quickly as it was co-created with the listing of the resources and the testing through commitment to begin the new story at work on the following day.
- The Solidification Dance occurred as the coach celebrated the smallest approximation of success with Ray and explored with him how he was able to do that. It occurred also when the coach tested Ray regarding whether he would remember it back in the workplace.

Summary

- *Narrative*, as a model and metaphor, offers us another way to look at, talk about, and deal with our experiences. What if we viewed our life as *a story*? If we did, what kind of a story is your life? What is its plot? Its nature? Are you living a drama, melo-drama, comedy, tragedy, horror, detective, hero journey, etc.?

- The Narrative approach enables us to ask many empowering coaching questions: Who storied you? Do you like the story? Does it serve you to enhance your life or empower you as a person? Would you like a new story? If so, what story would you like to have narrated?

- A Narrative Conversation enables us to playfully talk about life in some new and surprising ways, enabling us to facilitate transformation.

End Notes:
1. The sources of *Narrative Therapy* include Brief Psychotherapy, Solution Oriented Therapy, and Ericksonian hypnosis. In using it here in the context of coaching, we use it not for the healing of old hurts and traumas, but for creating new orientations for future transformations.

Chapter 17

TIME-LINE

CONVERSATIONS

"To have a present [moment] . . . someone must speak. The present is then indicated by the coincidence between an event and the discourse that states it. To rejoin lived time starting from chronicle time, therefore, we have to pass through *linguistic time,* which refers to *discourse.*"
Paul Ricoeur (1971)

- How do we handle *time* in Coaching Conversations?
- How can we use time-line conversations in the coaching situation to facilitate transformation?
- How do we structure a time-line conversation?
- What does it look like or sound like?
- How can a coach travel through time with a client, especially to the past and to past hurts without turning the coaching into therapy?

The Theoretical Framework
While we live the *times* of our life, we don't notice until we begin to live in *time* as a concept. To do that we have to step back from the event. "Time" is one of those meta-frames that we bring to the events of our lives. It doesn't exist on its own, it doesn't exist "out there." It's part of our mental Matrix, the Time Matrix. As a meta-frame, it is a conceptual and semantic reality.

Yet we experience the time matrix in our body as real. We hardly notice that time is a construct at all. We are so much embedded inside of this conceptual matrix that it is even difficult to imagine life without it. Yet, *time* is a concept and not an entity at all. This becomes really clear when we ask a few sensory-based questions about it:
What does time look, sound, feel, smell, or taste like?
Have you ever opened your refrigerator and asked, "Who left some *time*

in the fridge?"
Can you put *time* on a chair or in a wheelbarrow?

What we call *time* is actually *our mental computation of the difference between events.* In the actual world, events occur. The planet spins every day, the planet moves around the sun, a person runs a mile (or kilometer) on the planet, etc. We then compare one event in terms of another event. We sub-divide a day into hours, into minutes, into seconds and then we "measure" how long in "time" it takes a person to run a mile (or kilometer). The clock and the calendar are ways that we distinguish events and to come up with units of time.

Time arises then as a human construct created by our reflective consciousness. As we reflect on events that have happened, events that are happening, and events that will happen—we create the temporal concepts of past, present, and future. This allows us to not only *remember* past events, but to use those events to color the present and future. In this way we enter into the *temporal dimension.* In this way we create and use narratives to structure, form, and even determine our future.

Time and *time-line*[1] *conversations* include the narrative conversations that we have with ourselves and others by which we define ourselves, the story of our life, the story that we are currently living out, and the desired stories that we long for as we noted in the last chapter.

Coaching the Today-Tomorrow Gap

When we have a conversation we can, and do, travel in "time." But where? Are you in the moment? Is your conversation about the past? Are you forecasting a new future? These *time distinctions* are always present within our conversations and if we tune our ears to hear them they can give us critical information about the Matrix that a client lives in and about his or her Time Matrix.
- Where are you in time?
- What kind of a *temporal* conversation are you having?

Those who are forever talking about *the past,* and living there in their mind-body system, will tend to describe *why* things are as they are, and the *causes* of their current situation. They may be in a state of feeling defensive, survival, nostalgia, victim, etc.

Those who live in the *now,* talk in *the present* moment are more likely to be active in their conversations. They will be either in sensory awareness of the now and appreciating the moment, grabbing the opportunity, or describing present reality and the gap between that and where they want to go.

When you notice that the conversation keeps turning to the past, the way to most effectively use the past is to focus on it, pull from it all of the possible learnings, and use it to establish the connections and resources which then allow the person to move forward. Those who talk in *the future* tense are generally in the domain of possibility. Perhaps they feel anticipation and excitement about charting their path into the preferred future. Perhaps, they are anticipating the worst, worrying, fretting, dreading, and feeling anxious about all of the bad things that could happen.

While conversing about an exciting new future is important, it isn't enough. The conversation has to lead the client to taking such ownership that the person will take effective action to implement the compelling future imagined.

Kim Krisco (1997) writes:
> "It's a good idea to explore and understand the future, because that's where you'll spend the rest of your life. The future is always in the making. The future is not a place, cannot be encountered or discovered, it is created in conversation." (p. 39)

Consciously and intentionally, conversing enables us to become more effective in our use of time, energy, and focus. Everything we create actually begins with a conversation. As we nurture that conversation and guide it, it develops our visions, incorporates our values, and activates our energies. The actions that follow are based on the new possibilities that we give birth in dialogue.

If coaching bridges the gap between the present and future, it does so by calling forth our dreams and visions, amplifying them with the resources that empower us to make them happen, and then activates our highest potentials to rise up to the challenge. In this process, the coaching conversations transforms our experiences in and through time.

Time-Lining Questions
> What has played a determinative influence in the way you think, feel, and relate today?
> How do you recall those memories?
> What cinematic features and qualities, making up the past movies that you play and reference, make them compellingly real to you?
> Do you use any memories to interfere with your full development today?
> Are there any old stories, events, or decisions that are so familiar that they seem current and keep you attached to them?
> When you think about the future and make a movie of where you are going, how bright or compelling is that movie?
> If you were to step back from the time-line of your life, what does it

look like?

Does it work for you or against you?

How much *time* does your time-line give you?

A Time-Lining Conversation

Coach: So where are you today? [*Exploring to find an away from or move toward state.*]

> *Client:* It looks like I have an extraordinary career opportunity that I have been offered, but I am really nervous to say yes to it. I want to work out what is holding me back, I feel stuck where I am, as though I can't move forward.

Coach: What would you like to achieve by the end of this session? [*Questioning to awaken the client to an outcome.*]

> I want to feel confident that I have made the right decision for my future and for the future of my family.

What else would you like to experience by the end of this session? *(More awakening for an outcome.*]

> I want to know that I can move on from where I am and all that happened in the past. I feel as though I wear that around my neck and drag it everywhere with me.

How will you know when you can move on from where you are and that you have let go of the past? [*An awakening question exploring what the client will consider as evidence of success.*]

> I will see myself easily resigning my current job and this knot inside here [touching chest] will be gone. I will feel calm and certain and know that I have done my very best, and that my existing team will be all right without me in the future.

Is there anything else that is important to you from today's session? *(Continuing to awaken outcome and value frames.*]

> No, if I get this today, I will be a very content man.

What is the opportunity you are wanting to explore? *(Probing present situation.*]

> It is to become the President for the Asia Pacific region [smiling]. You know these American companies, they have these big titles. Well, this job deserves it. I will be the big guy for the whole region.

Congratulations! [smiling] What does this opportunity mean to you, Richard? [*Celebrating the success and probing its meanings.*]

> Ohhh . . . [big sigh] . . . it means I will have achieved a goal that I set

for myself many years ago . . . actually a goal that I did not know I would necessarily achieve after all that has happened. It means that I will be on a very big salary, we will be able to move house, the kids will be able to go to private schools after all. And Sally [client's wife], if she wants to, can give up work. She won't want to, but, as you know it is something that I wanted to make available to her.

As you think about yourself in this role in the future, what else do you see and feel? [*Continuing to probe.*]

A lot of challenge. I will be dealing with immense cultural diversity, it also means a lot of travel and a lot of time away from home. It means the buck stops with me, it could, or I guess if I am truthful with myself, it will be a great deal of pressure. As I say this to you that feeling in my chest gets tighter.

How does the knot relate to your future, your past or where you are now? [*Probing to understand relationship between frames and physiological experience.*]

Ohhh [big sigh] . . . I have not forgotten what happened last time I took a role that was a big challenge to me. I was very excited about the role, there was a lot of change that I had to implement. It was a big job and it really took its toll on all my relationships, particularly with my boss at the time and Sally. Our marriage nearly ended over it. I just could not balance the stress of the role and the stress I had with my boss. I would bring it home with me, I wasn't able to turn off at night . . . [Richard's eyes de-focus and glaze over].

Where are you right now Richard? [*Probing to find where Richard has gone inside.*]

I am remembering one night that I came home, I will never forget this image. It was 11 at night, and I had been having a hell week . . . [big sigh]. I had to lay off 45 people over three days—it was during the Tech crash. Even after having done all of that I thought I could have been laid off myself. We were mortgaged up to our ears on the home we were in, we had my mother living with us, because Dad had died six months before and I was getting home late every night, 10 and 11 o'clock. Sally was pregnant with our third child Ethan, our second child Alissa had been sick for 48 hours and was suffering from a vomiting and diarrhea virus. They wanted to hospitalize her. Sally and I had not spoken all week, with the exception of me yelling at her. [Long pause, eyes tear up] . . . I walked in and Sally was on the ground sobbing, she had Alissa screaming in her arms while Talia our oldest daughter, who was four, was also crying while trying to wipe Alissa's vomit off Sally. I looked her in the eyes and knew then that I had pushed it all too far.

She looked straight in my eyes and said she was leaving me. [Big sigh]

[Long pause] . . . How does this experience relate to where you are now in your career and life? [*Exploring for connection between that past event and what's going on now.*]

> It has taken a lot, but I made many changes, and Sally and I saved our marriage. We are now very happy. What I found out, at that time, was that my family is the most important thing in my life after my own health and I manage my life and career to protect both of those parts of my life. But I always have this fear in the back of my mind. If I want to achieve my career goals, I will cause that to happen again. I feel like I carry that past job, and what it did to us, everywhere I go as a reminder of what will happen if I don't watch out.

How is carrying that past event everywhere you go working out for you? [*Provoking question to check ecology and provoke readiness for change.*]

> [Laughter] For the most part I think it is a really good reminder of where I don't want to be, so it forces me to make choices that I otherwise might not make. But, it also causes a lot of anxiety. And I realize as we speak that it keeps me stuck, I feel like it's not okay to move on because what I put Sally through.

How far into your future do you need to continue carrying that event around your neck before you let it go? [*A provoking question that explores the use of the frame and old game.*]

> Good question! . . . I had never thought about *when* the best time would be to give it up. It's starting to sound really silly how I have been doing that [Laughter]. But I want to protect Sally and the kids from it ever happening again.

So you want to protect Sally and the kids from that experience? [Richard nods]. Where do you fit into all of this? [*Pacing and exploring further.*]

> Well . . . this is part of the problem. I don't think about myself until it is too late. I know the correct answer should be that I want to protect myself from this happening, but the truth is I don't think about it that way. [*Identification of a missing resource that Richard recognizes as a problem.*]

What would happen if you did? [*Directly challenging the current system of frames to invite a new co-creating of a better game.*]

> [Pause] . . . What do you mean? . . . Think about *myself*?

Yeah, what happens when you include yourself in your deliberations? [*Exploring the possibilities around that missing resource.*]

Well, I don't know. Let me try this—I don't know how to do that . .

How do you think about things when you came home to Sally at 11 at night? [*Probing Richard's frames about his current behavior.*]
> I think about what I did *to* Sally and the kids by not dealing with the pressure. I think about all the people that I laid off that week, and how they must have felt. [*Identify the problems, the things he moves away from.*]

If you were to step inside your body, and remember about how you thought and felt at the time, what were you experiencing about yourself? [*Using a hypothetical question to explore the inclusion of the missing resource.*]
> [Pause] . . . Wow . . . that was when I started to have this pain in my chest, and I just felt so much pressure. I felt rushed all the time, I felt like I had no time for anybody or anything. I felt like I was a useless husband and father.

Great, well I don't mean "great" that you felt like a useless husband and father [Richard laughs], but *great* that you *can* think about yourself. [*Using humor to lighten things up and cheerleading his ability to access the missing resource.*]
> Yeah, I can.

So, if you were to go back to the beginning of that job, before it got to be so much pressure and just notice when you started to realize it was getting hard, how did you know it was getting hard? What let you know that you were under pressure? [*Co-creating by bringing into conscious awareness of feeling "under pressure."*]
> I started to feel tired in the mornings, I couldn't turn my mind off at night . . . I started snapping at Alissa and Sally. And I started to feel criticized by my boss about things I would not normally take offence at. I started skipping lunch and coming home later at night, after Sally had fed the kids. Then I got this pain in my chest.

So, you felt tired in the mornings, were snapping at Sally and Alissa, taking offence from your boss and starting to skip meals? [Richard nods] And you got that knot in your chest? [*Summarizing and confirming the cues for the pain and the pressure.*]
> Yes, and I stopped going to the gym and playing tennis with Gary. I just was too tired.

With all that awareness in mind from the past, what do you now realize about your ability to recognize when you are under pressure? *(Actualizer and tester)*
> Well, I guess I am discovering what the signs are and, more

importantly, what the triggers are. If I am going to skip meals and stop exercising, this is not going to help me deal with the stress and pressure.

Thinking about this, and looking forward to you taking the new role, how will you recognize if you are not coping well with the pressure? [*Confirmation of the awareness to respond more resourcefully, and future pacing it to actualize and test things.*]

> I will notice that I am having trouble switching off at night, or that I am waking up tired. I will notice I want to reschedule my social and fitness activities, and I will notice myself not eating well and coming home passed dinner time. I will also notice that there is distance between Sally and I. The biggest thing I learned from that experience was that I stopped talking to Sally. She pointed this out then, but at that time I did not listen, I just had to keep going.

What will you do differently about this if you take the new role? [*Exploring future differences to actualize the new game.*]

> I will talk through the pressures with Sally, that will help me and also help us go through stresses together, and she will feel more supported too. She won't feel like she is all on her own looking after the kids and me.

Is there anything that could interfere with this? [*Testing the new game and how he will play it.*]

> No, not now, not after what I have been through. I get a feeling inside when we are not talking, and Sally lets me know too. So if I use that feeling and act upon that as a signal, there should be nothing that gets in the way.

Can you do that? Think about doing that now, and how does it feel? [*Further testing.*]

> [Pause] Yeah, fine.

Are there any other leanings you can gain from that past experience? [*Checking for the need of other resources.*]

> In many ways, I'm glad it happened. I would never have thought I would say this, but if that did not happen to me when I was young enough to bounce back, I could have lost Sally and the kids and never learned how to balance my life. You know when I look back now on the time since then, I have really learned how to deal with pressure and stress, and from today I can now recognize those signs before it is too late, and how to respond to those signs.

Realizing these leanings from the past what opens up to you about your future? [*Awakening Richard to his future.*]

> Well, it is very different. I can see that I do have good skills that I have already developed for stress management, and realizing this means I can handle the future, have this new role, with all the challenges it holds knowing I can maintain my lifestyle, my relationship with Sally and be the father that I want to be. I know there will be difficulties, but I now feel confident to handle them and my home life. [Big sigh] What a relief.

If you check in with what you feel now when you think about the future, what do you notice inside your body? [*Invitation to further actualize the new game in his body so it becomes the outer game.*]

> That relief . . . calm, confidence . . . and that knot has gone [Smiling]. It really has! [Big sigh] How did that happen?! [Laughter] Oh, a relief.

[Laughing] What is all that relief about? [*Exploring.*]

> That the knot has gone. And that I can take this role and maintain my family. I can't tell you how that has been eating away at me all these years since that night I was telling you about. I think I was really holding back from going for career opportunities, because I doubted myself.

How do you think and feel about yourself now? [*Questioning self-identity to strengthen the new inner game, to test, and to future pace.*]

> I feel like I have taken a really terrible experience in my life and finally got some good from it. I feel like I have learned something, so I feel really confident that I can move on because I learned from it. In my career when I have learned something I have always been good at maintaining that skill and teaching others, so you never know, maybe my story can be an example to some of the other young guns coming up who want to have it all. And if I can help another person, I am always a happy man.

Is there anything else you need to consider about taking this role? [*Probing for any doubts that might be unexpressed.*]

> No, I have already spoken with Sally about it. But what I will do is speak to her about what I have learned today, and ask her what she learned from that time, so as a couple we can learn new strategies too. You know how I love to go back to her after our coaching sessions. I think she ends up getting just as much out of them.

I want to just check a couple of things you mentioned at the beginning of the session. First, you said you wanted to know that your team would be alright without you in the future, where are you with this now? [*Testing against an outcome set at the beginning of the session.*]

> I was concerned that they would repeat some of the same mistakes they made before I was their boss, but if I can sit down with them like we have just done and help them learn from their past, which I am sure I can, there is no problem there at all. In fact, given they get those leanings, I can see them doing really well in the future. And after all, I will still be their boss. So I am feeling good with that.

And you will do that? [*Testing the new outer game.*]

> Oh, of course. It gives me that sense of certainty, so it is very important to me.

When will you do that?

> After I let them know I am taking the President role. I will sit down one on one with each of them.

So, will we make this, and talking with Sally, two of your actions from this session? [*Actualizing through tasking for the coming week.*]

> Yes. I want to do both of those in the next week.

You also said that it was important that you knew taking this role was the best thing for your family. So when you think about the family's future, how do you feel? [*Testing against session outcome and getting confirmation and a "yes" set.*]

> Well, knowing Sally and I have the skills form the past for dealing with this now, I am not concerned about losing anybody, because I now know I can catch things before they get bad and that feels great. It really does feel like a relief [pause . . . and another big sigh]. So, the only thing to check in on is around the amount of travel . . . and given the flexibility I will have when I am in the country, I am really okay with that. And Sally is okay with that for a period of two-to-three years, so this fits fine with me. I will track up a great number of frequent flyer points, so we will all benefit from the overseas holidays we will all take as a family. We love Club Med for the family—the kids love the entertainment.

Given all of this, how do you know this is the right direction for *your* future? [*Continual testing to make the new decisions real.*]

> Because I feel confident about my abilities in the role, they were never really in question. My only question was around coping in the times of enormous pressure. I respect this company. The role is what I have always wanted, so there is nothing else to explore there. The boss I will now report to directly in the US has an excellent reputation for leading

form afar, so will give me room to do what I need to do in the role, and will mentor when needed. I will need to improve my written leadership skills, as I will have many more reports in all of the region, but this is just a development area. I feel great about it.

Meta-Debriefing

This conversation abundantly illustrates that a coaching conversation is a dance. Even in establishing the particular objective of that day's coaching session, Michelle danced from awakener to tester, to prober, and celebrator. She then danced back into probing . . . and probing and probing as she danced around the states about readiness to change, commitment and leverage for knowing how to do it, and trusting oneself to do it. In this dance, she kept exploring Richard's current frames regarding his perspectives, feelings, understandings, and beliefs.

The actual co-creating of a new inner game didn't occur until she asked a hypothetical question, "What would happen if you did?" That seemed a shock to Richard. It took him a moment to even try on the new frame. That, by the way, is typical when we invite a person to step out of the old box of thinking which created the pattern of behavior and emoting that's now in the way.

Also, because it is to some extent a paradigm shift, we frequently have to back step to the provoker role for more readiness and leverage. That happened in this conversation. Michelle provoked Richard repeatedly as she facilitated him to step into the role of expanding and enriching the new belief and value frame they were co-creating. Once the new inner game plan had been developed it was just a matter of shifting the conversation to how to actualize it in everyday life and actions.

We have included Time-Line Conversation as a coaching conversation even though it can tempt, seduce, and test the coach to step out of coaching and into a therapist's role. Even in this coaching conversation with Richard about a business move that was originally focused on making an important career move, emotional conflicts from a past hurt emerged. Yet Michelle did not engage him in a therapeutic conversation even though it brought about a healing.

> How did she maintain a coaching conversation focused on today and the future, on solutions rather than problems, and on generative change rather than remedial?
> How did she not let his tears, sadness, fears and even the physical "knot" become the focus?

She did something very simple. She simply accepted the emotions for what they were. As she became a crucible for his emotions, he was able to look at the past hurt, and face it with an ego-strength that looked for solutions. She probed that experience using meta-questions that allowed Richard to re-map his understandings and create a new map for the new inner game. This stimulated his own creativity and self-confidence.

She used the *past* hurt as a rich opportunity for new learnings and resources. She facilitated him taking those learnings into the *present* and then into the *future* where he had been feeling anxiety. By simply facilitating the reframing and the positive learnings, the *past* hurt event transformed into a positive resource for his future.

Did you catch *the coaching conversation dance* as it occurred in this Narrative Conversation? Did you identify how did the coach and client *danced* around the four meta-program axes of change?

- The Push—Pull Dance where the client described the very personally painful events that occurred from the job stresses and pressure, the threat of losing his family, the fear of repeating the past. Only after expressing that was he able to dance into describing what he wanted, and create a vision of having a solid foundation at home to moving into his dream job.

- The Readiness—Leverage of Decision Dance occurred through the coach exploring and probing Richard's current frames about things and identifying the missing resource. By identifying the missing resource, Richard was able to begin to construct a new game plan.

- The Inner—Outer Game Dance took longer as the coach not only asked co-creation questions, but also questions about application and translation to everyday life. This induced more and more of a sense of assurance and conviction as Richard identified the signs of pressure and pushing too hard and how that new awareness would protect him in the future.

- The Solidification Dance occurred through the reinforcements and testing questions.

Summary

- Every coaching conversation begins in the *now* and explores *future* hopes, dreams, and visions. It does so by tapping into the learnings, wisdoms, experiences, and resources of the *past*. In every coaching conversation we engage in time traveling.

- The skill and art of coaching lies in how we handle the trips we make back and forth between what has been, and what can be, and how we bring it back to *today*—what we are going to do today to make our preferred future possible.

- In a Time-Line Conversation, we dance into one of the key matrices of our mind, the Time Matrix. We do so because we are creatures of "time." We construct it in our anticipation of what we desire and in how we map out a new inner game for living there.

End Notes:

1. The idea of *time* encoded as a *line* has been around for hundreds of years. From our early school days we study time-lines of historical events. Bandler discovered that we structure our sense of time by putting past, present, and future events in different places in space that we can link together. When we do, this leads to the domain known as Time-Lines. See *Time Line Therapy* (Woodsmall and James), *Time-Lining* (Hall and Bodenhamer).

Chapter 18

THE NEURO-LOGICAL CONVERSATION

During the last thirty years, *Robert Dilts,* one of the original co-founders of NLP has stayed on the cutting edge of NLP developments and applications. In this chapter and the one on the Hero Journey, Robert presents two models for coaching conversations. Here Robert *coaches to a pattern,* which differs from the more freestyle conversations in this book.

This chapter presents *the Neuro-Logical Levels model* which is a powerful tool for leading clients through a set of different perspectives of an experience. As you will see, this conversation allows us to coach a person for an expanded perspective, personal transformation, and for enhancing behavioral performance. As an overview of this model, the following distinctions which describe the key elements of the Neuro-Logical Levels model:

6) Spirit	—	Awakening
5) Identity	—	Sponsoring
4) Values and Beliefs	—	Mentoring
3) Capabilities	—	Teaching
2) Behavior	—	Coaching
1) Environment	—	Guiding / Caretaking.

The Theoretical Framework
One of the most useful NLP models for coaching is that of *Neuro-Logical Levels.* Coaching interventions and conversations frequently need to address multiple levels of issues to be successful. According to the Neuro-Logical Levels model (Dilts, 1989, 1990, 1993, 2000, 2003), there are influences on our lives which come from a variety of different levels: environment, behavior, capabilities, values and beliefs, identity, and spiritual.[1]

A particular *environment,* for instance, is made up of factors such as the type of external setting, weather conditions, food, noise level, etc., that surround an individual or group as they attempt to reach a desired state. Environmental level of influences usually determine the opportunities or constraints a client has to contend with. They relate to the questions *Where?* and *When?*

Behavior relates to the specific physical actions and reactions through which we interact with the people and environment around us. Specifying behaviors comes from asking the question "*What* are you doing and what do you want to do?"

Capabilities have to do with the mental maps and strategies and maps people develop to guide their specific behaviors. These mental maps and internal guidelines become clarified by asking the question *How?*

Values and beliefs relate to fundamental judgments and evaluations about ourselves, others, and the world around us. They determine how events are given meaning, and are at the core of motivation and culture. Our beliefs and values provide the reinforcement (*motivation* and *permission*) that supports or inhibits particular capabilities and behaviors. Beliefs and values relate to the question, *Why?*

The level of *identity* relates to our sense of *who* we are. It is our perception of our identity that organizes our beliefs, capabilities, and behaviors into a single system. Our sense of identity also relates to our perception of ourselves in relation to the larger systems of which we are a part, determining our sense of "role," "purpose" and "mission."

Spiritual level experience has to do with our sense of being part of something, on a very deep level, that is beyond ourselves. It is the awareness of, what Gregory Bateson called, "the pattern which connects" all things together into a larger whole. As individuals, we are a subsystem of this larger system. Our experience of this level is related to our sense of purpose and mission in life. It comes from asking the questions: *For whom?* and *For what?*

Levels of Processes Within Individuals and Organizations
In summary, coaching conversations can address several levels of factors:
Environmental factors
> These determine the external opportunities or constraints which clients must recognize and react to. They involve considering *where* and *when* success occurs.

Behavioral factors
> These are the specific action steps to be taken by clients in order to reach their desired states. They involve *what*, specifically, must be done or accomplished in order to succeed.

Capabilities

> These relate to the mental maps, plans, or strategies that lead to desired states. They direct *how* actions are selected and monitored.

Beliefs and values

> These provide the reinforcement that supports or inhibits particular capabilities and actions. They relate to *why* a particular path is taken and the deeper motivations which drive people to act or persevere.

Identity factors

> These relate to a client's sense of his or her role or mission. These factors are a function of *who* the client perceives himself or herself to be.

"Spiritual" factors

> These relate to a client's view of the larger system of which he or she is a part. These factors involve *for whom* or *for what* a particular action step or path has been taken (the purpose).

Why do I call these various levels of factors the "Neuro-Logical Levels" model? Because each level can be associated with progressively deeper and more encompassing neural "circuits." The level of neurology that is mobilized when a person is challenged at the level of mission and identity, for instance, is much deeper than the level of neurology that is required to move his or her hand.

To experience the environment, a person can passively adjust his or her sense organs. To take action in a particular environment, a person needs to mobilize more of his or her nervous system. In order to coordinate those actions in a complex sequence, such as dancing or driving an automobile, a person has to utilize even more of the nervous system. Forming and manifesting beliefs and values about capabilities, behaviors, and the environment, require an even deeper commitment of neurology (including those related to the "heart" and "guts"). A sense of self arises from a total mobilization of the nervous system at all of the other levels. In general, then, higher levels of process mobilize a deeper commitment of the nervous system.

Supporting Change at different Neuro-Logical levels

A central task of effective coaching is to provide the necessary support and "guardianship" which help clients to identify, address, and align factors at all of these levels in their lives. Depending on the situation and needs of the client, the coach may be called upon to provide support at one or all of these levels, requiring that he or she take on one of several possible roles (see *From Coach to Awakener*, Dilts, 2003).

Guiding and Caretaking

Guiding and caretaking have to do with providing support with respect to the *environment* in which change takes place. Guiding is the process of directing a person or group along the path leading from some present state to a desired state. It presupposes that the "guide" has been there before, and knows the best way (or at least a way) to reach the desired state. Being a caretaker, or "custodian," involves providing a safe and supportive environment. It has to do with attending to the external context and making sure that what is needed is available, and that there are no unnecessary distractions or interferences from the outside.

Coaching

Traditional coaching is focused at a behavioral level, involving the process of helping another person to achieve or improve a particular *behavioral* performance. Coaching methods at this level derive primarily from a sports training model, promoting conscious awareness of resources and abilities, and the development of conscious competence. They involve drawing out and strengthening people's abilities through careful observation and feedback, and facilitating them to act in coordination with other team members. An effective coach of this type observes people's behavior and gives them tips and guidance about how to improve in specific contexts and situations.

Teaching

Teaching relates to helping a person develop *cognitive skills and capabilities*. The goal of teaching is generally to assist people to increase competencies and "thinking skills" relevant to an area of learning. Teaching focuses on the acquisition of general cognitive abilities, rather than on particular performances in specific situations. A teacher helps a person to develop new strategies for thinking and acting. The emphasis of teaching is more on *new* learning than on refining one's previous performance.

Mentoring

Mentoring involves guiding someone to discover his or her own unconscious competencies and overcome internal resistances and interferences, through believing in the person and validating his or her positive intentions. Mentors help to shape or influence a person's *beliefs and values* in a positive way by "resonating" with, releasing, or unveiling that person's inner wisdom, frequently through the mentor's own example. This type of mentoring often becomes internalized as part of a person, so that the external presence of the mentor is no longer necessary. People are able to carry "inner mentors" as counselors and guides for their lives in many situations.

Sponsoring

"Sponsorship" is the process of recognizing and acknowledging ("seeing and blessing") the essence or *identity* of another person. Sponsorship involves seeking and safeguarding potential within others, focusing on the development of identity and core values. Effective sponsorship results from the commitment to promote something that is already within a person or group, but which is not being manifested to its fullest capacity. This is accomplished through constantly sending messages such as:

> *You exist. I see you. You are valuable. You are important / special / unique. You are welcome. You belong here. You have something to contribute.*

A good "sponsor" creates a context in which others can act, grow, and excel. Sponsors provide the conditions, contacts, and resources that allow the group or individual being sponsored to focus on, develop, and use their own abilities and skills.

Awakening

Awakening goes beyond coaching, teaching, mentoring, and sponsorship to include the level of *vision, mission and spirit*. An awakener supports another person by providing contexts and experiences which bring out the best of that person's understanding of love, self, and spirit. An awakener *awakens* others through his or her own integrity and congruence. An awakener puts other people in touch with their own missions and visions by being in full contact with his or her own vision and mission.

Neuro-Logical Questions

The basic coaching conversation relating to Neuro-Logical Levels involves defining and aligning the various levels of factors affecting the client's ability to reach his or her desired state. A common pattern is to start at the level of environment and work your way up to the higher levels of identity and spirit.

Environment
- What is the *environment* in which you want your goal?
- When and *where* do you want to enact the goal or behavior?
- What will be the external context surrounding your desired goal and activities?"

Behavior
- What is the specific *behavior* associated with your goal?
- What, specifically, do you want to do in the context you have selected?
- What is the new behavior associated with your desired state?

Capabilities
- What *capabilities* are needed to reach the goal within your chosen context?

- How will you accomplish the goal and the behaviors associated with your desired state?
- What capabilities and cognitive processes are needed or presupposed in order to direct or guide your desired actions in the context you have defined?

Beliefs and Values
- What *beliefs* and *values* are expressed by or will be validated by reaching your desired state in the context you have selected?
- What values are expressed by your goal and capabilities?
- *Why* will you use the particular cognitive processes or capabilities you have identified to accomplish your goal?
- What beliefs provide the motivation for your thoughts and activity?

Identity
- What is your *identity* or role with respect to the goal and the beliefs and values associated with it?
- *Who* are you if you engage those particular beliefs, values, capabilities and behaviors in that particular context?
- What is your mission in that context?

Spiritual
- What is your sense of the *larger system* in which you are operating?
- What is your *vision* of the larger system in which you are pursuing that mission?

Moving from Vision to Action
Another coaching conversation involves beginning with vision first, and then moving down to the level of action. This involves a series of questions that help clients to identify their larger purpose, and then to identify and organize the individual capabilities, actions, and resources they will need to mobilize in order to achieve it.
- What is your vision?
- What is your role (mission) with respect to that vision? What role model will you follow as an example?
- What values and beliefs motivate you to take on that role and vision?
- What capabilities are necessary to reach the vision? Which ones do you already have? Which ones do you need?
- What action steps will you take in order to reach your vision?
- What environmental opportunities and constraints will you have to take advantage of, or contend with, in order to reach the vision?

A Neuro-Logical Conversation
Coach: What is the context in which you would like to be more personally

aligned and resourceful? [*Initial outcome question to set the direction and orientation of the conversation.*]

> *Client:* Well, I'm a manager, and I would like be more aligned in my job. [*Client identifies a value that pulls on him.*]

What are some of the environments that you work in as a manager? Where and when do you function as a manager? Describe some specific times and places that you engage in your job. [*Probing the environment contexts.*]

> Usually I'm in my office at our headquarters. I could also be in a meeting room, like this one, but a little bit smaller. There are a number of people that come and go. I primarily interact with about a dozen key people on a daily basis. Usually it is during the week, sometimes on the weekends.

What do you want to do more of in this environment? What are the actions and behaviors you would be engaging in, at the times and places you have mentioned, if you were more aligned and effective as a manager? Would you describe the kinds of things that you do when you are effectively managing those people in those places and times? [*Exploring the client's goals in the environment that awakens a vision.*]

> I could be standing, sitting or walking around. Sometimes I'm talking, sometimes I'm presenting ideas or negotiating with people. Sometimes I'm trying to support people by asking questions, saying things to them, and writing things down. So I'm listening, asking questions, trying to make sense out of what people are saying and doing, and then trying to give them guidance or keep them on track.

Would you pay attention to your body for a moment to get a sense of how your posture would be if you were aligned while you were sitting, standing, or walking in your office environment? How would you be holding your body? [*Exploring the physiological qualities using a hypothetic frame and testing it in the present moment.*]

> [Client becomes more erect and symmetrical.] I'd be balanced and centered. I guess my head would be back and slightly up.

What would you be doing with your hands? What kinds of gestures do you make when you are aligned? [*Hypothetical frame and questioning around the desired physiology which invites the client to try on elements of the outer game.*]

> [Moving his arms.] I think I would be reaching out to people more, and making more eye contact.

Do you notice anything different or special about your breathing when you are aligned? [*Co-creating the outer game to embody in the client's neurology.*]

> Yes, it is slower and deeper.

What about your voice? How does your voice sound when you are aligned?

> It's softer; a bit more resonant and inquisitive. It also seems clearer and more even.

I can hear that. So, *how* are you going to be able to maintain those behaviors in the environment you have chosen? What is the know-how, or the mental strategies and skills, you need in order to listen, ask questions, and guide people in a way that's balanced, centered, clear and even? [*Inviting the client to create or identify the strategies and frames of the inner game.*]

> Well, I need to use my capability to structure things and to organize information. I need my professional knowledge to put that structure into words, action, and behavior. I also need my capability to put myself into the shoes of others and see things from their perspective.

Okay. What mental abilities do you need in order to maintain the physical expression of your aligned state? What are the inner capabilities that allow you to be balanced and centered, reaching out to people, breathing more deeply, and speaking more softly and clearly? [*Inviting more construction of the inner game in terms of skills and abilities.*]

> The ability to hold my personal goals clearly in mind and to see how they fit the situation. Also, the capability to maintain a feedback loop with myself, and between myself and others. I guess primarily it would be my ability to be aware of myself and what I want, and the quality of my relationship with my collaborators.

Great. Now, why do you want to use those particular capabilities to act in those ways in those environments? Why do you choose to use your abilities to structure, to put things into words, to look at things from other perspectives, to picture what you are going to do, to be aware of yourself and others and to get feedback? What sort of beliefs and values lead you to use that know-how and to take those actions in those times and places? [*Validation of the client's response. Exploration of supporting beliefs and values for the inner game.*]

> Well, I believe in respect; respect for other people. I also believe in having good relationships. I believe in support for other people and myself, in order to enrich what we can do together. I believe that it is important to have integrity, and that it's good to have a lot of skills in order to accomplish things.

So you value respect, relationships, support, skill, and integrity? Those are important and powerful values. I am curious what kind of person would respect the lives of others, want good relationships, support people, value lots of skills and believe in integrity? Who are you that you would use your mind to create structure, to put things into words, to take multiple perspectives, visualize the future, and maintain an awareness of yourself and your goals? What kind of a

manager are you? What is your metaphor for yourself and your mission?
[*Pacing with a question and leading with identity questions to build supporting self-definition frames.*]

> [Pause] Well, one metaphor would be that I am like a lighthouse. I am a lighthouse that shows people the way and helps them to get there.

So, you are like a lighthouse that gives support and direction to people? This is a metaphor or symbol for your sense of identity and mission. Take a moment and think about your vision and purpose as a "lighthouse." Imagine you could see beyond your own life and your own identity for a moment. What is your purpose? What are you serving in this identity as a lighthouse? A lighthouse for what? What is the vision that your mission supports? [*Shifting into a metaphor conversation, using the metaphor to develop resources for the new game.*]

> [Long pause] It has something to do with congruence and integrity, but I don't know how to put it into words.

Take your time. These words are very important. There's no need to rush them. Let them emerge or flow from your unconscious. Just describe what's going on as you experience it. Maybe it's just colors or an image of some kind. [*Giving permission and direction to let the metaphor come alive and create more supportive mapping.*]

> I'm seeing something that looks like a vast globe or planet. The planet is mostly in the light, but there are certain parts of that planet that are dark or are in the shadows. Some parts are in the shadows a lot and some are only temporarily dark. But in the times and places of darkness, people need lighthouses to help them find their way out of the shadows. I am not the only lighthouse. There are many of them, but because they are spaced just out of reach of one another to best serve the travelers, they aren't always aware that the other lighthouses are out there. But I'm hearing a kind of noise, like a fog horn, that lets the lighthouses know that other lighthouses are nearby.

Wonderful. Now, take a moment and just be fully in the state of awareness of this planet of light and shadows, and of the lighthouses that communicate their presence to one another through their foghorns. Notice how the awareness of this larger vision strengthens and enriches your experience of who you are. [*Cheerleading and inducing state.*]

> I can feel it but, it's hard for me to put into words. It's like adding excitement to it all, and the awareness of being part of something bigger.

You have an awareness that you are part of a network of lighthouses that provide guidance to travelers. And there's a feeling of excitement that emerges out of that vision when you bring it into your sense of identity and mission. [*Mirroring statements that confirm and validate.*]

> It's also a sense of being thankful . . . experiencing gratitude. And at the same time, it's getting much more energy.

That vision can mobilize your nervous system in a powerful way and fill it with new energy and commitment. Bring the sense of your vision and mission into your heart. How are your beliefs and values solidified or enriched? [*Induction, and presupposition question of actualizing the new frames.*]

> Well, on one level, I am able to concretely feel the sense of the integrity of the whole system and the importance of relationship and support. There is also the belief that growing is good, without needing any further purpose than to grow . . . as if growth is a natural result of integrity and support. It can have a purpose, but there is a sense that growing is good even without having any purpose. That's one thing. There is also a realization that I am supposed to be here at this time. That I also have support, and can relax, enjoy, and appreciate what I am doing more.

Connect your vision, your mission, your sense of identity, and your heart to your mind. Realize that your skills and capabilities are a reflection and expression of those beliefs and values, of your identity, mission, and vision. Your mind is the way in which you manifest these deep structures. As you fully sense all of these levels of yourself, how does it solidify or enrich your perception of the capabilities you have for manifesting your values, beliefs, identity, and vision? [*Extending the state induction and applying to skills and aligning all of the levels.*]

> I have more of a capability of being in my own shoes and respecting my own point of view. Also, it's easy to see other points of view and take wider and wider perspectives. It's easier to understand other maps of the world, and other ways of thinking. It is as if I have fewer boundaries. I have more of the capability of perceiving where people and events are flowing and of giving direction to that flow.

Re-experience those specific actions that you mentioned earlier: listening, asking questions, giving verbal guidance to people from a state that is balanced and centered, reaching out to people, breathing more deeply, speaking more softly and clearly. Take this total sense of your capabilities, beliefs, identity, and vision into those behaviors and connect your strengths as a manager to your mind and to your heart and to your mission and your vision. How might you experience these activities differently? How would having this hologram of your total being enrich these very specific, concrete actions that you take? [*Using the co-creation of the inner game by using an induction and ending with application at the behavioral level—the outer game.*]

> It changes a lot. I am more aware of all that's going on around me, of what I'm doing and hearing. If I explain something, I have the "why" of doing it. I experience much more of a sense of confidence and meaning about my job.

Now think of the various environments in which you act: the headquarters, your office, the meeting rooms, the twelve people you interact with every day. Align your vision and sense of purpose with your identity, your heart, and your mind with your actions in this environment. How would you re-perceive, re-experience, and re-state your sense of your environment if you brought your sense of being part of a network of lighthouses giving guidance to others into this environment? Also bring your beliefs that relationships are important and that growth is good in and of itself, your realization that you belong here at this time, your valuing of respect, support, skill, and integrity. Take your ability to maintain feedback with yourself and others, to understand other maps and take a wider view, to have fewer boundaries, and direct the flow of your experience. Also bring in your aligned physiology, your soft but clear voice, and the sense of awareness, confidence and meaning that you have with respect to your actions. Notice how your experience of the environment changes and enriches. [*Extensive summary induction applied to the environment.*]

> One difference I experience is that would be much less of doing a job. I feel like I can be much more in contact with the environment and my collaborators. I get more of the sense that I belong there. I feel that I can be much more creative in my work.

You can also notice that this environment is a place for respect, support, skill, and integrity. It is a place for wider perspectives, where different maps are understood and where growth is valued, whether it has an obvious purpose or not. It is a place where you belong and where you can go beyond old constraints and boundaries. It is a place in which you can manifest your vision and your values. [*More induction.*]

> Yes . . . Thank you.

Meta-Debriefing

Did you catch the key structure to this conversation? Robert started at the lowest level of the model (behavior) and used his questions to move the client up the levels. As he did, the questions and suggestions *coached* the client to attach more and more meaning to the original behavior. Specifically, the coaching conversation invited the client to access higher supportive frames using the Neuro-Logical Levels—frames that would enrich the behavioral performance.

After the coach took the client up the levels from behavior to beliefs and values, and to identity and mission, he then coached the client by various inductions to fully experience those states. The questions invited the person to bring the highest resources back down. As this connected the highest visions and meanings with the most immediate behaviors, it demonstrated how the Neuro-Logical levels Coaching Conversation reflects a powerful pattern utilizing the "levels" or dimensions of our mind.

Did you catch *the coaching conversation dance* as it occurred in this Neuro-Logical Conversation? Did you identify how did the coach and client *danced* around the four meta-program axes of change?

*   The Push—Pull Dance in this instance involved only the Pull, what the client wanted for himself in his work environment. There was plenty of motivation. He wanted more alignment and more refinement of his skills as a manager.
*   The Readiness—Leverage of Decision Dance occurred as the coach explored how the client represented and would hypothetically represent being at his best in that environment. Again, he was ready to change, so there was no need to gain or work a leverage point.
*   The Inner—Outer Game Dance was the dominant part of this conversation as Robert coached the client through each level accessing and applying each to the managerial task. The coach here asked many co-creation questions, and then provided induction statements applying the resources to his everyday work life.
*   The Solidification Dance occurred only briefly when the coach validated the client's new mapping in his inner game.

In this particular conversation the coach and client mainly danced around the *Pull* (toward) step of the Push-Pull dance. The *Readiness —Leverage dance* occurred on the way "up" the Neuro-Logical Levels which simultaneously evoked and facilitated the client creating his or her *inner game*. From there the *inner game* became richer and richer as the application suggestions invited the client to actualize the frames to become the *outer game*.

This *Coaching Conversation* differs from the others in this book in that it runs an NLP pattern and invites the client to experience it. As a conversation it is more procedural in style and feel, giving the coach a specific set of instructions about what to do. This is *process coaching* and so it coaches the client to experience the pattern. By way of contrast, *freestyle coaching* follows the energy of the client, and is more optional in style and feel.

Summary
*   The *Neuro-Logical Levels model* provides a way to use and coach the meta-levels of the mind to move from primary state to these higher meta-states to bring fullness of representation and support and alignment.

- This model can be used both inductively and deductively. As a coach, we can begin at the bottom and develop an entire belief that will support a beginning activity in a given environment (inductive) or we can begin at the top with some great "spiritual" awareness and bring it down the levels (deductive).
- Because the Neuro-Logical Levels model provides a structured form it enables us to conversationally meta-state a client and works powerfully to create personal alignment and congruency.

End Notes:

1. The use of the terminology of "logical levels" here by Robert Dilts differs from the way we use it in Neuro-Semantics. In our perspective, the first three or four levels of *Neuro-Logical Levels* is part of the primary state: Behavior, Environment, and Behavior. *Capability* could also be part of the primary state if we think of it as the ability, or potential ability to act, or it could be a meta-level if it is our *belief* in our potential ability. Above the primary level, this model has three to five "logical levels:" Capability, Belief, Value, Identity Purpose and Spirit.

Robert presents a description and history of *Neuro-Logical Levels* in the first appendix in *From Coach to Awakener.* In that model Robert uses fixed and unmoving metaphors to describe the "logical levels"—hierarchy, steps, a jungle gym. By contrast, in Neuro-Semantics we put the concept back ("logical levels") into verb form (the *layering* of thinking-and-feeling) and think of them using fluid and dynamic metaphors—spirals, eddies, whirlwinds, etc.

Chapter 19

THE
METAPHORICAL
CONVERSATION

- Can coaching occur with or around a metaphor?
- Is so, how does metaphor affect the coaching experience?
- How can a conversation around a metaphor influence the way we map things in changing or in making transitions?
- How do we initiate a metaphorical conversation and structure the change process to enhance a client reaching his or her goals?

The Theoretical Framework
To a great extent our mind works by thinking in metaphors. In thinking, knowing, and comprehending we compare one thing with another. We think about one thing in terms of another. This is how language works. All language is metaphorical because we use symbols that *stand for* something else. Language, in fact, arises directly from metaphors. For these and many other reasons, using metaphors in coaching conversations is a natural and powerful way to converse, to get to the heart of an issue, to set new and transformational frames, and to facilitate a desired transformation.

To conduct a metaphorical conversation in the context of coaching for more resourcefulness, clarity, self-responsibility, etc. we have to first tune our ears to hear the metaphors that our clients directly use and those that are presupposed in their words. Once we do that, we can play with those metaphors. Doing this enables us to enter into the matrix of our client and to use a key aspect of the way they have structured their thinking, feeling, and perceiving. By turning a metaphor over again and again, by looking at it from many perspectives, and by testing and probing it in various ways, we are able to more fully explore our client's inner world and bring the structures and assumptions of their metaphors to their own awareness.

Metaphors represents one of the ways that we construct meaning. Every time we use something that we know in order to understand something else, we *"bring over"* (phrein, "to carry over") to the new subject ideas and images as frames from something we already know. In that way we can then think *about* ("meta") things with more understanding (hence the term, *meta-phor*). Not only are all explanatory frameworks metaphors, but all metaphors operate as explanatory frameworks. That's what makes them so important and impactful. We use metaphors as short-and-quick theories about life, ourselves, others, work, success, failure, etc.

Metaphorical Questions
*   What is this experience like for you?
*   What does this remind you of?
*   If, in this context with your boss, you were an animal, what animal would you be?
*   What empowering symbol, or emblem, would best represent this resource to you?
*   If we take what you mentioned literally, and played with it as a metaphor, what would it suggest to you?
*   What books, images, ideas, etc. have influenced you about this subject of control?

A Metaphorical Conversation
We pick up the following conversation at the beginning of a session. The client is a leader in his field. He is a chairman who sought coaching for leadership and work/life balance. Regarding this, he said, "I have built an armor around myself so that I can be self-reliant." Michelle, the coach in this conversation, began to explore this, and as she does, another metaphor arose, and then another. She then used those metaphors to guide the coaching conversation.

Coach: For what purpose do you need to be self-reliant? [*Opening outcome question to establish the direction of the coaching conversation.*]

> *Client:* The world can be a lonely . . . harsh . . . and disappointing place. The armor is maybe the rhinoceros skin that I have always been striving for. [*He presents the reason for the Push that he senses and a metaphorical vision that Pulls him forward.*]

What does the rhinoceros skin mean to you? [*Exploring and probing the meaning of this statement.*]

> It means being bulletproof. You can still go down an extraordinary path in an ordinary world and be able to handle the attack. I read the leadership book about the rhinoceros in university. The cows are happy

to be in the pastures and to not go out to find new territories. But rhinoceroses know where they want to get to, and they don't care about the cows putting shit on them because they are going in a different direction. They head straight for their goals ... the doctrine around this book is partly good, but also misleading and destructive. [*He specifies some of the values in his Push—Pull system.*]

How so? [*Open-ended exploring question.*]
I think maybe you can still proceed down a path without having to have such a tough skin ... maybe you can. I am not sure. I am still fairly young to know, and I have not been under a huge amount of attack.

Haven't you? [*Testing the last statement.*]
[Laughter] Well, I suppose I have ... yep. [Lots of laughter and pause for smiling at each other]

Considering that, what do you now think about being cloaked with the rhinoceros skin? [*Playing with the metaphor and exploring how it now serves the client.*]
Hmmm ... I think other people see that. And people like to hang out with other cows like themselves. It is more comfortable. For them having a friend that is a cow is easier ... even though they admire having the friend who is the rhinoceros, they do not necessarily want to spend all their time with them, because they feel a bit inadequate when they are around them. [*More of his Push—Pull system.*]

What does this mean for you then? [*Probing for meaning frames.*]
One or two things. It is potentially a lonely existence or it is a mediocre existence because you start to settle.

"Mediocre" being the cow or the rhinoceros? [*Seeking clarification.*]
The cow.

So it is lonely being the rhinoceros and mediocre being the cow? [*Seeking clarification.*]
Yes.

Considering what you know now compared to when you read the book, by the way, how old where you then? ["I was 21."] So at 21 did you take on board the need to be apart from the cows, to be bulletproof, to have a skin around you that would make you bulletproof ... so that you can go outside the paddock and head for your goals because you didn't want to have a mediocre cow life? [*Exploration of how the client has used the metaphor to understand and act.*]
Yep. There's also something else that defines my personality. I was

always the youngest kid in my class, and because I came from a farm, I was fairly naive. So while in sports and academics I was in some ways a leader, in everything else I was not.

You were the youngest?

Yes, yet the problem was mostly about my lack of experience. Even when I went to university, I was a naive country boy going to the big city. It was not till I left university that some of those shackles fell away, I was more of an observer than an individual then. [*Descriptions about his sense of Self in relation to Others.*]

What do you feel you learned about yourself? Who makes you who you are today from those experiences? [*Continuing the probing in the Self matrix.*]

I guess wanting to keep up with the Jones' and to have an opinion about something.

What is important about keeping up with the Jones' and being ahead of the cows? [*Playing the Prober role.*]

I guess until you have a very good sense of yourself, then keeping up with the Jones's is nearly everything! That's really what life is about and I think people get caught in that trap. What was the second part?

Staying ahead of the cows ...

Yes, not being a cow is the second bit. It is a hard job just being a cow and I was being a cow for quite a long time, and then I realized that being the top cow, or even a decent cow, is not all that fantastic. So I wanted to be a rhinoceros.

It fit it very well, didn't it? [*Pacing and questioning the frame.*]

Yes. But I didn't have my self-assuredness till that period of time. That's when it started. Peers, relatives and teachers would often say that I would be a future leader. People even would mention that they thought I would be a future Prime Minister, but I had never worked out what they saw in me because I always saw myself less than other people who I looked up to at the time. I thought, "Wow! They know everything." [*The client's narrative of the awakening of the vision of becoming a leader.*]

And how do you think of yourself now? [*A time-line question moving from the past to the present.*]

I guess I see myself as having had a lot of experience in the last ten years and understanding the experiences I had before, going through those experiences which I didn't really understand. I now understand them and a lot more about life. I feel I am wiser. I think I am better equipped to be an individual.

And in relationship to the metaphor you described of feeling less than others, or looking up to others, how does that feel now? [*Exploring Self/ Others matrices in relationship to the client's metaphor.*]

> It is still a little unreconciled because when I first went through the rhinoceros stage I didn't respect the cows. Now I have a lot of respect for the cows, the people who want to have kids, grow old, and die. I have a lot of respect, but that does not mean that I want to do that. There are some things inside of that, which I am surprising myself that I am starting to want, you know, cow related activity. [Smiling]

[Laughter] How does that fit with the identity of the rhinoceros? [*Probing to find leverage frames.*]

> Well, I now understand that a rhinoceros is not enough. [*He identifies a Push value that has begun to create a leverage for change in his life.*]

So when you think about the fact that others saw you as a rhinoceros before you saw it yourself, and they were saying you could be Prime Minister, and that you could be a leader—

> Well no, they did not see me as a rhinoceros, they saw me as a head cow.

Did you see yourself as a head Cow? [*Probing self identity.*]

> Actually, I had already attached to being the Prime Minister from the age of six.

Because it sounded good or because it was innately in there?

> I guess my underlying personality at that age was something to do with power and control. At the time Prime Minister seemed to be the most powerful and in-control kind of person, and that is what I wanted to be. [(Laughter] [*A narrative conversation about the leadership vision that Pulls on him.*]

Is this the kind of leader you want to be or is it because that's what was suggested? [*Probing for ownership of frame.*]

> No, I think I wanted it more than those people's observations of me. But those observations have been validated along the way.

So you got external feedback to validate what you already felt? [*Seeking confirmation.*]

> Yes, that's part of it, there is also the drive. That's one of my underlying things, and probably why the rhinoceros analogy works really well for me. I am somebody who is just happy to go straight for

something [slapping hands together] without concern of the personal cost or personal emotion. I don't feel those sort of things. [*He describes his assertive, go-at, full-on personality style.*]

You don't feel? You have learned not to feel them? [*Provoking and probing.*]
   Yeah. It is like when I work sometimes with my dad. I often don't even know that I have injuries until night. I work so hard, and while some of the injuries can be bleeding profusely, I don't even notice them because I am driving so hard. I guess I believe I am indestructible so I push my body beyond its limits. [*Describes the pushing and demandingness of his style that pushes beyond limits .*]

The metaphor of the rhinoceros has worked well for you up till now in that you have felt as if you were bulletproof, you feel like you are a tank? [*Exploring and testing the metaphor and its effect in his life.*]
   Yes, although Trisha [wife] has shot down some of those myths. Without having somebody to sympathize with, you have no choice but to be like that. But as soon as you have somebody like Trisha who is very sympathetic and giving, and very caring, I have to be less of a rhinoceros with her. I beat myself up about this sometimes. I think, What is this giving up? For example, I had never slept-in until I met Trisha. My friends couldn't believe it. [*Describing the current situation and some of the limits of the metaphor.*]

What do you mean? [*Probing for meaning frames.*]
   No matter what day it was, I would never sleep beyond six or seven in the morning. I felt it a bit of an affront if people wasted the day sleeping.

And now? [*Probing for relevance to today's experience.*]
   If I have an afternoon sleep or a nap, it kills me.

So you make yourself wrong for this, because it does not fit the identity of the rhinoceros? [*Probing to see how it fits within the metaphor.*]
   That's right.

How do you now feel about this metaphor of cows and rhinoceros? Being the rhinoceros has helped you to feel indestructible, to be able to be bulletproof, not letting other people's thoughts and feeling disturb you externally, and heading straight for your goals. You said you have had a tunnel focus and have achieved many of your goals. But how is this working out being the rhinoceros? Are you having all of the life experience you want to have? [*Quality controlling the metaphor, and provoking to see if the client is ready for a change.*]
   Not exactly. There's loneliness ... well, the *fear* of loneliness because

I tend to move away from my friends a little bit more. [*He describes what he Pushes away from.*]

And we have talked a bit about this over the journey, haven't we?
>Yes, whether they are the wrong friends. Because Arians are known for keeping attachment of old relationships. I keep contact with my old girlfriends and my old friends from whichever part of my life, even though they have very different lives to mine. I make a huge effort to do that. That might be a limiting belief prohibiting me from going to the next thing.

So being a rhinoceros means there is a risk of being lonely? [*Probing for leverage frame.*]
>Yes.

What else does it prevent you from having? [*Provoking for readiness to change by challenging his current reality about what's not enhancing his life.*]
>Well, feelings . . . I guess.

How so?
>Well, you get conditioned to not acknowledge feelings when they hit you.

As a rhinoceros, what's the purpose of not acknowledging feelings when they hit you? [*Exploring the positive intentions behind the failure to acknowledge feelings.*]
>Because feelings divert you from your goals.

What is the most important thing to the rhinoceros?
>Goals.

What is the most important thing for the cows?
>Eating grass in the moment. Just living, just existing, and being in a community.

What do you reject from the cows that you don't want to have? [*Probing further into his Toward and Away From values.*]
>That every day seems to be a bit of the same, so lack of variety. You won't be able to look back on your life and say what difference did you made.

What else? [*Probing to explore other frames that govern the metaphor.*]
>Lack of being in control of your own destiny. The farmer is the one who sees what they do and when they do it. The cows don't fit a lot of

things into life, they do a lot of winging.

Tell me about this "winging."
> Well, they have a life, but they spend a lot of time complaining about how bad it is. They sort of enjoy sitting round and talking about how bad it is, rather than do anything about it.

Is there anything else?
> They are not *individuals* . . .

Are you in the same paddock as the cows?
> Oh no . . . I am on the road.

What are you doing on the road?
> I don't know. I am heading on a journey somewhere, passing lots and lots of paddocks of Cows!

Are there any rhinoceroses on the road, or is it just you?
> No. I haven't seen any.

As you go passed all these paddocks full of cows, and you are on the road, what speed are you moving? [*Pacing the metaphor.*]
> I am moving right along, pretty fast, powering down the road at a slow jog . . .

[Laughing] I can just see this rhinoceros moving down the road in a slow jog! [*Inducing a state of humor regarding the metaphor.*]
> He is still looking around, saying, "I don't want any of that!" and is still charging ahead.

Now that Trisha is with you, is there a female rhinoceros with you?
> No, I am just on my own.

Where is Trisha then?
> I don't know, the whole rhinoceros thing has slowed down since we got together.

Where is she?
> She is separate from the whole rhinoceros and cow thing. [*The client here identifies something outside of his map, something beyond the metaphor.*]

If she is not part of this, what is she a part of?
> Well, she could be my guardian angel. [*Introducing a new metaphor.*]

Tell me about that . . . you are on your slow jog . . . and . . .

> She is getting me to be healthy, or experience life a bit and smell the roses.

Does that mean going into the paddock with the cows?

> No, the rhinoceros does not fraternize with the cows!

But in life you do. What would happen in this metaphor if the Rhinoceros fraternizes with the cows? [*Probing and provoking to see the edges of his maps.*]

> He might turn into a cow.

How does that feel for the rhinoceros? [*Probing to find leverage frame.*]

> Anxious. It's dangerous. Also a feeling of being distracted because I think I should really be moving on.

Not much choice for him to be present to the cows, is there? [*Challenging his metaphorical map.*]

> No.

What are some of the things you look at when jogging passed the cows that you look at and say, "I want a bit of that?" [*Using the metaphor to identify some of his desired outcomes.*]

> Well, just living life in the moment is good, the humor, the emotion, just allowing yourself to do bugger all. To not be so goal driven, because it is much harder to be goal driven.

What else do these cows have that you don't?

> I guess there is more community.

So there is living in the moment, having humor, and emotions . . .

> And enjoyment, just sitting there enjoying it. [*Elicitation of lots of things to move toward that creates leverage for change.*]

So, what are the things about the rhinoceros that you reject and really do not want?

> The aloneness, the ugly duckling syndrome, just knowing that you are different; reaching goals and knowing there is only more to do. You have to keep traveling and knowing that you never actually arrive . . . having no people to share the experience with. [*Elicitation of all the undesirable facets of the rhinoceros life.*]

What about your feelings?

> There are no feelings. Well, I don't know if I want them or not. I think

I should and that it would be better, but I don't really know.

What are the benefits of being the rhinoceros?
All the anti-cow stuff of being different and being an individual.

Those are benefits? [Client nods]   So at the moment the cows and rhinoceros are very separate, and there is not much choice, is there? [*Summary of situation.*]
No. I don't think the solution is more rhinoceroses either. The easy solution is like the ugly duckling, saying he should hang out with all the swans, but I don't see that as the solution at all.

How is that *not* the solution?
Because most rhinoceroses do not have it quite worked out.

Tell me about that. [*Probing the meaning.*]
As far as their feelings go, or how to live life, or how to be successful in the right way.

What are some examples of this?
Kerry Packer is a rhinoceros, and his image is respected, but the persona that he gives off is that he is rude and obnoxious, and that he buys people. Richard Branson is another; he is the same sort of person. He comes under the fire of riding on other people's backs.

Are there *any* rhinoceroses that you feel an affinity with?
Yeah, Dick Smith. He seems to have that rhinoceros ability to be very driven, but has a good heart about it.

"Has a good heart about it"—is that the key things missing for you? In the other rhinoceroses, do you perceive them as to not having a lot of heart? [*Probing to get a leverage frame.*]
That is probably why I don't want to go and hang out with the other rhinoceroses; maybe they are too superficial.

What about the cows? What about them?
I guess they are more in touch with their emotions.

I wonder what would happen if we took the rhinoceros, and all your thoughts and feelings about the rhinoceros, and brought that together with all the cows and all your thoughts and feelings about the cows? I wonder what you could create with all *the qualities* that you have wanted from the rhinoceros and all *the qualities* that you have wanted from the cows, but have not now had permission to have? [*Co-creation by invitation to integrate the best qualities of these*

metaphorical parts to create a new game in life.]
> Well, that would be good.

Okay. I want to invite you to let a visual image come out that represents the rhinoceros. What does it look like and feel like?
> It is powerful and feels healthy.

Now invite out a visual image that represents all the cows. What does it look and feel like?
> I see a housewife who is fed up with the world and feels negative.

I am now going to show you with my hands how you can swap the image of the rhinoceros and put it where the image of the cows is, and then move the image of the cows so that it moves to where the rhinoceros is. How's that? [*The coach is here using the Spinning Icon pattern facilitating the client to hold each hand out in front of him with the palm up..*][1]
> Good. I can do that.

Now continue to move these two images back and forth until they start to spin. Faster and faster ... that's right ... until ... that's it ... until they start to merge together and a new image starts to emerge from them. You can even close your eyes if you need to really get the speed up so that they can fully merge now. ... [*A coaching induction to co-create a new "image" thereby creating a new metaphor.*]
> Hmmmm.

What image have you got? What emerged?
> A random cross.

A "random cross?" [Yes.] What does it mean to you?
> It is like a biblical cross.

What is the story behind this cross? [*Eliciting a fuller description to amplify the new resource.*]
> There is a bright star above it. It is helping other people. It has a lot of respect.

What else?
> It is stable.

What else do you notice and what else does it mean to you?
> It is about leadership. Something that people can attach to, understand, and respect. It is communicative ... it is in the desert. There are no people around. It can be seen from a long, long way away.

It can be seen from "long, long way away"—what does that mean to you? [*Eliciting more description to facilitate the client creating his new game.*]
> It has a lot of reach. It is makes a difference. [Client's eyes water.]

What is *that* feeling, that feeling that you had after you said, "makes a difference." What came to mind then? [*Further expanding awareness.*]
> Jesus Christ. He was a mortal and yet a deity.

What does that mean?
> Being a mortal you get more respect because you are one of the people and being a deity means that you get to leave behind some kind of legacy.

As you breathe in the idea of the cross and the representation of it for you, of being a mortal and a deity, of leadership and of leaving a legacy, is there anything else that appears now as you look at it? [*Inviting an integration of the new metaphor and mapping to try it on and actualize it.*]
> Humanity— helping other people and being humble.

Allow your body to be filled up by those feelings and what else do you see ... [*Co-Creating with the client's integration.*]
> While the cross is in the desert I can see vegetation growing and becoming more and more lush.

What does this mean to you?
> Being able to help people become lush and green where they may feel dry.

As you take this inside of you now, what does this mean to you in your life? What significance does this metaphor hold for you?
> I have a higher purpose that can combine being a mortal and a leader.

How do you think and feel about being able to be a leader and a mortal?
> It feels very comfortable.

What opens up for you now? [*Co-creating a new game by bringing awareness to the present experience.*]
> Being able to be more giving to the people around me, being able to share my experiences and what I have to give now, rather than only in the future.

How do you feel about sharing more of yourself now? [*Bringing resources into the present.*]
> It feels good.

What else opens up for you now?
>Time is not so urgent; I know things will happen as they happen. The pressure has come off.

How does this change your experience of time? [*Testing to see what are the effects of the new mapping and frames.*]
>I know things are more likely to happen with patience than with too much action.

What is the relationship between time, action, and Jesus?
>Since I'm not a religious person, I don't know.

Well . . . what comes to mind?
>Circumstances happened that he did not instigate himself that caused religion to be born.

When you think about this for yourself, what comes to mind? [*Co-creating new inner frames and game.*]
>Things can happen without *me having to make* them happen.

What opens up to you about control in your life?
>Simply having faith in myself and others.

So just be with this belief, and breathe it inside of you, as it fills up you and your life . . . notice what opens up by having this belief now?
>It is harnessing the power of other people rather than just being an individual only. It means what I can achieve is a lot more and have a lot more fun.

So you can achieve a lot more with others than on your own? [*Co-creating new frames in Others matrix.*]
>It is a sense of belonging.

What opens up to you now being able to harness the power of others? [*Co-creating new frames in Power matrix.*]
>Being the type of leader I want to be.

What type of leader is that? [*Co-creating new frames in Self matrix.*]
>Being pushed up by other people and also inspiring them.

How does that relate to Jesus from what you know?
>He opened people's eyes to a different part of who they could be and where they could go.

And if you were to step inside Jesus, what do you think it was inside of him that was able to open people in this way? [*Eliciting him to actualize this new frame even further.*]

> He had no tags on himself. He had the ability to give without needing to receive. He did not necessarily want to be a leader, he wanted to help people, and through that he become a leader.

So it was not about him, it was about others? [Nodding] As you imagine being inside of him, what was his relationship to his feelings? [*Co-creating by inviting stepping into another's experience.*]

> Very in touch with his feelings and the feelings of other people. By being able to understand other people's feeling you are able to help them a lot more. [*Description of a new inner and outer game.*]

So when you apply this to yourself, what does this mean for you now?

> It feels good.

Do you now have permission to feel your feelings and to acknowledge the feelings of others? [*Testing co-creation of permission frame.*]

> Yes, I do. It feels nice.

Just welcome those feeling inside, and the possibility of making a difference to others by opening themselves up to a part of themselves they could be. Just breathe that in and be with that. Is there anything more important to you than helping others? [*Checking if there are more resources still needed.*]

> No. It is just being comfortable with who I am as well.

If we look at this new metaphor with Jesus, what was Jesus' relationship to being comfortable with himself? [*Continuing to co-create from the client's metaphor.*]

> He was able to handle this retribution and did not let it change who he was. He did not resist it.

What allowed him to do that? [*Probing to find resources from the metaphor.*]

> Partly his vision, and partly his ability to not reflect it, but just absorb it and turned it into his own power.

So being able to take what others give you and turn it into your own power. What does this mean to you? [*Co-creating by more probing.*]

> It means being a different kind of rhinoceros, having a porous skin that absorbs things rather than deflects them. [*Integrating his new frames with his original metaphor.*]

What are the qualities that allowed him to turn that absorption into energy?

[*More probing for additional resources.*]
> Knowingness and a belief in others. That when they are giving the retribution they can be saved.

So what does that mean for you? [*Strengthening the new resources.*]
> I can take their energy and give them some positive energy back.

How does that feel?
> It feels very powerful.

Do you have permission to feel that powerful? [*Checking his permission frames for this.*]
> Yes.

Let's take this out into the next days and weeks to come and see how this feels. What is different? [*Testing against future activities.*]
> I feel connection with others, and am sharing my feelings.

How does this feel?
> Very good.

Do you want this? [*Provoking.*]
> Yes!

Are you sure? [*Provoking and teasing.*]
> Yes!

Are there any objections to you having this? [*Testing congruency.*]
> No.

So this is yours? [*More testing.*]
> Yes it is. Thank you.

Meta-Debriefing

In this coaching conversation the metaphor arose from a leadership book that the client had read when he attended university—a book that became a powerful metaphor for business and leadership. Yet while the metaphor enabled him to map some things so that he could pull off certain behaviors (i.e., goal setting, achievement, leadership, handling criticism bull-proof) it also created difficulties in other areas of life (i.e., relationship, emotions, emotional intelligence and comfort, intimacy, closeness, etc.).

Structurally, Michelle spent a lot of time just exploring the ins-and-outs of the metaphor, what it meant to him, how he experienced it, what it led to in terms of skills, what it prevented him from experiencing, the price it cost him, etc.

This exploration part of the conversation essentially paced and validated the client's model of the world as it tested to check for ecology of the metaphor and to find entry points for provoking readiness for change. It was also the part of the conversational dance where they stepped in and out of the *Push—Pull* dynamics of what to move toward and what to move away from. Only after that did she begin to engage in a more robust conversation about the rhinoceros skin, testing his *readiness* to make a change, and developing some new frames that would serve as *leverage* points for the changes that he wanted to make.

It was then that she shifted into the role of a meta-coach as she began asking meta-questions. Here she used the meta-questions to quality control the metaphor and the experiences it elicited.

> How do you *feel about* this metaphor of the cows and a rhinoceros? Being the rhinoceros has helped you to feel indestructible, to be able to be bulletproof, not letting other people's thoughts and feeling disturb you externally, and heading straight for your goals. You have had a tunnel focus and have achieved many of your goals. But how is this working out being the rhinoceros? Are you having all of the life experience you want to have?

The structure of this conversation moved back and forth regarding the strengths and weaknesses of the metaphor, the good things and the not-so good things about thinking about self and others in terms of cows and rhinoceroses. This was the *Push—Pull* dance in the conversation of challenging and awakening.

At this point the conversation shifted increasingly to dealing with the incongruencies and limitations of the metaphor, and how to create some kind of alignment or meta-agreement. This allowed Michelle to work with him to get his neurology *ready* for a change, to threshold the need and to find the frames that would negotiate such. That was the *Readiness—Leverage* dance in this conversation.

The shift to *Co-Creating* the new frames of the *inner game* came when she presented a united frame that would maintain the best of both worlds:

> I wonder what would happen if we took the rhinoceros and all your thoughts and feelings about the rhinoceros, and brought that together with all the cows and all your thoughts and feelings about the cows? I wonder what you could create with all *the qualities* that you have wanted from the Rhinoceros and all *the qualities* that you have wanted from the cows, but have not now had permission to have?

As a way to then bring about a unifying frame (the *inner game*), Michelle gracefully introduced into the conversation the *Spinning Icons* pattern. This facilitated in the client new metaphors which, in his model of the world, worked as a solution to his inner conflicts. In this way she coached a Metaphorical Conversation and facilitated an ecological resolution. The Solidification dance came last as it always does as she reinforced and tested the strength of his resolve.

Summary

- Because we think and set frames metaphorically, and because all kinds of wild and wonderful metaphors occur in our everyday language, a Metaphorical Coaching Conversation utilizes our metaphorical thinking as a powerful coaching technique.
- The difference in metaphorical thinking and languaging is that the images and meanings are less overt and explicit and much more covert and implicit. This means that a metaphorical conversation is going to tap into more of our mind-body-emotion system that is outside of consciousness.
- We can dance in and out of the Axes of Change metaphorically as we watch the client's motivation energy become clearer and more focused. We can then engage in the awareness dance around the frames that create the current situation and prod and provoke and tease using the metaphor until the client reaches a threshold and is fully ready for a new game. Then we can dance into co-creation and actualizing.

End Notes:
1. You can see the *Spinning Icons* pattern in the books *Secrets of Personal Mastery* (1999), *Source Book of Magic, Volume II.*

Chapter 20

THE HERO'S JOURNEY

CONVERSATION

By Robert Dilts

- Can we take an archetype like the hero's journey and build a coaching conversation around it?
- How do we engage in such a conversation and how do we think about it so that it fits into the larger frame of becoming more resourceful and translating our dreams into reality?
- What is an archetype, and what is the Hero's Journey?

The Theoretical Framework

Not infrequently, effective coaching involves helping people to deal with transitions and crises in their lives. These are the events that seem to turn everything upside down. Interestingly, the term "crisis" comes from the Greek *krisis*, literally means "decision" (from *krinein* —"to decide"). It's a time for major decisions about self, direction, style, belief, and much more. This perspective is also reflected in the Chinese character for *"crisis"*—a synthesis of the characters for both "danger" and "opportunity." Crises put us at choice point.

- Is it an opportunity?
- Is it dangerous?
- What should we do?

Psychologically, the notion of crisis is typically applied to an emotionally significant event or radical change of status in life. A "midlife crisis," for example, refers to a period of emotional turmoil in middle age characterized especially by a strong desire for change. An "identity crisis" may be a personal psychosocial conflict or an evolution in one's growth. It usually involves confusion about one's social role and often a sense of loss of continuity to one's personality.

How do we coach in the face of such crises? Such situations require a special type of conversation, one that is related to our larger life path or "Hero's Journey." That's the subject of this chapter.

The Hero's Journey
Managing the process of life change and crisis can be likened to what Joseph Campbell called the "Hero's Journey" (*The Power of Myth*, 1988). Campbell spent years searching for patterns in the myths and stories of change that cross cultural boundaries. He discovered that certain themes are repeated in many cultures and appear to be deeper threads connecting all of humanity, reflecting the overall path that we take from birth to death regardless of our individual circumstances. Just as we are born the same and die the same, there are other deep patterns held in the collective memory of our species.

Campbell described the commonalities of our overall life path in terms of the steps of the "Hero's Journey"—the sequence of events that seem to be shared in the epic myths of every culture. According to Campbell, these steps include:

1) *Hearing a calling*
 This is a call or "call to action" that relates to our identity, life purpose or mission. We can choose to either accept or ignore the calling.

2) *Accepting the calling*
 This involves making a *commitment* that leads us to confront a boundary or threshold in our existing abilities or map of the world.

3) *Crossing a threshold*
 This crossing propels us into some new life "territory" outside of our current comfort zone. It's a territory that forces us to grow and evolve, and requires us to find support and guidance.

4) *Finding a guardian*
 Finding a guardian or mentor is something that often comes naturally from having the courage to cross a threshold. "When the student is ready, the teacher appears."

5) *Facing a challenge (or "demon")*
 Finding a challenge is a natural result of crossing a threshold. "Demons" are not necessarily evil or bad; they are simply a type of "energy" or "power" that we need to learn to contend with or accept. Often, they are simply a reflection of one of our own inner fears and shadows.

6) *Transforming the "demon"*
 Transforming the "demon" into a resource or advisor is typically

accomplished by either:
a) Developing a special skill.
b) Discovering a special resource or tool.

7. Completing the task

Completing the task for which one has been called, and *finding the way* to fulfill the calling is ultimately achieved by creating a *new map of the world* that incorporates the growth and discoveries brought about by the journey.

8) Returning home

Returning home as a transformed person, and sharing with others the knowledge and experience gained as a result of the journey.

While the hero's journey is clearly a metaphor, it captures a good deal of the reality that faces us as we seek to build a path to a successful future and contend with the uncertainties of change.

Calling:

The notion of a calling, clearly symbolizes the vision and mission that we individually or as a family, team, or company are pursuing.

Threshold:

The threshold represents the unknown and uncertain elements that we must confront in order to bring the vision into action.

Demon:

The symbol of the demon reflects the challenges of upheaval, competition, internal interferences and other obstacles and crises which emerge from circumstances beyond our control.

Resources:

Our resources are the values, behavioral skills, and capabilities we are able to put into action in order to deal with complexity, uncertainty, and resistance. This is the area where the client must grow in order develop the flexibility and increased requisite variety necessary to successfully navigate the new territory and overcome the obstacles which arise along the way.

Guardians:

Guardians are the sponsors, and relationships we develop, that support us to build skills, believe in ourselves, and stay focused on our objectives.

It is sometimes tempting to think that the client is the "victim" and the coach is the "hero" who will slay the client's demon with his or her wonderful coaching techniques. It is important to keep in mind, however, that in the coaching model *the client is the hero and the coach is the guardian.* Our job as coaches and sponsors is to help the client recognize his or her own hero's journey and to support him or her on that journey.

The Hero Journey Questions

To be an effective guardian, a coach needs to ask questions that lead clients to recognize that they are not victims, but are rather on a Hero's Journey. The fundamental questions leading to this conversation relate to the various stages of that journey:

1) Hearing the calling:

> What is your calling?
> What is your life purpose or mission?
> What is the "call to action" in your life circumstances now?
> (It is often useful to encourage clients to answer this question in the form of a symbol or metaphor; e.g., "I am being called to become an eagle / warrior / magician, etc.")

2) Committing to the calling:

> What is the commitment you need to make in order to achieve your calling?
> What is the decision that you must make?

3) Crossing the threshold:

> What is the current boundary or threshold in your existing abilities or map of the world that need to be stretched in order for you to move forward with respect to your calling?
> What is the unknown or new life "territory" outside of your current comfort zone that will cause you to grow and evolve?
> What is your "point of no return" with respect to your calling?

4) Finding a guardian or mentor:

> Who will be your mentors or guardians on your Hero's Journey?
> Who can you rely on for insight, support, and nurture?
> Who will help you to remember and use the resources you need in order to complete your Hero's Journey?

5) Facing the crisis or challenge:

> What is the crisis, challenge, or "demon" you must confront or face in order to achieve your calling?
> What are some of the inner fears and "shadows" that come up for you when you think about crossing your threshold and going for your calling?

6) Transforming the crisis or challenge:

What *resources*, *skills*, or *tools* do you have that can help you to face and transform your challenge (or "demon")?

Which resources do you need to strengthen or develop more fully?

7) Completing the journey:

What do you need to do in order to complete your journey?

How will you complete the journey?

What rituals or ceremonies will give it closure?

What is your new map of the world that incorporates the growth and discoveries brought about by your calling and journey?

8) Returning home.

What do you need in order to return home?

What knowledge and experience have you gained as a result of your journey that is important for you to share with others?

How will you know when you've returned home?

While Campbell's description of the journey begins with hearing and accepting a "calling," our real life experiences often call us to the hero's journey by presenting us with the challenge or crisis first. The many heroes who emerged as a result of the September 11 terrorist attacks on the World Trade Center, for instance, were thrown into their journey by a direct confrontation with the "demon." They had to face their threshold and recognize their calling within the crisis they were facing.

Frequently, this is also the case with our clients. A crisis presents the calling. Certainly, dealing with any sort of crisis is a type of hero's journey in and of itself. To help clients explore and prepare themselves for some of the key aspects of their own heroes journeys, pick a project, transition or initiative that they are currently involved in, or planning, and ask the following *Hero Journey questions:*

1) What is the "demon" (challenge) you must face?

What is a situation in which you feel more of a "victim" than a "hero?"

2) What is your threshold?

What is the unknown territory, outside of your comfort zone, that either a) the crisis is forcing you into or b) you must enter in order to deal with the crisis?

3) What's your "demon?"

Given the demon you are facing and the threshold you must cross, what is the "call to action"—what are you being "called" to do or become?

(Again, it is often useful to answer this question in the form of a symbol or metaphor.)

4) What resources do you have or need?

What resources do you need to develop more fully to face the challenge, cross your threshold, and accomplish your calling?

5) Who are (or will be) your "guardians" for those resources?

The Hero Journey Conversation

Coach: What is the challenge or crisis you are facing? What is the situation in which you feel more of a "victim" than a "hero?" [*Awakening the client to the hero journey and challenging him to boldly look at the current situation for what it is.*]

Client: There is a difficult transition happening at my office. Things have been down economically for the past couple of years. Recently, my old boss retired and was replaced with someone new, a guy who is basically just a "bean counter" with no vision. He does not communicate well and has fired some people that have been here a long time. Morale is down and I am worried that our whole office may fall apart. [*Identifies a lot of Away From values that create the Push for him.*]

So, your new boss is a kind of a "demon" for you? [*Paces client and elicits the "demon" of the Hero Journey frame.*]

I guess so [laughing]. I hadn't thought of it that way before, but he certainly is a challenge. I know he means well and is trying to do the best for the company. But a number of the things he has done seem counter-productive. It seems like we are losing some of the core values and focus that have been driving the company since it started. [*Identifies even more Away From values.*]

What is the area, outside of your comfort zone, that this challenge is forcing you into? Is there something different that is not so usual or comfortable for you that you find yourself having to do in order to deal with this situation? [*Probing into the challenges and the "call" of the Hero Journey.*]

I find myself being more confrontative than I'm used to being. I have to stand up for myself and what I think is right and kind of "get in the face" of my boss. That is definitely not something that I am used to and its pretty risky for me. So far, he seems to at least take what I say into account. He does not always act on it, but he seems to put up with it for now. [*Identifies the area of challenge.*]

So you are kind of having to "put your foot down" with respect to your boss?

You need to really say what is right, and especially what is right for you, even if it goes against what your boss thinks? [*Summarizes the situation and checks understanding.*]

> Yes, I guess so. I am not used to that. I don't like confrontation. It is more my style to work cooperatively with others to reach shared goals and objectives. In this case I feel like I am having to be more of a balancing weight to keep things from going too much in the wrong direction.

Okay, so given this challenge of the new "bean-counting" boss without vision, who is making some counter-productive decisions that are negatively affecting morale and threatening your office; and given that you are finding yourself having to "get in the face" of your boss, and stand up for yourself, and what you think is right to keep things balanced, what are you being "called" to do or become? What is the "calling" for you within this crisis? [*Co-creating questions to awaken the point of challenge and the crisis to be deal with.*]

> I guess I am being called to take more of a leadership role in our office, though I've never seen myself as much of a leader.

It does sound like this crisis is calling you to lead "upwards," which is probably the most difficult type of leadership. I'm curious, what type of symbol or metaphor would you use to represent that calling? [*Pacing and setting frame about leadership. Shifts to begin a metaphorical conversation.*]

> [Pauses] I'm being called to be a "co-pilot" [voice becomes stronger and more confident] I've been with the company a lot longer than my new boss and, for whatever reason, I at least have his ear for the time being. I think I've been more of a passanger up to this point. I feel like I need to be a type of co-pilot to keep the plane from crashing in rough air. [*Inner game —> outer game*]

Wow! A co-pilot is a special type of leader, and no matter how much flying time a pilot has, he or she always needs a good co-pilot. I think that would be something very important for your boss and your company. What resources are you going to need in order to be a good leader or coach for your own boss, to go successfully into the new territory of standing up for yourself, and to stand up to others and become a better and better "co-pilot?" [*Cheerleading. Co-creation questions to elicit supporting resources.*]

> I need confidence and conviction. I also need the ability to be subtle but firm, to be clear about what direction we need to go, and what I believe will bring us there. I need to be able to read the same "instruments" my boss is looking at and relate my advice to those measurements. I need to have enough vision to make up for my new boss' lack of it. [*Offers lots of specific resources that describe the new Game.*]

Who could be your "guardians" for those resources? Can you think of people in your life who helped you to develop any of these resources or who helped you recognize that you had them already? [*Co-creating through eliciting the guardian element of the Hero Journey.*]

> My old boss would be one. Another would be an important teacher I had in business school. [Pauses] . . . Oh yes, there is one of my friends who is really good at saying what she feels and needs.

What would those guardians advise you to do in this situation? As you put yourself into the shoes of each of your various mentors for a moment, what would be their messages to you? [*Co-creating using second position to elicit a resource frame.*]

> My old boss would say, "Keep your eye on the horizon. Remember where you are trying to get to." My teacher would tell me, "You've got what it takes. You've got a good head on your shoulders. Use it!" My friend would say, "Say what is true for you. It gets easier and easier once you get into the habit." [*More frames for the inner game.*]

Now let's revisit that challenging situation with your new boss. How do you feel about it now? [*Shifting to the Actualizer role to apply the resources of the hero to the Hero Journey.*]

> It is completely different. I don't feel like a victim anymore. I know what I need to do and feel that I can do it. I am the best one to be in the position that I am in. I am kind of excited to see my boss again. I think I can help him to be a better pilot.

Great!

Meta-Debriefing

This coaching conversation plays with the metaphor of a journey, a Hero's Journey. Doing so enables us to formulate a coaching conversation around the eight steps or stages and to inquire about each of those facets of the Hero Journey: call, commitment, threshold, guardians, challenges, transformations, completion, and returning home. This coaching conversation presupposes that the crises and challenges, even the "demons" that arise are but steps in the process of exploring and transforming a new world and becoming a hero.

Structurally the Hero Journey Coaching Conversation frames the client as the emergent hero with inner resources to be called forth. It also frames the everyday life challenge of self-discovery as a heroic venture.

In terms of the Axes of Change, it began with the *Push—Pull* dance as he moved back and forth between the values that he wanted to move away from and those that he wanted to move toward, that would fulfill his criteria for success. He mostly knew what he wanted to avoid, what he didn't like about the current situation. The coach paced and summarized these and then began asking about what he wanted instead. The Hero Journey began with the energy of the *away from* values since that's what started the "call" and challenge of the journey.

The Hero's Journey continued in terms of the *Readiness—Leverage* dance as the coach asked questions that facilitated the awareness of the frames that governed the current game. As the readiness energy increased, the conversation moved into the *Inner/Outer Game* dance. In this the client began identifying the resources for being a co-pilot leader at work, the frames that made up the new game. The Solidification dance involved the validation of the coach ("That's great!") to reinforce the new game. The coach finally tested by recalling the original challenging situation to see how the new game would handle it.

Summary
- Framing life as a Hero Journey enables us to use that as a framework for discerning where we are in the process.
- Because the Hero Journey is an archetypical experience, we can all relate to it and easily use it to develop new resources.
- What heroic journeys have you already made? Which are even now at the door beckoning you on to a new adventure?

Chapter 21

THE ARCHETYPAL

CONVERSATION

"Archetypes are the architects of our lives"
Caroline Myss

- How do we coach a client in discovering greater purpose and meaning?
- What framework supports such a conversation?
- What questions can awaken a client to see and realize more of his or her potential?
- How do we support a client moving from *seeing* potential to *taking* the relevant *action* to unleash it?

The Theoretical Framework
We have several metaphorical conversations among the coaching conversations in this book. The Matrix is a metaphor, so is the Hero Journey. These are conversations in metaphor. We now turn to another metaphor—the Archetypal Conversation.

An *archetype* refers to an original pattern or model of which all things of the same type are representations or copies. Carl Jung popularized *archetypes*. He referred to them as a metaphorical pattern that succinctly summarizes a major theme or motif in life. Jung described an archetype as "an inherited mode of psychic functioning . . . in other words, it is a 'pattern of behavior'" (Whitmont, 1991, p. 104).

Because an archetype functions like a prototype idea that's present in all cultures and ages, Jung postulated "the collective unconscious." In his original writings Jung detailed Shadow, Wise Old Man, Child and Child Hero, Mother (Primordial and Earth), Maiden Animal (Female pattern) and Anima (Male pattern).[1]

Jung noted that there is a light and dark side to each archetype. Within these patterns we find our strengths and our weaknesses, typically our weakness, or shadow side, is our strength over-done. That is, we have played so much to our skills, talents, and strengths that we have gotten out-of-balance. In terms of coaching, an archetypical conversation enables us to work with facilitating a client to discover or create higher levels of purpose and meaning in life and work and to create new balances as we work with a metaphor that calls forth thinking about life's themes. This conversation also enables us to work in the coaching relationship with behavior patterns that create limitations or sabotages to effectiveness.

List of Common Archetypes[2]

So what are some of the most common archetypes that we can build a conversation around? Here's a sample list you can use:

Advocate (Attorney, Defender, Legislator)	Addict
Alchemist (Wizard, Magician, Scientist, Inventor)	Coward (Bully)
Artist (Musician, Author, Dramatist, Actor)	Gambler
Beggar (Homeless Person, Indigent)	God and Goddess
Child (Orphan, Wounded, Innocent)	Lover
Jester (Clown, Fool, etc)	Midas/Miser
Prince(ss) (Includes Damsel etc)	Martyr
Destroyer (Mad Scientist, Serial Killer, Spoiler)	Father-Mother
Detective (Spy, Double Agent, Sleuth)	Prostitute
Seducer (Don Juan, Femme Fetal)	Servant
Networker (Gossip, Communicator, Messenger)	Storyteller
Wise Woman (Guru, Sage, Preacher, Mentor)	Thief
Healer (Therapist, Nurse, Caregiver)	Victim
Judge (Critic, Examiner, Mediator)	
King-Queen (Leader, Ruler)	
Pioneer (Explorer, Settler, Pilgrim, Innovator, Entrepreneur)	
Rebel (Anarchist, Revolutionary, Political Protester)	
Rescuer (Hero, Heroine, Knight, Warrior)	
Student (Disciple, Devotee, Follower, Apprentice)	
Trickster (Puck, Provocateur)	
Visionary (Dreamer, Prophet, Seer)	

Archetypal Questions

- Using the list of common archetypes, which archetype do you feel a relationship to and/or see as a theme in your life?
- What does this archetype represent to you?
- How has it represented itself in your life?

- How have you lived this archetype in your life?
- What do you understand about this archetype?
- What does this archetype open up for you?
- What permissions does this archetype give to you or take from you?
- What learning and wisdom have you learned from this archetype?
- What strengths and talents do you associate with this archetype?
- How have you demonstrated the "dark side" of this archetype?
- What is the highest potential of this archetype?
- How can you now realize this potential?
- What opportunities have come into your life that you can relate to this archetype?
- What fears do you relate to this archetype?
- What choices have you made while being guided by this archetype?
- What is your current opportunity for learning?
- How has your perception of this archetype limited your growth?
- What would happen if you let go of this archetype as your life theme?
- What are the opportunities for you outside of this archetype?
- What is the relationship between this archetype and other archetypes you relate to?
- What have you not yet embraced about this archetype that, if you did, would transform your life?
- How does this archetype support you as a leader (e.g., mother, father, lover, etc)?
- How does this archetype support you in your work (health, work, career, relationships, etc.)?
- How does this archetype influence your self identity?
- How does this archetype influence your sense of power and resourcefulness?
- How does this archetype influence your relationship with others?
- How does this archetype influence your outlook of the world?

Archetypal Conversation

This coaching conversation occurred midway during Erica's coaching program. Erica engaged me (MD) with the intention of finding a meaningful purpose and direction for her professional life. At the age of 50, Erica had never felt intentional or purposeful about her work or creative activities. She had started many projects and business partnerships only to be disappointed time and again. Since they seldom came to full fruition, she felt she was not realizing her professional potential. Many of Erica's business relationships had ended abruptly with hostility, confrontation, and much disappointment for her.

In preparation for the coaching, Erica studied a list of Archetypes and brought to the first session those Archetypes with which she had an affinity, connection, or relationship. While the following coaching conversation could have been directed in many different directions, the conversation was coached to Erica's specific outcome of finding meaning and purposefulness in her professional life. It began with Erica choosing the Queen as her Archetype.

Coach: What does the Queen Archetype mean to you? [*Exploring the meaning of the archetype as a frame for her life.*]

> *Client:* She is where my power lies—the power to succeed, the power to alienate and frighten, the power to achieve and to sabotage.

How do you think and feel about being a Queen? [*A question to explore self-identity and the archetype.*]

> I love her. She is the fearlessness that allows the pioneer in me to go forward. She is the strength and optimism that has kept me from sinking into everlasting depression. . . . She is also the source of my aloneness . . . with this much power I stand apart and hold off people from approaching.

How have you been using this power? [*Probing the use of this frame.*]

> In many of my relationships I have frightened and controlled others. At first I believe I used it to intimidate others. I thought this was just a cultural thing, since I am both American and Jewish. But it has been there throughout my entire life. And I have wielded that power in conjunction with the Seductress to get what I want and subjugated people and hurt others too . . . although I don't think I do this very much any more. [*Identifying some of the away from values of the archetype as well as another archetype, the Seductress.*]

What has it cost you, using the power of your Queen in this way? [*Pacing the misuse of the archetype to fully play the role of challenger to her.*]

> It has cost me accessing my full potential. From looking at the light and dark side of the Queen I was able to see for the first time why others feel intimidated around me, and why many of my creative relationships have ended. It has cost me business, personal relationships, and it has cost me the satisfaction of achieving in the world. [*Identify more away from values which increases motivation to change.*]

If you were to access your Queen's power in it's highest form, what would that be like? [*Eliciting the toward values to fully awaken the archetype's potential value.*]

> I believe at heart she is the "Philosopher King" Plato spoke about, the one that combines knowledge, heart, spirit, and power. I want her to soar, to take wing, and to fulfill her destiny. I believe she holds what I am truly capable of. I do know that the Queen wants to assume her

throne and rule magnanimously and benignly, and with the wisdom of the Teacher–Wise Woman, and I don't know how to create that for her yet. [*Identifying many Toward values, another archetype, and the awareness of not-knowing yet how to create the new game she desires.*]

What is the relationship between your Queen and your Teacher–Wise Woman? [*Probing the relationship between these archetypes.*]

For me this is the ultimate reward of a life time searching. When I'm teaching, I have touched the reality of being this— what I don't know is if it has touched me. Am I what I teach?

Are you? [*Following up on the question to test where Erica is.*]

Well, my Teacher is a legacy from both my parents. My mother was the gifted and much loved teacher and my father was the feared and admired teacher. The Teacher seems to be what I have been doing, what I have been effortlessly drawn to do and what has presented the least obstacles along the way. [*The archetype morphs into the Teacher.*]

How do you describe yourself as a Teacher? [*Probing the self identity frame of the teacher.*]

I am the synthesis of my mother and father with true heart and spirit flowing through me.

And have you become this now? [*Probing to understand the process of how this occurred.*]

When I stand in front of my students, I truly am [tears]. And in my work, this is the only place this happens for me. I truly feel God speaks through me.

[Smiling] What is the relationship between you as this Teacher and your power as Queen? [*Probing the relationship to invite the client to create the new frame.*]

I can now see it is using my power as the Queen truly can. Truly combining knowledge, heart, spirit, and power.

[Long pause] You also mentioned the Seducer. What is your relationship to the Seducer? [*Exploring and probing.*]

From very early on, I knew I could get others to do what I wanted, or think like I thought, or go along with my agenda. I do believe that my drive to do this was based on a belief that I knew what was best for everyone. So what motivated me was the good of all. Yet I have been told by others that this has not always been the case. [*Identifies the power and problems of the Seducer and so accepts the challenge of facing her personal reality head-on.*]

How has it served you using your Seducer in this way? [*Probing for the positive values of this archetype.*]

> I think my ability to enthuse and inspire is a great quality. I guess I am accustomed to getting my own way and have difficulty letting go, or accepting when my seduction skills fail to produce the desired effect. My dismay is partly because I genuinely believe I want what is best for everyone, or I have decided that what I want will end up being the best. I have seduced in the literal sense and I have seduced in the spiritual and intellectual sense. Looking back, I am probably not as proud of my physical seductions, but at the time I believed this was my one and only real power.

As you step back here again, looking at your Queenly power, what do you now understand about your power to influence others? [*Co-creating by invitation to construct new learnings.*]

> Until now I have had no conscious awareness about how powerful and influential I am! I had no idea that I had all of this power to influence others. But, of course, it has always been there, but in a covert way. I was using it to protect myself. Growing up in my family I never felt powerful, I never felt seen, I never felt they really understood me. Particularly my father. I saw him, and still do, as very powerful. With him and then others, I learned to fight to take power [tears].

What does this realization mean to you? [*Continuing the co-creation of new frames.*]

> It means that I don't have to stay stuck in my self identity. I can feel the sadness of being a young child, locked out in the hallway [Crying]. . . . locked out from my mother and father's room and refused by my sister to go into her room. I can see how I have carried this forward as a theme of being dis-empowered which has caused me to feel that I had to fight for power.

[Smiling] Hmmm . . . and as you stay with those feelings for a moment, Erica, what opens up to you? [*Allowing the awakening to occur and inviting her into the co-creator role.*]

> A true vision and true possibility ... that with this awareness I can finally step fully into my true power. I don't have to take power from others to be powerful.

[Long pause with smiling and long eye contact] Are there any other archetypes that you also feel have a relationship to the Queen? [*Further exploring.*]

> Well, the Truth Teller and Judge.

So, what is your relationship to the Truth Teller and Judge?

I believe this is my mission, the light I am meant to carry into the world. The tendency to share and hear the truth has always been with me. Yet I have not always told the truth, but somehow I have always known in myself when I've lied—even when I didn't know it . . . my challenge has been to find a way to tell the truth that others can hear. Often I have spoken or acted or reacted with the justification of the truth in ways that did not communicate or served to alienate, frighten, or incense.

What is important to you about truth? [*Probing for positive intentions.*]

Truth is my highest value. I long to know the truth about things, about the world, about spirit, about people. But the truth in my mind and heart rises above the ego. Fears drive it. It is paramount. I don't know if I value anything higher because I believe that in the truth resides in all knowledge and all wisdom, in all that we ever need.

Have you always lived the Truth Teller and Judge in its highest form? [*Probing the use of this frame and challenging the absoluteness of her description.*]

My Judge, and judgment side, has often hurt others. It has created anger in me, and perhaps a lack of compassion. With family and friends, I have set high standards and expectations and have been disappointed and angry when others failed to live up to my expectations. [*Identifies away from values and problems.*]

What has your imposed expectations cost you? [*Playing the challenger role to intensify the motivation for change.*]

That is a good question . . . I had never thought of it in this way. I only thought of it terms of what others lost by not living up to *my* expectations. I guess it's the classic Judge at work here, isn't it? In presupposing that I know what is right and what is wrong for everybody else . . . [laughter at self, shaking head and long pause] . . . it had made me very difficult to work with . . . [another long pause]. In looking at it from this position, I would say it has probably cost me a successful career in working with others. I feel like nobody wants to help me or work with me.

What does this realization now mean to you? [*Provoking her to use the answers for change to co-create a new game.*]

I don't like being that kind of a Judge! I have only been living the Judge in a very limited way, and I now want to know how to use the Judge in her highest form, but what would that be like?

So, how could you experience the Judge in her highest form? [*Inviting her to co-create the new game.*]

Hmmm   . . . [big exhalation]. I don't know if I know. What do you think?

If you did know [smiling], what is the highest expression of a Judge or Truth Teller? [*Refusing to take the bait of giving advice and using a hypothetical question to awaken her co-creator.*]

I think it would be being fair and compassionate . . . at heart it is helping people become more of who they want to be. It is being willing to point the truth to others . . . but the significant difference is—*their own truth*. It is helping others evaluate what is right and wrong against their only values, their own criteria. It is being willing to stand up for justice and for protecting others for themselves and hurting others. Oh my goodness! It is putting my opinions aside and evaluating against an agreed criteria. Only giving my opinion when I am asked for it . . . now that would be very different for me! [*As the coach held the space for the client to discover and create her own answers, she suddenly creates many wonderful frames for her new game.*]

When you try these frames on, how do they feel? [*Taking the creation of her frames and inviting her to actualize them in her body and life.*]

[Pause] Different! Very different! It is no longer about me . . . it now feels like when I teach and I feel like God speaks through me . . . [tears]. I feel like I really can make a difference this way.

Given this, how have you fully accessed in the Truth Teller and Judge in the past? [*Inviting her to further identify how she accesses a resource.*]

I don't know if I have very much. But I do believe it has allowed me to easily set boundaries, be assertive, speak my mind, have an opinion. It has fuelled my passion for ideas, creations, activities, and sometimes causes. I love being the Truth-Teller, and being able to express my opinion. I am very comfortable with this.

Is there anything else you feel you need to explore about the Judge and Truth-Teller in relationship to your work and future direction? [*Inviting more actualizing.*]

I don't think so. I can see now that the Judge and Wise-Woman a very similar to one another.

We have explored your relationship to power through the Queen, Seductress, Teacher—Wise Woman and now the Truth Teller and Judge. As you step back from all of these archetypes, what do you see is the inter-relationship between them all? [*Inviting an integration and alignment of this archetype as a resource.*]

[Pause] . . . well . . . I am in that place of the Teacher—being the channel for the knowledge, I have always felt most at home. The Queen is in control . . . the Seducer is at her best...the Pioneer has found purpose and expression . . . the Truth Teller has a forum . . . and the Dreamer/Artist an outlet. (Long pause) Do you know . . . If at the end of my life I could be and know that I had found wisdom, all would be well.

Good, so go there now . . . to the end of your life, and step into that experience. What do you think and feel? [*Shifting into a time-line orientation to elicit more co-creating and actualizing.*]

I feel complete. [Tears and a long pause, smiling at each other, Erica legs jumping up and down with energy.] This is just all too exciting!

And *I* am also very excited for you! You mentioned just now the Dreamer and Artist—what do they mean to you? [*Cheerleading and celebrating the new game and decisions.*]

It is through the Dreamer that the child stays alive in me and finds expression. It was she who I first remember when I think of myself as a child—gazing out the window of our car as we drove across America—letting my mind and my heart invent stories that were more real than my family in the car or the scenery floating past. In the Dreamer lies my heart's desire, the invented world in which I am all that I am meant to be. The Dreamer brought me to acting . . . the Dreamer wanted to create a reality in which I could soar as the Queen and Teacher as the Wise Woman and Pioneer new ways to help and heal and love and be loved.

How have you lived out the Dreamer and Artist in your life? [*Exploring the use of this archetype.*]

The Dreamer has caused me to live in a dream, to tell myself lies about what was true and what was not—to stay locked in a cycle of hope, sabotage, victim, and hope.

How else have you lived the Dreamer / Artist?

The Dreamer together with the Seducer has been a powerful force in convincing not only me, but those who care about me that I know what I'm doing, that acting or moving to Japan or Australia or being with this man or that—will bring me that happiness and fulfilment I seek. It is how I have lied to myself and others . . . And it is the Dreamer that creates the stories that I write and is the source of my creativity. She is utterly free and knows no boundaries.

Given this, and what you have discovered today about your power, what opens up to you? [*Inviting more application and integration of the resources.*]

That I have enormous influence, and that I can use it powerfully. That I can now be purposeful and embrace this aspect of me, that I have never known before. So much is possible for me now.

What are some of those possibilities? [*Inviting specific application to actualize.*] My Dreamer and Artist can intentionally share the messages of my Teacher and Wise Woman. What I am now realizing is that there is a body of knowledge inside of me to share—that is already written. It is now ready to come out. I am now ready to share it. To take my throne and to hold court with compassion, love, and to help others to share in the truth of the human experience. I feel for the very first time that I can step into this fully as a direction with purpose [smiling and laughing].

[Smiling and laughing] What will this look like? [*More questioning to elicit more actualizing.*] First, I will write a book on the acting classes that I have taught over the years. Do you know, believe it or not, I already have all the transcripts from my acting classes. I have not known what to do with them. I now realize that this book is almost already written. I can easily get this done. And that book is just the beginning. I want to go out there right away and start now!

How do you know that this is the best path for you? [*Eliciting her evidence criteria and testing it.*] Because for the first time I can see how I got here, how I have been living in the dark sabotaging my pure power. The possibilities for my future now seem clear. I have never believed I could handle the obstacles and challenges because I never felt I was on a path. I now feel I am actually on a path, I have been all along but could never see it before. Thank you!

Meta Debriefing

Archetypal Conversations are very powerful in teasing out personality and life themes or patterns. Why? Because inherent in it is the ability to step outside of one's story to identify the stories's theme or form, the Archetype. *Archetypal Conversations* become truly transformational when we invite a client to reflect on their personal themes and patterns with the intention of identifying the highest potential in each theme. Through discovering one's archetype and probing into its strengths and weaknesses clients are enabled to step back and identify specifically how and where they are not realizing their fullest potential, and the consequence of not doing so.

In using an archetypal framework and language, we ask a client to continually step in and out of first position (experiencing the archetype's presence in their own life), second position (how others experience the archetype's presence), third position (observing the archetype's possibilities outside of self) and fourth position (the current effects and possible effects of this archetype's presence in their history and future). This simple process illuminates the gap between where they are and the potentials not yet identified. In doing this, developmental steps miraculously appear while identifying a compelling pathway that pulls them to realizing more of their potential.

The first step of *identifying* core archetypes *challenges* the client to explore his or her current self identity and to face that reality in all its grandeur and darkness. The *Archetypal Conversation* structure requires the client to accept and take responsibility for *all* behaviour of the archetype, positive and negative. In Erica's case, she had not before accepted the full power and influence of her Queen and Seducer nor taken responsibility for the consequences of using their presence destructively with herself and others.

The second step of *exploring* each archetype through *probing and provoking,* activates the archetypal energy being explored and illuminates current behaviour and its effectiveness. In Erica's case she was able to see for the very first time how placing her Judge's expectations upon her colleagues had sabotaged her from creating productive working relationships and ultimately prevented her from achieving career fulfilment and satisfaction.

The third step of *accessing* the grandest potential of each archetype occurs through co-creating and awakening new awareness of the archetype's "highest form" and in the process identifying and accessing those new resources that the "highest form" suggests. In this session Erica discovered her highest potential of leading as the Queen and the highest potential of communicating as a Judge. She accessed and accepted new resources in both contexts: compassion, wisdom, fairness, love, etc.

The fourth step of *experiencing* the grandest potential of each archetype occurs through *actualizing* and *testing* the new resources and the consequent behaviours in different contexts. With Erica, the coach tested her Teacher, Judge, and the future of all the archetypes against her specific coaching outcome of finding meaningfulness and a direction for her professional life.

Summary
- Archetypes, as a collection of *metaphors,* offer a coach a framework for looking at, talking about, and developing new potentials in our personality and behaviors by using a global and thematic portrait of life.
- As a coaching tool, archetypes give us multiple external perspectives for viewing the themes and patterns of our lives, and for identifying

unrealized potentials.
* Archetypes also give us a way to identify and try on new resources for enhancing performance and for gaining more meaning and fulfillment from our lives.

End Notes:

1. C. G. Jung. (1970). *The structure and dynamics of the psyche.* Collected works of C.G. Jung, Vol. 8, edited and translated by G. Adler and R.F.C. Hull. "The Archetypes and Collective Unconscious," NJ: Princeton University Press.

2. Caroline Myss, *Sacred Contracts* (Bantam 2001).

Chapter 22

PUTTING IT
ALTOGETHER

"Any conversation that gives the person being coached more confidence in their ability to perform and leaves them poised to act, is a coaching conversation."
                    Kim H. Krisco

"Coaching bridges the gap between the present and future. Coaching changes, focuses, and intensifies human behavior."
                    Kim H. Krisco

"Coaching is about change. Most people are good at starting to make changes; but not in carrying through and maintaining transformative changes. Most people are not intrinsically lazy or weak willed, but they are very busy. They forget, they get distracted."
                    Grant and Greene, *Coach yourself* (2002)

In *Coaching Conversation*s we have portrayed and analyzed the conversation between a client and coach as *a dance*. This metaphor has enabled us to look at the form of the conversation as involving the coach dancing in and out of eight steps and eight roles to facilitate the experience of change. On the client's part, the dance involves changing in eight dimensions. Together the dance takes them through *the Axes of Change* which uses four explicit meta-programs that we have used to describe *how change occurs*.   The axes occur on four continua and so involve an oscillation between eight poles. As we have highlighted time and again, this gives us the following *dances* within Coaching Conversations.

- Toward / Away From meta-program:
    The Push—Pull Dance
    Challenger and Awakener
- Active / Reflective meta-program:
    The Readiness—Leverage of Decision Dance
    Provoker and Prober

- Internal / External meta-program:
  The Inner—Outer Game Dance
  Co-Creator and Actualizer
- Match / Mis-Match meta-program:
  The Solidification Dance
  Reinforcer and Tester

We could also take into consideration there other meta-programs, filters that are inherent in each dance. These include the following:
- Global / Specific meta-program:
  The Meta-Detailing Dance
- Options / Procedures meta-program:
  The Pattern—Alternative Dance

As a model, *the Axes of Change* give us eight essential coaching roles. These are the eight roles and states which the coach transverses again and again. As such, they that involve the following activities which imply numerous coaching skills.

The First Dance
In *the Push—Pull dance* the coach oscillates in his or her movements between the attractor values (*toward*) and the aversion dis-values (*away from*). In this coach and client dance around motivation, desire, passion, direction, the future, how to live, what to live for, meaning, and purpose.

In the first, the coach is the *Awakener* who inspires, stimulates, seduces, and plays. What skills does a coach need here? He or she needs to be able to arouse, motivate, model, tell stories, and inspire. Typically, this dance step is the first one. It's where everything begins. Yet it is also a dance step that the coach must be ready to move back to. That's because this is the step that invites and elicits the client to *move forward* to a new and exciting vision.

In the second part of the Push-Pull dance is the *Challenger*. Here the coach puts the spotlight on the client's current state and where things are going unless a change is made. As *Challenger,* the coach provides the push, the prod, and the confrontation. Here the coach holds the focus on the unpleasant facets of reality to induce anger, fear, frustration, stress, intolerance, and other "negative" emotions that creates a move *away from* what's should not be tolerated: mediocrity, unrealistic fears, procrastination, selling oneself short, excuses, and anything that settles for less.

The Second Dance
In *the Active—Reflective dance* the coach oscillates between the two pole extremes of awareness. Feeling motivated to change (Axis I) doesn't inform

anyone about *what* to change, *how* to change, or what frames of mind to change. With the motivation to change, we next need to raise awareness of the content of change.

When some people feel the need to change, they immediately start acting. They do something different. It is only after acting that they then reflect on what they are changing and the results they are getting. That's the active mode. Others move into a more reflective mode first. They think about their thoughts, feelings, beliefs, history, understandings, expectations, and other frames. When they have a more well-thought out plan about what to change, then they act. We describe this second Axis as the *Readiness* and *Leverage* axis, the Axis of Decision since deciding involves both knowing what to change, considering and weighing alternatives, and then committing to it.

In the *reflective* state or stage, the coach plays the role of the *Prober*. Here the coach gets rapport by seeking to understand, by matching, by pacing, and by using all of his or her curiosity to empathetically enter into the client's matrix. How does it work? What does the person think, feel, understand, believe, expect, want, remember, imagine, etc.? Here the coach dances with the client as an explorer of the frames of mind that create the current reality and vision for the future. The coach as *Prober* moves into the client's frames and possible new frames to detect the structures and patterns that govern his or her present life.

In the *reflective* dance, the coach is looking for the *leverage* point in the belief, understanding, decision, and identity frames. Where is the leverage point in the system? What frames are holding the client back? What frames need to change? What does the client need to believe, decide, know, remember, imagine, etc. in order to breakthrough to a new level of success? What are the pros and cons, the advantages and disadvantages in the client's decision-making strategy?

In the *readiness* state or stage, the coach plays the role of *Provoker*. Here the coach provokes, teases, coaxes, taunts, and even torments. Why? To get enough energy to actually make the decision to change. After the coach and client dance into the reflective mode, the coach then moves back to the active mode to provoke, challenge, and test to see if the client is ready, if he or she has the ego-strength to handle the coaching, to make a decision, to make a commitment, to get to threshold, and to take action.

The Third Dance
In *the Internal—External reference dance* the coach oscillates again between two poles. Now the coach and client moves back and forth between the inner

and outer games. Together they swing back and forth between referencing the inner world of understandings, decisions, beliefs, expectations, etc. and the outer world of action and performance. This gives us two more coaching stages.

First, the coach and client work as co-creators of the change. The coach plays the role of *Collaborator* and *Co-Creator* to the client. After all, it is the *client's* outcomes, talents, values, beliefs, etc. that the coach holds and nurtures. It is the client who will ultimately play the new game. The coaching skills needed here include that of eliciting and evoking, nurturing, brainstorming, and exciting. The coach also needs to be able to set the creation in motion and let go of his or her agendas. After all, it is not about the coach. As coaches we have to embrace ambiguity since we never know what the client will give birth to in the process.

The dance then shifts as the coach takes to playing the *Actualizer* role. This refers to encouraging and enabling the client to take the construction of the inner game outside and to begin to enact it in real time in the real world. The coaching skills involved in this stage of change involves reassuring, supporting, giving permission to try things out, experimenting to see what works, learning from failures, etc. Here we are seeking to see and understand what *actually* brings the inner game out and makes it real or actual in the client's life and world.

The Fourth Dance
The final dance is the *Dance of Solidification*. Our focus here is on the continuance of the change to sustain the new inner and outer games. Will it last? Will it fade away? Will it fit into the rest of life ecologically?

In this dance, there are again two poles and two roles. These are built around the coach and client looking to *match* what fits and corresponds to the inner game—even in its smallest development and approximation and then when that new behavior, attitude, belief, etc. becomes robust enough to *mis-match* what does not fit. This gives us the *Reinforcer* and *Tester* roles for the coach.

The coaching skills involved in the *Reinforcement* stage of change involves validating the client, cheerleading any and every approximation of what works, celebrating change, development, and effort, acknowledging spirit and attitude, and finding first approximations to build upon.

Finally, the coach moves into the role of *Tester*. In this role the coach seeks to test things, to monitor and see if the game works, if the new frames have translated into new behavior (i.e., communicating, relating, negotiating, listening, questioning, etc.) has been activated, and how things are going. In testing, the coach will be confirming, checking, and holding the client accountable. The coach will also be giving tasking assignments and feedback for refinement and debriefing the client on the next step of development. The coaching skills needed here are monitoring, giving feedback, facilitating performance reviews and appraisals, encouraging, challenging, inviting redesign, and tasking.

And then the Dance

Putting these *dances* and *roles* together enables us to see coaching and coaching conversations as a dynamic, non-linear, systemic, ever-evolving, and fluid process. There is no "one right way" to do it. There is not even a single beginning place. You can start at any of these places and you will start at any one of these steps with various clients. Nor is there an end-game to the process. Even when we are in the outer game of performance, we can even view that as just the beginning of moving toward even higher goals.

In a formal coaching relationship, the coach will fully assess four things with regard to the desired change. These are the four areas around which we have built *the Axes of Change model*.

> 1) *Motivation:* The level of motivation for the change.
> 2) *Decision:* The level of readiness and decision strength for the change.
> 3) *Creation:* The creation of a plan in the mind and the degree to which the plan has been created.
> 4) *Solidification:* The degree of sustainability of the change and the degree to which the change has become ecologically habituated in life.

Depending on the amount of energy available at each stage, we will start the coaching dance at the point where the energy needs to be access and directed. So if there is low motivation for change, we start as an *Awakener* and *Challenger*. If there is already high motivation that's compelling, then the coach will probably start as *Prober and Provoker* to explore what specifically needs to be changed and when. On other occasions, clients, colleagues, lovers, and friends will come already feeling totally compelled and clear about what and when to change. With them, we will probably start the dance as a *Co-Creator* and *Actualizer*. As the person translates the new game into actual behavior, we play the roles of *Reinforcer* and *Tester* to see how it's developing, and what yet needs to be refined.

Does it discourage you that the change process does not operate as a linear step-by-step process that guarantees that you will always move a conversation forward in just the right way? Or do you find it exciting and freeing to know that this gives you a fluid model that you can adjust precisely to where the client is? As a dance, you and your client are *inventing the new game* as you go. We call it a *co-creation* because like creation, it's an evolving and developing process. Sometimes we don't have a clue as to what dream or vision we will give birth to.

So, above and beyond the science of how our mind-body-emotion system works, there is an *art* to the process of change. There is the art of using your love and knowledge and all of your coaching skills to dance with another in co-creating more possibilities, new potentials, and even possible life transformations.

For this we must practice and train our intuitions about human experiences. For this we have to develop our confidence in the basic skills of coaching—in listening, supporting, questioning, meta-questioning, giving and receiving feedback, inducing states, exploring, facilitating, etc. For this we have to trust ourselves and our intuitions as we match and pace the person we're coaching, holding his or her agenda front and center, and moving into a caring and empathic role. This is what makes coaching such an exciting endeavor.

As we move from *Performance Coaching* around the outer game that increases the skill set and level of our clients, we move to *Developmental Coaching*. This coaching invites them to step out of the box of their current thinking into new and unexplored boxes. Here we invite them to the possibilities of human experience at higher levels. Yet that isn't the end. After that we invite clients to move up into the highest form of coaching, *Transformational Coaching*. In Transformational Coaching it is not only about performance that improves or self that develops, but a whole new way or direction of life that transforms.

Along the way we have many robust and breakthrough conversations, breaking through one level to the next. We dance between the key Coaching Conversations that we have mentioned in this book: Outcome, Resource, Possibility, Fierce, Matrix, Narrative, Time-Line, Neuro-Logical Levels, Hero Journey, Archetypal, etc.

Conversational Distinctions
We know that there's something special about people with expertise, but what?
- What distinguishes those who develop *mastery* in a field or discipline?
- What do skilled *masters* have, or know, that sets them apart?

People who move to mastery are able to make more distinctions than those who perform at a more mediocre level. What does this mean for coaching? It highlights a important realization: *Distinctions create mastery.* Therefore, the more *critical distinctions* that you have, and that you can make, regarding the key variables of an experience, the more you can become masterful in your field and in your performance. It's as simple as that. That's important to know as a coach when you coach for performance, it's also valuable to know to improve your performance as a coach. To now build on our ability to make valuable distinctions in our conversations, we offer the following.

As a conversation, coaching works as *a self-actualizing tool or methodology*. By the conversation, we create a climate, environment, and context that invites individuals and groups to feel more confidence as we excite them to take action on specific goals which they own and are committed to achieving. Ultimately, the effectiveness of a coach lies in the positive difference that occurs in the client's life, does it not? In the end, we judge good coaches by the results which *their clients,* loved ones, team, friends, and associates achieve.

What are some of the *critical* distinctions regarding the conversations and coaching conversations that are crucial? What are the key distinctions we should be making that will enrich the dialogues that we initiate? To focus on them we offer the following questions.

1) What is the conversation's quality, intent, and nature?
All conversations are not created equal. Conversations come in a variety of flavors. Some are high quality, others are trivial, they are worthless, mere chatter or noise. Some are actually harmful.
• What is the *quality* of your conversation at any given moment?

Making distinctions about the *quality* of a conversation is vital if we want to raise the impact and power of our coaching. Actually, it's possible to be engaged in what we consider a life-changing conversation *and* the other person not even realize it. Have you ever had a conversation (or thought you were having that kind of conversation with someone) and later discovered that they thought you were just chatting with them, just "shooting the breeze?"

To have a high quality coaching conversations, typically it is best to frame the communication as that. We do that by simply highlighting the nature and purpose of the conversation. Why? Because how we frame our talk will influence and govern how the other person will listen and what they think we are doing with our words.
• Is the person being coached even listening to what I'm offering as "coaching?"

Since it is the frame that structures the mental context, be explicit about what you are doing. It certainly is possible to do this covertly, and oftentimes successfully, but that carries its own problems and challenges.[1]

2) Are you distinguishing facts from interpretations?
If there's any distinction that's absolutely critical for being a professional communicator, it is this one. Why? Because facts, and interpretation of facts,

are very different animals and occur on completely different *levels*. They are not the same at all and do not even exist in the same dimension. Further, all kinds of problems arise in communication and relationship when we confuse levels. So, as a coach, make this distinction.

- Am I distinguishing the facts and the interpretations of my client (colleague, lover, friend)?
- Is my client recognizing this distinction and can tell the difference between these levels?

What's the difference? *Facts* are the events, actions, and things that happen in the outside world. These are the sensory-based observations and descriptions that we make about what actually happened that we can perceive with our senses. *Interpretations* are all of our meta-level frames about such—our ideas, beliefs, understandings, conclusions, meaning attributions, explanations, expectations, memories, imaginations, etc.

What happens if we don't make this distinction in conversation? We can be seduced into the story with the client and fail to see new possibilities or unleash new potentials. At the level of facts and events, we experience the triggers and stimuli to which we respond. At the level of meaning and interpretation, we experience our frames and all of the embedded frames of our matrix. This is where we can *change our world.* So as a coach we can ask ourselves:

- Does the client's interpretations (frames) open up new possibilities for him or her?
- What questions can I ask that will invite my client to step out of those frames and try on, experiment with, and create new frames?

It's not enough that we separate fact from interpretation, from there we move to frame, deframe, and reframe in ways that evoke the client's mental and emotional powers, the client's creative powers, to open up new options and possibilities for a brighter future.[2]

Can we clearly and effectively distinguish between the brute facts, the things that exist in reality which has substance from those that only exist in language—in the inner reality of their neuro-semantic system? Here's another way to do it. Use the difference between a true noun and a false one to linguistically test this distinction. How? By recognizing that a true noun refers to an actual, empirical thing. You can put it in the refrigerator. You can drop it on the carpet or leave it on the sidewalk to stumble over. It's a person, place, or thing.

Then there are the actions and verbs that we try to elevate to the status of an actual thing, but which only exists in the mind, in language, in the inner matrices of our consciousness. You cannot put these things in the frig. You cannot put meaning, relationship, love, honor, pleasure, motivation, pride, satisfaction or a thousand other things.

3) Is your client translating his or her best ideas into practice?
This distinction enables us to sort our *mere* talk to *transformational* talk.
- Is this talk leading anywhere?
- Does it empower and enrich the client so that things change?
- Is the client translating the inspiring ideas and critical knowledge into practice into effective actions that make a difference in the needed contexts?

This is where coaching hits the road, isn't it? Are we actually evoking and coaching within the client a willingness to take full ownership and commitment to do something about what is being discussed? Or, is the conversation *just* talk? Are we seeing behaviors change? New life emerging? Higher performance results occurring?

It is to this end that we use *tasking* in coaching. It is to this end that we use all kinds of things in the *actualizing stage* of coaching as well as in the continuance stage. We task our clients so that they actually *act on* and *with* the insights and awarenesses from the coaching. We also use feedback, monitoring, accountability, tough questions, and fierce conversations. We may use various Neuro-Semantic patterns like the Mind-to-Muscle pattern to coach the body how to feel an idea.[3]

Making the distinction in a conversation about whether the client is fully on board with *owning* his or her power, accepting responsibility to make a change in thinking, feeling, speaking, acting, or relating, and feeling "at cause" as an agent of change is critical in order to ensure that the coaching doesn't degenerate into just a nice chat. In this, coaching invites clients to step up into both management and leadership roles.

Whether the client is a manager or leader isn't the point. Nor is it whether you are doing personal coaching rather than business coaching. The point is that growth, change, and transformation necessitates clients accepting the role of a *leader* and *manager* of self—of his or her own vision for life, values, beliefs, actions, relationships, etc. Ultimately, *leadership* is about vision and framing. It's about taking the risk to identify a passion and pursue it. And ultimately, *management* is about translating that vision and values into everyday actions and managing the process of implementation.

This calls upon us to become a self-leader and manager. The ultimate in leadership and management is *self-leadership* and *self-management*. Why? Because when you can lead and manage yourself, then you can make your dreams come true. You can translate your great ideas, the ideas that inspire you, into reality.

*   What is your vision for your life, your health, your business, your relationships, your creativity, your contributions, etc.?
*   How are you managing your mind, emotions, heart, body, speech, actions, and relationships?
*   What opportunities for leadership do you see in this situation?
*   What are the potential opportunities for you to create a vision and lead out?
*   How can you make a difference as a leader in this situation? What legacy would you like to leave?

4) Is your client changing, growing, developing, and transforming?
Coaching is all about change—altering our thinking or feeling, changing our income, our health and fitness, our hopes and dreams. Coaching is about actualizing our potentials. This is another critical distinction.

Because coaching is for the well, it differs significantly from counseling and therapy. Since therapy is designed to bringing healing to the wounded, it is more about "finishing the business" of the past. That's why it often involves the therapist playing a re-parenting role and empowering a person to complete the developmental tasks so that he or she can come into the present. That's why transference and counter-transference are key considerations for therapy, even in the best cognitive behavioral and brief psychotherapy. The goals and roles of therapy mostly center around trauma. Therapy is mostly for the unwell. It's to bring healing and sanity to otherwise dysfunctional parenting errors.

By contrast, coaching is for the mentally and emotionally healthy. Coaching is most ideally suited for people who want to break boundaries, set records, and push themselves in a variety of ways. Coaching is for people with the ego-strength to look reality in the face, even the most challenging problems and accessing belief in self and the power of self-efficacy to take effective action to make the impossible possible.

People who are not goal setters, and who do not feel driven, will find coaching distasteful. It will not be their cup of tea. People who are very much wedded to their excuses and complaints, who hold on to resentful bitterness, will not like the "optimism" of coaching. Coaching is suited best for those who want to be the best they can be and find utter joy in giving it their all.

In the meta-coaching style, we focus much more on the person than on the results. We do so because we believe that it is the person who focuses on the result and that we, as the coach, operate as the facilitators of that focus. That's also why, as a meta-coach, we focus primarily on the frames—on the thinking patterns, meaning patterns, states, intentions, beliefs, and behaviors which create the results. For us, we know that here lies the leverage for change.

5) Are we breaking through problems and constraints with our conversations and questions?
Coaching is not only for the well, but for the top-performers, for those who refuse to live life just getting by, just surviving. Coaching is for dreamers and visionaries. That's why the coach plays the role of *Awakener*—to wake up the possibilities and potentials that are sleepy in the client and invite the client on a bigger vision that he or she even dreamed about when they started the coaching relationship.

In this coaching focuses on *breakthrough performances*. It's about creating and living a world-class life—a life to write home about, a life to have a biography written about. It's about making a difference and leaving a legacy that will contribute to the generations to come.

Do you make this distinction in your coaching conversation? Are you asking breakthrough questions of your clients?
- What stops you from getting through this barrier?
- What's in the back of your mind that you need to release?
- How clear and compelling is your desired outcome? What if you doubled it?
- What are you willing to do to achieve this?
- What are you willing to give up?
- What would happen if . . .?
- Have you made a decision to do this yet?
- When you break through this barrier, what's beyond it?

6) Is your client having "Aha!" experiences?
We can expect a sense of *"Aha!"* at every level of change. At the first levels, the "Aha!" will be more matter-of-fact, "Oh yes, that's a much better idea, frame, interpretation." At the highest levels, the "Aha!" can become such a celebration of insight that it can transform everything. And because coaching is about facilitating conversation, dialogue, and experience so that the client *discovers* and therefore owns the insights, the insights come from within the client.

In the Matrix of our frames, "Know thyself" is the ancient wisdom that calls us to step back, and to reflect and to create the best kinds of frames. Does the client have more life force energy from the conversations? Is there more energy to live more fully, to take on more passionate goals, to have more, become more, and contribute more?

7) Are you as a coach growing, evolving, and changing.
Let the coach who thinks coaching is all about the client changing take notice, and beware. Effective and powerful coaching that brings transformation to others will inevitably change the coach. There's many reasons for that, not the least of which is the fact that in coaching the coach uses his or her own thinking, feeling, relating, conversing, and experiencing as a key transformation process. That means that the coaching will bring changes and even transformations to the coach. To coach is to be changed.

Summary

- If ultimately coaching is a *conversational* dance, then it's about finding a client's rhythm in his or her beliefs, hopes, dreams, visions, emotions, and passions . . . entering the rhythm of that energy and working with it to help channel it in the direction that the client sets.

- As coaches, we assume that there are all kinds of incredible potentials to be unleashed in the minds and hearts of our clients and that coaching is the adventure of discovering how to make that unleashing possible.

- Change is not only possible, it is inevitable. Whether we will or won't change is not the choice or question before us. Our choice has to do with the kind of changes we make, the quality of changes we make, whether we have fun along the way, and whether the changes brings out our best to fulfill our best dreams.

End Notes
1: For more about *framing* and the many forms and facets of framing see *Frame Games* (2000) and for more on communication and all of the things we can do with words and language, see *Communication Magic* (2001).

2: For more about framing, deframing, and reframing *conversationally*, see *Mind-Lines: Lines for Changing Minds* (2001). Mind-Lines is a model for how to conversationally frame and reframe meaning; it presents the seven directions that we can "send a mind" as we speak that gives more choice in our attribution and construction of meaning.

3: For more about the Mind-to-Muscle pattern, see *Secrets of Personal Mastery,* or check it out on the www.neurosemantics.com website. Also the spiral book, *Make It So!* (2002) is a whole book about the are of implementation so that we execute what we say is important.

Appendix A:

META-COACH TRAINING

Under the auspices of the International Society of Neuro-Semantics® (ISNS) and the Meta-Coach Foundation (MCF) we have a coach training track for certification and levels of professional coach accreditation. The *Meta-Coaching Taining and Certification*™ system involves extensive study and training while the accreditation process involves extensive competency testing, validation of coaching experience, and achievement of other professional standards.

If you are brand new to Neuro-Semantics (NS) and NLP, then the "Fast Track" (below) gives you a way to get started. This lets you discover your commitment and passion for coaching and if you want to become a professional in the field. We recommend this track and/or the Internal Coach training for those who simply want to add coaching skills and an introduction to Neuro-Semantics (NS) to their repertoire of skills. This is excellent for business owners, managers, CEOs, entrepreneurs, etc. The *Internal Coach Certification Training* (below) is specially designed for business. The "Ultimate Coaching Track" (below) describes the process for anyone who plans to open up a coaching practice.

THE FAST TRACK. For those just new to NLP and who want to quickly get on board and get started with NLP and Neuro-Semantic coaching.
1) *Coaching Essentials*
>   A 3-day introduction to the essential coaching/communication skills of NLP that begins the process: rapport, pacing, anchoring, state management, resourcefulness, precision questioning, and some basic patterns.

2) *Coaching Genius* (also APG *Accessing Personal Genius*)
>   The 3-day introduction to Meta-States that focuses on developing your powers of "focus" and intentionality, in texturing your coaching state with the prerequisites of personal genius and offering you 14 coaching patterns.

3a) **ICMC**: *Internal Certified Meta-Coach*
>   This is a 5-day training for managers, business owners, CEOs, and others in leadership and management to add to their repertoire of skills. ICMC covers the Axes of Change model, Matrix model, Matrix Business Plan, benchmarking of skills, lots of experiential hands-on practice, and much more.

3b) **ACMC:** *Associate Certified Meta-Coach*
> The 7-day intensive training using the best of Meta-States and Neuro-Semantics, a three-fold focus: Yourself as a Coach, Your Skills for coaching, and your Practice as a business. Structured to enable you to Coach to the Matrix, this training involves lots of experiential hands-on practice in coaching, benchmarking skills, the Matrix Life/Business Plan, Axes of Change model, and much more.
>
> Pre-requisites for attaining ACMC and ICMS credentialing is a minimum of *Coaching Essentials* and *Coaching Genius*— Meta States Certification. While this is *the fast track*, more typically those who become ACMC certified realize the importance of becoming full qualified in the foundations of NLP and so return to complete the Practitioner and Master Practitioner courses.

THE ULTIMATE COACHING TRACK
1) NLP Practitioner or Meta-NLP Certification.
> NLP Practitioner or Meta-NLP practitioner which occur between 7 and 21 days of training that covers the Practitioner course.

2) Master Practitioner or the Meta-Masters.
> In the *Meta-Masters* format this involves a 14 day accelerated training of NLP Master Practitioner training and includes training in Living Genius, Meta-Programs, Mind-Lines, and Modeling.

3) Coaching Genius (same as above).
4) ACMC
5) **PCMC:** *Professional Certified Coach*
> With 400 hours of verifiable paid coaching experience, ACMC Certification and NLP/NS Master Practitioner Certification you are eligible to attend a 3 to 5 day training and competency testing for the PCMC accreditation. To obtain this credential you will successfully pass PCMC competency assessment in a written examination and coaching demonstration.

6) **MCMC:** *Master Coach Certification Training*
> With 1000 hours of verifiable paid coaching experience and PCMC accreditation and having successfully completed 3 to 5 days of Master Coach Certification Training, a person is eligible to apply for MCMC accreditation. To obtain this, a person has to successfully pass MCMC competency assessment.

For more information contact on of the following websites:
> www.meta-coaching.org
> www.neurosemantics.com

To find a meta-coach in your country, contact:
> www.meta-coaches.com

Appendix B

INTERNATIONAL SOCIETY OF NEURO-SEMANTICS (ISNS)

www.neurosemantics.com

Neuro-Semantics® began as a field of study within the cognitive-behavioral movement in psychology, from NLP, General Semantics (Korzybski), Bateson and the Mental Research Institute, Cognitive Linguistics, Meta-Cognition, etc. It arose originally from a research project on resilience from which the *Meta-States model* arose (1994). Studying the structure and process of how mind works *reflexively* to reflect on itself, and does so repeatedly, Meta-States traced out the reflexive nature of human experience. This led to other models in Neuro-Semantics—

    Frame Games (2000)
    The Matrix Model (2002)
    The Axes of Change (2003)
    The Self-Actualization Quadrants (2004)
    The Benchmarking Model (2005)

From these models, key developers and leaders in Neuro-Semantics began creating numerous applications of these models:

    Selling Excellence (1999)
    Wealth Building (2000)
    Games Fit and Slim People Play (2000)
    Games for Mastering Fear (2000)
    Games for Mastering Stuttering (2001)
    Games Business Experts Play (2001)
    Games Great Lovers Play (2003)
    Meta-Coaching (2002)

Today the International Society Neuro-Semantics has an international influence in over 30 countries with hundreds of Trainers and Coaches listed on the primary website, and many more on websites in South Africa, the United Kingdom, Australia, Japan, Holland, Germany, France, Belgium, and so on.

BIBLIOGRAPHY

Bechtell, Michele L. (2002). *On Target: How to Conduct Effective Business Reviews.* San Francisco: Barrett-Koehler Publishers

Belf, Teri-E. (2002). *Coaching with Spirit: Allowing success to emerge.* San Francisco, CA: Jossey-Bass/ Pfeiffer.

Campbell, Joseph. (1988). *The power of myth.* Gardencity, NY: Doubleday and Company.

Cooperrider, David L., and Srivastva, S. (1988). "Appreciative Inquiry in Organizational Life." In *Research in Organization Change and Development,* vol. I, edited by W. Pasmore and R. Woodman, pp. 129-169. Greenwich, CN: JAI Press.

Cooperride, David. L. (1996). "Resources for Getting Appreciative Inquiry Started: An Example OD Proposal," *OD Practitioner*, vol. 28, nos. 1 & 2, pp. 23-33.

Covey, Stephen. (1987). *The 7 Habits of Highly Effective People.* NY: Simon and Schultzer.

Dilts, Robert; Hallbom, Tim; Smith, Susie. (1989). *Beliefs: Pathways to health and well-being.* Portland, OR: Metamorphous Press.

Dilts, Robert. (1990). *Changing belief systems with NLP.* Capitola, CA: Meta Publications.

Dilts, Robert; Bonissone, G. (1993). *Skills for the future: Managing creativity and innovation.* Capitola, CA: Meta Pulications.

Dilts, Robert; DeLozier, Judith. (2002). *Modeling and coaching.* Ben Lomond, CA: Dynamic Learning Publications.

Dilts, Robert. (2003). *From coach to awakener.* Capitola, CA: Meta Publications.

Dotlich, David L.; Cario, Peter C. (1999). *Action coaching: How to leverage individual performance for company success.* San Francisco: Jossey-Bass: A Wiley Company.

Downey, Myles. (2003). *Effective Coaching: Lessons from the coaches' coach.* Sydney, Australia: Thomson.

Druckman, Daniel; Bjork, Robert. (1991, editors). *In the Mind's Eye:*

Enhancing Human Performance. Wash DC: National Academy Press.

English, Gary. (1998). *Phoenix without the ashes: Achieving organizational excellence through common sense management.* NY: St. Lucie Press.

Flaherty, Butterworth. (1999). *Coaching: Evoking Excellence in Others.* Boston: Henemann.

Gallwey, W. Timothy. (1974). *The Inner Game of Tennis.* NY: Random House.

Gallwey, Timothy; Kriegel, Bob. (1977). *Inner Skiing.* NY: Random House.

Gallwey, W. Timothy. (1979/ 1981). *The Inner Game of Golf.* New York: Random House.

Gallwey, W. Timothy. (2000). *The inner game of Work: Focus, Learning, pleasure, and mobility in the workplace.* New York: Random House Trade Paperbacks.

Gardner, Howard. (1983). *Frames of mind: The theory of multiple intelligences.* NY: BasicBooks.

Gardner, Howard. (1991). *The unschooled mind: How children think and how schools should teach* NY: HarperCollins.

Gardner, Howard. (1983). *Multiple intelligences: The theory in practice.* NY: BasicBooks.

Grant, A.M.; and Greene, J. (2001). *Coach Yourself: Make Real change in your Life.* London: Momentum Press.

Grant, Antony. (2002). Dissertation, *"Towards a Psychology of Coaching: The impact of coaching on meta-cognition, mental health and goal attainment,"* University of Sydney, Australia, www.psycho.usyd.edu.au/coach.

Green, Barry; Gallwey, W. Timothy. (1986). *The Inner Game of Music.* Garden City, NY: Anchor Press, Doubleday.

Greene, Jane; Grant, Anthony. (2003). *Solution-Focused Coaching: Managing people in a complex world.* England: Pearson Education Limited.

Grinder, John; (1993) *Precision: How to get the Information you need to get Results.*

Hall, D.T. (1999). *Behind Closed Doors: What Really Happens in Executive*

Coaching. Organizational Dynamics. 27 (3) 39-53.

Hall, Michael. (1995/2000). *Meta-states: Managing the higher levels of your mind's reflexivity.* Grand Jct., CO: Neuro-Semantic Publications.

Hall, Michael. (2000). *Dragon slaying: Dragons to princes.* Grand Jct. CO: Neuro-Semantic Publications.

Hall, Michael. (2001). *NLP: Going meta—Advance modeling using meta-levels.* Grand Jct., CO: Neuro-Semantic Publications.

Hall, L. Michael; Bodenhamer, Bob G. (1999). *Sub-Modalities going meta.* Clifton, CO: Neuro-Semantic Publications.

Hall, L. Michael. (2000). *Secrets of personal mastery: Advanced techniques for accessing your higher levels of consciousness.* Wales, UK: Crown House Publications.

Hall, L. Michael. (2001). *Games slim and fit people play.* Grand Jct., CO: Neuro-Semantics Publications.

Hall, L. Michael; Bodenhamer, Bob. (2001). *Games for mastering fear.* Grand Jct. CO: Neuro-Semantics Publications.

Hall, L. Michael. (2001). *Communication Magic.* Wales, UK: Crown House Publications.

Holman, Peggy; Devane, Tom. (Eds.) (1999). *The change handbook: Group methods for shaping the future.* San Francisco: Berrett-Koehler Publishers, Inc.

Hudson, Frederic M. (1999). *The Handbook of Coaching: A comprehensive resource guide for managers, executives, consultants, and human resource professionals.* San Francisco, CA: Jossey-Bass Publishers.

Kilburg, Richard R. (2000). *Executive Coaching: Developing Managerial Wisdom in a World of Chao. Wash DC.* American Psychological Association.

Lenhardt, Vincent. (2004). *Coaching for Meaning: The culture and practice of coaching and team building.* London, UK: Palgrave Macmillan.

McDermott, Ian; Jago, Wendy. (2001). *The NLP Coach: A comprehensive Guide to Personal Well-Being and Professional Success.* London: Platkus, Action Printing.

McLeod, Angus. (2004). *Performance Coaching: The handbook for managers, H.R. professionals and coaches.* Carmarthen, Wales, UK: Crown House

Publications.

Phillip McGraw (1999), *Life Strategies: Doing What Works; Doing What Matters.* New York: Hyperion.

Mink, Oscar; Owen, Keith; Mink, Barbara. (1993). *Developing high-performance people: The art of Coaching.* New York: Addison-Wesley Publishing Com. Inc.

Myss, Caroline. (2001). Myss, *Sacred Contracts.* New York: Bantam.
Nigro, Nicholas (2003). *The Everything Coaching and Mentoring Book: How to increase productivity, foster talent, and encourage success.* Avon, MA: Adams Media Corporation.

Rosinski, Philippe. (2003). *Coaching across cultures: New tools for leveraging national, corporate and professional differences.* London: Nicholas Brealey Publishing.

Scott, Susan. (2002). *Fierce Conversations: Achieving success at work and in life, one conversation at a time.* New York: Viking: Penguin Press.

Self, Teri-E. (2002). *Coaching with spirit.* San Francisco: Jossey-Bass/ Pfiefer.
Senge, Peter. (1990). *The fifth discipline: The art and practice of the learning organization.* New York: Doubleday Currency.

Shula, Don; Blanchard, Ken. (1995). *Everyone's a coach: You can inspire anyone to be a winner.* New York: Harper Business.

Starr, Julie. (2003). *The Coaching Manual: The definitive guide to the process, principles, and skills of personal coaching.* London: Prentice Hall Business: Pearson Education.

Stowell, Steven J.; Starcevich, Matt. M. (1987/ 1994). *The Coach: Creating partnerships for a competitive edge.* Salt Lake City: UT: Center for Management and Organization Effectiveness.

Whitworth, Laura; Kimsey-House, Henry; Sandahl, Phil. (1998). *Co-Active Coaching: New skills for coaching people toward success in work and life.* Palo alto, CA: Davies-Black Publishing.

Whitmont, E.C. (1991). *The symbolic quest: Basic concepts of analytical psychology.* Princeton, NJ: Princeton U.

Whitmore, John. (1992/ 1998). *Coaching for Performance.* (Second edition). London: Nicholas Brealey Publishing.

Zeig, Jeffrey. (1985). *Experiencing Erickson*. NY: Brunner/Mazel.

Zembe, Ron; Anderson, Kristin. (1997). *Coaching Knock Your Socks Off Service*. New York: AMACOM: American Management Association.

Zeus, Perry; Skiffington, Suzanne. (2000). *The complete guide to coaching at work*. Sydney/ New York: The McGraw-Hill Companies.

Zohar, Donah. (2002). *SQ: Spiritual Intelligence: The ultimate intelligence*. Boomsbury: Ian Marshall.

INDEX

The Authors:

L. Michael Hall, Ph.D.

Neuro-Semantics® International
P.O. Box 8
Clifton, Colorado 81520 USA
(970) 523-7877

www.runyourownbrain.com   www.neurosemantics.com

L. Michael Hall is a visionary leader in the field of Neuro-Semantics and today works as an entrepreneur, researcher/modeler, and international trainer. His doctorate is in the Cognitive-Behavioral sciences from Union Institute University. He was working as a psychotherapist in Colorado when he found NLP in 1986 and then studied with Richard Bandler. When studying and modeling resilience, he developed the Meta-States model (1994). Soon he began traveling nationally and then internationally, co-created the field of Neuro-Semantics with Dr. Bob Bodenhamer. *The International Society of Neuro-Semantics* (ISNS) was established in 1996. As a prolific writer, Michael has written more than 30 books, many best sellers in the field of NLP. Michael first applied NLP to coaching in 1991, but didn't create the beginnings of Neuro-Semantic Coaching until 2001 when together with Michelle Duval co-created Meta-Coaching training system. In 2003, the Meta-Coach Foundation was created.

Books:

1) *Meta-States: Mastering the Higher Levels of Mind* (1995/ 2000)
2) *Dragon Slaying: Dragons to Princes* (1996 / 2000)
3) *The Spirit of NLP: The Process, Meaning and Criteria for Mastering NLP* (1996)
4) *Languaging: The Linguistics of Psychotherapy* (1996)
5) *Becoming More Ferocious as a Presenter* (1996)
6) *Patterns For "Renewing the Mind"* (w. Bodenhamer) (1997)
7) *Time-Lining: Advance Time-Line Processes* (w. Bodenhamer) (1997)
8) *NLP: Going Meta — Advance Modeling Using Meta-Levels* (1997/2001)
9) *Figuring Out People: Design Engineering With Meta-Programs* (w. Bodenhamer) (1997)
10) *A Source Book of Magic* (with Belnap) (1997)

11) *Mind-Lines: Lines For Changing Minds* (w. Bodenharmer) (1997/ 2002)
12) *The Secrets of Magic* (1998) Retitled: *Communication Magic* (2001).
13) *Meta-State Magic: Meta-State Journal* (1997-1999).
14) *The Structure of Excellence: Unmasking the Meta-Levels of "Sub-modalities."* (Hall and Bodenhamer, 1999). Second edition: *When Sub-Modalities Go Meta.*
15) *Instant Relaxation* (1999, Lederer and Hall)
16) *The Structure of Personality:* Modeling "Personality Using NLP and Neuro-Semantics (Hall, Bodenhamer, Bolstad, Harmblett, 2001)
17) *The Secrets of Personal Mastery* (Fall, 2000)
18) *Frame Games: Persuasion Elegance* (2000)

19) *Games Fit and Slim People Play* (2001)
20) *Games for Mastering Fear* (2001, with Bodenhamer)

21) *Games Business Experts Play* (2001)
22) *The Matrix Model* (2002/ 2003)
23) *User's Manual of the Brain: Master Practitioner Course, Volume II* (2002)
24) *MovieMind: Directing Your Mental Cinemas* (2002)
25) *The Bateson Report* (2002)
26) *Make it So!* (2002)
27) *Source Book of Magic, Volume II, Neuro-Semantic Patterns* (2004)
28) *Propulsion Systems* (2003)
29) *Games Great Lovers Play* (2004)
30) *Coaching Conversation, Meta-Coaching, Volume II* (2004 with Duval)
31) *Coaching Change, Meta-Coaching, Volume I* (2004, with Duval)

Michelle Duval, MCMC
Equilibrio
P.O. Box 2967
Sydney, NSW 2000 Australia

(02) 9363 9998   www.equlibrio.com.au

Michelle Duval is an inspiring international Master Coach, Speaker, Trainer, and founding CEO of *Equilibrio,* a Coaching organization specializing in performance, developmental and transformational Coaching.

Masterfully working with organisations, CEO's, senior executives, entrepreneurs, performers, parents and children, Michelle brings a unique flexibility and diversity into her coaching style.

As the developer of the renowned *Equilibrio Transformational Coaching Program*™ she has facilitated hundreds of people from ages 10 to 70 through this life-changing program to achieve exceptional professional and personal results.

In her commitment to building the professionalism of Coaching worldwide in 2001 Michelle co-developed with Dr. Michael Hall the *International Meta-Coach*™ Certification training system and *the Axes of Change* coaching model™. In 2003, she co-founded the *Meta-Coach Foundation* (MCF) accrediting Meta-Coaches in more than 24 countries under the auspices of the International Society of Neuro-Semantics and the Meta-Coach Foundation.

Apart from being a naturally gifted and intuitive coach, Michelle uses advanced coaching psychology from the Cognitive Behavioural Sciences, including Neuro-Linguistic Programming (NLP) and Neuro-Semantics (NS). Michelle is a Certified Trainer in both of these fields. She is also a certified Workplace Trainer and Assessor, Certificate IV, and holds advanced qualifications in Hypnosis and Values. Michelle was the founding Committee Chair for Professional Development for the International Coaching Federation Australasia (ICF) and the Co-President of the ICF Sydney, Australia 2000-2001.

In 2003 she was nominated for *Australian Business Women of the Year* and Equilibrio's innovative web site won the prestigious Golden Web Award, for *Best Web Site in the World 2003-2004.*